THE DAILY STUDY BIBLE
(OLD TESTAMENT)
General Editor: John C. L. Gibson

JEREMIAH II
and LAMENTATIONS

JEREMIAH

Volume II

and LAMENTATIONS

ROBERT DAVIDSON

THE SAINT ANDREW PRESS
EDINBURGH

THE WESTMINSTER PRESS
PHILADELPHIA

Published by
The Saint Andrew Press
Edinburgh, Scotland
and
The Westminster Press ®
Philadelphia, Pennsylvania

British Library Cataloguing in Publication Data
Davidson, Robert
  Jeremiah II, with Lamentations.
  1. Bible. O.T. Jeremiah II—Commentaries
  I. Title II. Davidson, Robert. Lamentations
224'.207 BS1525.3

ISBN 0-7152-0529-3

Printed and bound in Great Britain
by Bell and Bain Ltd., Glasgow

ISBN (Great Britain) 0 7152 0529 3

Reprinted 1990

GENERAL PREFACE

This series of commentaries on the Old Testament, to which this second volume on Jeremiah belongs, has been planned as a companion series to the much-acclaimed New Testament series of the late Professor William Barclay. As with that series, each volume is arranged in successive headed portions suitable for daily study. The Biblical text followed is that of the Revised Standard Version or Common Bible. Eleven contributors share the work, each being responsible for from one to three volumes. The series is issued in the hope that it will do for the Old Testament what Professor Barclay's series succeeded so splendidly in doing for the New Testament—make it come alive for the Christian believer in the twentieth century.

Its two-fold aim is the same as his. Firstly, it is intended to introduce the reader to some of the more important results and fascinating insights of modern Old Testament scholarship. Most of the contributors are already established experts in the field with many publications to their credit. Some are younger scholars who have yet to make their names but who in my judgment as General Editor are now ready to be tested. I can assure those who use these commentaries that they are in the hands of competent teachers who know what is of real consequence in their subject and are able to present it in a form that will appeal to the general public.

The primary purpose of the series, however, is *not* an academic one. Professor Barclay summed it up for his New Testament series in the words of Richard of Chichester's prayer—to enable men and women "to know Jesus Christ more clearly, to love Him more dearly, and to follow Him more nearly." In the case of the Old Testament we have to be a little more circumspect than that. The Old Testament was completed long before the time of Our Lord, and it was (as it still is) the sole Bible of the Jews, God's first people, before it became part of the Christian Bible. We must take this fact seriously.

Yet in its strangely compelling way, sometimes dimly and sometimes directly, sometimes charmingly and sometimes embarrassingly, it holds up before us the things of Christ. It should not be forgotten that Jesus Himself was raised on this Book, that He based His whole ministry on what it says, and that He approached His death with its words on His lips. Christian men and women have in this ancient collection of Jewish writings a uniquely illuminating avenue not only into the will and purposes of God the Father, but into the mind and heart of Him who is named God's Son, who was Himself born a Jew but went on through the Cross and Resurrection to become the Saviour of the world. Read reverently and imaginatively the Old Testament can become a living and relevant force in their everyday lives.

It is the prayer of myself and my colleagues that this series may be used by its readers and blessed by God to that end.

New College   JOHN C.L. GIBSON
Edinburgh   General Editor

CONTENTS

JEREMIAH (continued from Volume I)

Introduction   1

F. KINGS AND PROPHETS (CHS. 21–23)   7
Wishful thinking shattered (21:1–7)   8
The choice (21:8–10)   10
The house of David (21:11–14)   12
A palace sermon (22:1–9)   15
Shallum and Jehoiakim (22:10–19)   17
Jerusalem—friendless and desolate (22:20–23)   20
Coniah (22:24–30)   21
A brighter future (23:1–8)   23
A Note "concerning the prophets"   26
The meaning of adultery (23:9–15)   27
Prophets God did not send (23:16–22)   30
Lies, dreams and the word of God (23:23–32)   32
The "load" of the Lord (23:33–40)   35

G. WORDS OF HOPE AND JUDGEMENT (CHS. 24–25)
Good and bad figs (24:1–10)   37
Looking back and looking forward (25:1–14)   39
The potent brew of God's judgement (25:15–29)   42
On trial—guilty and condemned (25:30–38)   45

H. A MARKED MAN (CHS. 26–29)   46
That unpopular sermon again (26:1–16)   47
Three prophets—three responses (26:17–24)   50
An unpopular political stance (27:1–15)   52
More of the same (27:16–22)   55
A clash in the Temple—prophet against prophet
28:1–11)   57
A delayed word (28:12–17)   60
A surprising letter (i) (29:1–23)   61
A surprising letter (ii) (29:1–23) (cont'd), (24–32)   65

I. A FUTURE BRIGHT WITH HOPE (CHS. 30–33)   67

Punishment deserved—a future promised (30:1–11) ...   69
Curing the incurable (30:12–17)   72
A new community (30:18–24)   74
Love unchanging (31:1–14)   77
Weep no more, Ephraim—and Judah (31:15–26)   82
Personal responsibility (31:27–34)   86
The new covenant (31:31–34) (cont'd)   88
An unbreakable bond (31:35–40)   90
An act of faith (32:1–15)   92
A prayer and further words of hope (32:16–44)   95
A bright future for Judah and Jerusalem (33:1–13) ...   98
True kings and true priests (33:14–26)   101

J. THE STORMY PETREL OF THE JERUSALEM SCENE (CHS. 34–39)   103

Naught for your comfort—an interview with Zedekiah (34:1–7)   104
A brutally cynical act (34:8–22)   106
A shining example of faithfulness (35:1–19)   108
Banned, but not silenced (36:1–26)   112
Repeating the message—and more (36:27–32)   116
An urgent request—an uncompromising reply (37:1–10)   118
Arrest, imprisonment and a secret interview (37:11–21)   120
Arrest and imprisonment—another version (38:1–13) .   123
A secret interview—another version (38:14–28)   125
The fall of Jerusalem (39:1–18)   129

K. AFTER THE HOLOCAUST (CHS. 40–45)

Freedom for Jeremiah (40:1–6)   132
First steps in reconstruction—foiled (40:7–41:3)   134
Further bloodshed (41:4–18)   138
Is there a word from the Lord? (42:1–22)   141
Down to Egypt (43:1–13)   145
Some people never learn (44:1–14)   148
A clash of views (44:15–30)   151
A glimpse of Baruch (45:1–5)   154

L. RULER OF ALL NATIONS (CHS. 46–51)

Commentary on 46:1–51:58   156
Babylon is sunk (51:59–64)   160

M. EPILOGUE (CH. 52)
The curtain comes down (52:1–34)   162

LAMENTATIONS

Introduction......................................   167
Tragedy observed (1:1–11)........................   172
Tragedy relived (1:12–22)   176
What the Lord has done (2:1–10)   181
Grief and unanswered questions (2:11–17)   184
Appeal and response (2:18–22)   186
Suffering and despair (3:1–20)   188
Reviving faith (i) (3:21–39)   192
Reviving faith (ii) (3:21–39) *(cont'd)*   194
Tears of repentance (3:40–51)   197
The answer (3:52–66)   200
Misery abounds (4:1–16)   202
Last days and beyond (4:17–22)   206
A prayer of distress (5:1–18)   209
Certainties and questions (5:19–22)   211

Further Reading   214

INTRODUCTION

It is not easy to read through or to understand one of the lengthy prophetic books in the Old Testament. "The Book of Jeremiah" naturally suggests to us a book written by a man called Jeremiah. Yet anyone who sits down and seriously tries to read through this book from beginning to end must soon begin to doubt this. If this book was written by a sane man with an orderly mind, he has done his best to confuse us. It is scrappy, built up of many bits and pieces which do not always seem to follow on easily from one another. It is badly ordered. Chapter 21, for example, tells of an incident in the reign of the last king of Judah, Zedekiah, but chapter 26 describes a sermon preached by Jeremiah at the beginning of the reign of one of his predecessors some twenty years earlier. The first verse of the book begins with "the words of Jeremiah". Since the Hebrew *davar*, "word", can refer to something spoken, a word, or something done, a deed or event, this phrase could be translated "the story, or the biography, of Jeremiah". But it is an odd biography; and we are left with a biographer with an exceedingly untidy mind. He would have had his manuscript returned with a rejection slip from any modern publisher.

To understand the book we have got to remember one thing. Most of the Old Testament prophets were not primarily writers; they were *preachers* who spoke rather than wrote the word that God gave them. One of the best illustrations of this, curiously enough, is to be found in chapter 36 which speaks of a book or a scroll. It is the year 604 B.C. The prophet dictates a scroll to his secretary Baruch, a scroll that was to contain all the words that Jeremiah had spoken in obedience to God up to that moment.

Two things are interesting about this scroll:

(1) If, as seems likely, Jeremiah began his ministry as a prophet in the year 627 B.C., he had already been a prophet for over twenty years before he felt the need to put down in writing what he had been saying to his people. During these years he had been preaching and teaching, as many other prophets did,

1

and as Jesus did, by word of mouth. We must never forget that behind the written word in most prophetic books there lies the spoken word. We can feel this spoken word reaching out for us through the written word. It is characteristic of such preaching that again and again it comes back to the same themes and indeed uses the same illustrations, often in different sermons. Witness any popular preacher or evangelist today. Moreover, how we interpret the written word often depends on how we think the words were spoken, the tone of voice, the implied question, the hint of sarcasm. A good illustration of this is the different translations of 6:14 where Jeremiah is attacking prophets and priests for saying, according to the RSV:

> . . . 'Peace, peace,'
> when there is no peace.

But the NEB translates:

> . . . 'All is well.'
> All well? Nothing is well!

"Peace" and "All is well" are both reasonable translations of the Hebrew word *shalom*, but notice how when we come to the second *shalom* the NEB, perhaps rightly, implies a change of voice, a question.

(2) But why did Jeremiah feel the need to put his teaching into writing at this particular time? Probably because, as a result of his highly unpopular Temple Sermon (see chapters 7 and 26), he was *persona non grata* to the religious and political establishment. There were threats to his life; he was debarred from preaching in person in the Temple precincts. In this situation, and perhaps increasingly convinced of the urgency of his message of judgement, he dictates the scroll to Baruch. Baruch can read it to the people: the word must continue to be heard, even if the prophet himself is banned from speaking it. When the king confiscates the scroll, slashes it with a knife and consigns the pieces to the fire, Jeremiah redictates his words to

Baruch for inclusion in another scroll and adds a few further comments for good measure.

If the scroll of chapter 36 is the original spring out of which our present Book of Jeremiah flows, many other rivulets have made their contribution before the book reaches us in its present form. Let us look briefly at some of the richly varied material in the book.

(1) There are passages which are concerned mainly with the word that came to the prophet from God. They are usually fairly brief passages, poetic in form. We call them prophetic oracles. They are introduced by a phrase such as "Thus says the Lord" (6:6, 9, 16, 22) or "Hear the word of the Lord" (2:4; 10:1). Sometimes they end with a phrase which the RSV translates "says the Lord". Turn to the beginning of chapter 2 and you will find a very good example of such a brief prophetic oracle in 2:2–3:

> Thus says the Lord,
>   I remember the devotion of your youth,
>   your love as a bride,
>   how you followed me in the wilderness,
>   in a land not sown.
>   Israel was holy to the Lord,
>   the first fruits of his harvest.
>   All who ate of it became guilty;
>   evil came upon them,
>   says the Lord.

Notice the way in which Hebrew poetry achieves its effect by the use of balancing or parallel phrases. In verse 2, "the devotion of your youth" echoed by "your love as a bride"; "in the wilderness" echoed by "in a land not sown". In such oracles the prophet stands before us as God's messenger to the people of God. In the ancient world if you wanted to send a message to someone you could not pop it into an envelope and take it to the nearest pillar-box. You sent a personal messenger, who memorized the message you wished to deliver and then went and spoke it in your name and in your words, introducing the words by "Thus says my master". You will find a good example of this in Gen. 32:3–5. The prophet is just such a messenger, God's messenger.

(2) In addition to these brief poetic oracles there are longer prose passages, often in the form of sermons in a style and language very similar to that found in the Book of Deuteronomy, *eg* 7:1–8:3; 11:1–17. There has been much discussion among scholars as to whether these sermons in their present form come from Jeremiah himself or whether they are the work of later preachers, taking Jeremiah's ideas and adapting them to make them relevant to the changed situation of their own day when most of the Jewish people were in exile in Babylon. It hardly detracts from the value of these sermons if, in their present form, they do not come from Jeremiah: indeed it but serves to underline the vitality of his message. Far from being only for his own age, it was capable of being reshaped to speak to other situations—and it has done so ever since.

· (3) The Book of Jeremiah contains an unusual amount of biographical information, beginning with the account of a dramatic sermon which the prophet preached in Jerusalem in the autumn of 609 or the winter of 609/608 B.C. (see chapters 7 and 26) and continuing down to and including the fall of Jerusalem to the Babylonians in 587 B.C. In the last glimpse we have of him, we find him among Jewish exiles from that catastrophe in Egypt (chapter 44). In no sense is this information a complete biography. Rather it is a series of memoirs, mainly concerned with situations of conflict in which the prophet was involved. Some of these memoirs may come from the pen of Jeremiah's friend and secretary Baruch. Much of this material is to be found in chapters 26–45 of the present book.

(4) At various points in the book there are intensely personal autobiographical passages which, when taken together, make up what has been called Jeremiah's "Confessions" or "Personal

Spiritual Diary". Such passages—they include 11:18–12:6; 15:10–21; 17:5–10, 14–18; 18:18–23; 20:7–18—have no parallel in other prophetic books in the Old Testament. They seem to be modelled on—they may indeed have influenced—some of the Psalms, *eg* Psalm 73. For a few brief moments in these passages the veil which conceals from us the inner life of a prophet is lifted. We not only hear Jeremiah publicly preaching, we listen to him wrestling, agonizing in prayer. Not only may we admire the courage he displayed in the face of opposition, but we glimpse something of the uncertainties, the black moods of despair and bitterness which lie behind such courage. Above all we see a man baring his soul to God, locked in conflict with God, a man for whom the way of faith was not easy, a man who could accuse God of deceiving him. This is a very human prophet, touched with our weaknesses, haunted by the kind of doubts which plague us.

All this is but a sample of the rich tapestry which is the Book of Jeremiah. Many hands have woven its strands. We can see within the book certain clear patterns as deliberate attempts have been made to gather together material on related topics. Thus 23:9–40 is headed "Concerning the prophets", while chapters 27–29 recount incidents involving Jeremiah in conflict with other prophets. Chapters 30–33, often called "the book of consolation", gather together a series of passages whose dominant theme is hope for the future; while chapters 46–51 contain a collection of oracles against other nations. The book ends in chapter 52 with an extract from 2 Kings chapters 24–25.

ITS TWO FORMS

Not only is this not a book written by one man, Jeremiah, but it has come down to us across the centuries in two forms. The one, which we now read in our English versions including the RSV, goes back to what became the standard Hebrew text by the beginning of the Christian era. The other is found in the Greek version of the Old Testament, the Bible of the early Church, and behind it there lies a different Hebrew text. It is considerably shorter and the material in it is, at certain points, differently ordered. The collection of the oracles against other nations, for example, which in the RSV appears in chapters 46–51, comes in the Greek text after 25:13 following the words "everything written in this book, which Jeremiah prophesied against all the nations", and the separate oracles within this collection come in a different order. It is impossible to say which form of the text takes us closest to the original Book of Jeremiah, if there ever was one such book.

A GREAT PROPHET

There are thus many problems about the Book of Jeremiah and its composition. But it is not our task in this commentary to concern ourselves too much with academic matters. However the book got its present shape, we can be sure of one thing. Through all its pages there come to us the message and activities of a great prophet, courageous and vulnerable, sensitive and passionate, a man almost crucified by his contemporaries, but canonized by later generations. There is much to shame us here, much to inspire us, and much from which we can learn.

F. KINGS AND PROPHETS (CHS. 21-23)

At the end of volume 1 we left Jeremiah tenaciously holding on to faith in God in the midst of bouts of despair and recurring doubts. No other prophet has ever told us so much about his spiritual conflicts as Jeremiah does between chapters 11 and 20. This next section of the book throws light on one of the reasons for such inner conflicts: his uneasy relationship with two of the pillars of the establishment in his day, the monarchy (21:1; 23:8) and the prophets (23:9-40).

In this section, as elsewhere (see the Introduction), we must allow for the later editing and reshaping of material that goes back to Jeremiah. The order of some of the material in the chapters on the monarchy is very strange. To understand it we must briefly remind ourselves of the history of the period. When Josiah the patriotic reforming king died, tragically young, fighting for his nation's independence at Megiddo in 609 B.C., he was succeeded by his son Jehoahaz, called Shallum in 22:11-12. Within three months Jehoahaz was deposed by Pharaoh Neco, his Egyptian overlord, and banished to Egypt where he died. His brother Jehoiakim came to the throne to head an Egyptian puppet regime. He is the object of a slashing attack by Jeremiah in 22:13-19. He later switched his loyalty to the Babylonians, the new rising political star in the ancient Near East, but eventually rebelled against them. He died—he may even have been assassinated—a few months before the Babylonians occupied Jerusalem in 597 B.C. His son Jehoiachin—the Coniah of 22:24-30—surrendered to the Babylonians, was deposed and sent into exile to Babylon. The Babylonians placed on the throne his ncle Zedekiah who reigned for ten years, the last king of the Judean state. He fatally flirted with rebellion against his imperial overlord, and both he and his people paid a heavy penalty when the Babylonians ravaged Jerusalem in 587 B.C. It is with an incident in the reign of Zedekiah that this section on the monarchy begins; it ends looking forward to a king to come whose name is a barbed pun on the name Zedekiah. In between there are brief passages on the other three kings.

WISHFUL THINKING SHATTERED

Jeremiah 21:1-7

¹This is the word which came to Jeremiah from the Lord, when King Zedekiah sent to him Pashhur the son of Malchiah and Zephaniah the priest, the son of Maaseiah, saying, ²"Inquire of the Lord for us, for Nebuchadrezzar king of Babylon is making war against us; perhaps the Lord will deal with us according to all his wonderful deeds, and will make him withdraw from us."

³Then Jeremiah said to them: ⁴"Thus you shall say to Zedekiah, 'Thus says the Lord, the God of Israel: Behold, I will turn back the weapons of war which are in your hands and with which you are fighting against the king of Babylon and against the Chaldeans who are besieging you outside the walls; and I will bring them together into the midst of this city. ⁵I myself will fight against you with outstretched hand and strong arm, in anger, and in fury, and in great wrath. ⁶And I will smite the inhabitants of this city, both man and beast; they shall die of a great pestilence. ⁷Afterward, says the Lord, I will give Zedekiah king of Judah, and his servants, and the people in this city who survive the pestilence, sword, and famine, into the hand of Nebuchadrezzar king of Babylon and into the hand of their enemies, into the hand of those who seek their lives. He shall smite them with the edge of the sword; he shall not pity them, or spare them, or have compassion.'"

The situation in Jerusalem is increasingly grim. Zedekiah, having burnt his boats by rebelling against Nebuchadrezzar, can only watch helplessly as the Babylonian net is drawn ever more tightly around Jerusalem. This last king of Judah is a strange and fascinating character. He seems almost to have dithered into disaster, unable to resist pressure from the powerful anti-Babylonian lobby among the military in Jerusalem. Brutally cynical on occasion (see 34:8ff.), he nevertheless seems to have been haunted by the thought, or perhaps by the fear, that the true word for his day was to be found not on the lips of his political advisers or his official chaplains, but on the lips of that odd-ball Jeremiah. On several occasions during the last fateful months of the Judean state (see chs. 37-38) he asks for Jeremiah's diagnosis of the nation's condition and prospects. He is like a patient returning again and again to a doctor in search of reassurance, yet unwilling to take the medicine prescribed.

The passage describes a royal delegation... a request ... and a reply.

The delegation consists of Pashhur, son of Malchiah (not the Pashhur we met with in ch. 20), who features again in 38:1-6 as one of the state officials who seek to silence Jeremiah on the grounds that he is undermining the morale of soldiers and civilians; and of Zephaniah, son of Maaseiah, described simply as "the priest". Zephaniah appears in a similar delegation in 37:3. He must have held an important position in the Jerusalem religious establishment, since it is to him that one of the exiles in Babylon writes to complain about a subversive letter written by Jeremiah (29:25).

The delegation brings a simple request: "Inquire of the Lord for us" (verse 2). As a prophet Jeremiah is expected to approach God on behalf of the people to discover what God's will for them is. Hopefully it will be good news. After all, the past has been the story of the Lord's "wonderful deeds". There may be here a reference to the incident described in 2 Kings 19 which happened just over a hundred years earlier, when a powerful Assyrian army melted away from before the walls of Jerusalem. Why should it not happen again to the Babylonians under Nebuchadrezzar? (His name, by the way, is correctly spelled here with an 'r' in the middle; contrast chs. 27-29 where it has an 'n' instead of an 'r'.) If ever a miracle were needed, it is now ... and the Lord is a God of miracles, isn't he?

Jeremiah's reply is uncompromising and shattering. Verse 4 is not wholly clear, but "the weapons of war which are in your hands" probably refers to Judean troops or guerrilla groups still operating outside the city to harass the Babylonians. They are going to be withdrawn into the city to await the final attack. One thing, however, is clear. There will be no miracle. The real enemy of the city is not the Babylonians; they are merely the agents the Lord is using to carry out his inevitable and necessary death sentence upon a rebellious people. There is a grim irony in some of the words in this passage. God himself is fighting against his people "with outstretched hand and strong arm" (verse 5). A similar phrase is used frequently in Deuteronomy to describe how God fought on behalf of his people, giving them freedom instead of slavery in Egypt, bringing them to a land of their own: "you shall remember that you were a slave in Egypt and the Lord your God brought you out thence with a mighty hand and an outstretched arm" (Deut.5:15). But Deuteronomy always adds after such a statement "therefore", a "therefore" which spells out the obedience God expects from the people. Jeremiah is only too painfully aware that this "therefore" had been ignored; obedience had not been forthcoming. So the God who saved was now the God who must judge and destroy.

What we are listening to here is not the one-off angry response of a prophet who was having a bad day. It represents Jeremiah's consistent attitude and message during the dark months that climaxed in the end of the Judean state (see 37:3-10). His words lead him to be accused, justifiably, of high treason, a crime against the state which has always been regarded with distaste and anger. Many people have been perplexed by Jeremiah's attitude. It is worth looking at it a little more closely in the light of the next section.

THE CHOICE

Jeremiah 21:8-10

> [8]"And to this people you shall say: 'Thus says the Lord: Behold, I set before you the way of life and the way of death. [9]He who stays in this city shall die by the sword, by famine, and by pestilence; but he who goes out and surrenders to the Chaldeans who are besieging

you shall live and shall have his life as a prize of war. ¹⁰For I have set
my face against this city for evil and not for good, says the Lord: it
shall be given into the hand of the king of Babylon, and he shall
burn it with fire.'"

To the reply to Zedekiah there has been added a word to the
people. It confronts them with a choice, a stark choice between
"the way of life and the way of death". Again we are reminded
of Deuteronomy where the people are faced with the choice of
"life and good", theirs if they take seriously and live out their
new relationship with God; and "death and evil", the inevitable
result of ignoring the Lord's demands and worshipping other
gods (Deut.30:15–20). Jeremiah brings the choice up to date,
by spelling out its meaning in the contemporary crisis.
"Death"?. . . that is the fate awaiting anyone who remains in
Jerusalem and fights against the Babylonians: "life"?. . . that
may be had by deserting to the Babylonians. Anyone who so
deserts "shall have his life as a prize of war" (verse 9), a phrase
that occurs several times in the Book of Jeremiah (see 38:2;
39:18; 45:5). In a successful military campaign, a soldier could
reasonably expect to return home with booty. The only booty
to be had in this battle, says Jeremiah ironically, is survival,
"life", and that can only be had by deserting to the enemy.
     Alongside these words read chapters 37 and 38 and you will
see why the popular verdict on Jeremiah was "traitor". Yet
there are many odd things about this traitor. He did not practise
the undercover approach which is of the very essence of the
traitor's trade. He openly preached high treason in the streets of
Jerusalem. He counselled his fellow citizens to desert to the
enemy, yet he did not follow his own advice, but remained in the
city to share in the agony and suffering of those who had
refused to listen to what he was saying. There is no evidence that
he was influenced by misplaced idealism or by the often
incredible political naïvety which marks a traitor. He was not
part of a peace movement. He was not pro Babylonian; *he was
pro God.* He believed that, in the purposes of the Lord,
Jerusalem must be destroyed. Submission to Babylon was

nothing other than acceptance of the will of God—a view which must have been greeted with as much incredulity as the most die-hard, right-wing politician would bring to the suggestion that we should all toe the communist line.

Jeremiah is certainly an uncomfortable companion for anyone who believes that the noblest human ideal is expressed in the words 'for God and country'. Jeremiah was for God, and for that very reason against his own country. His fellow citizens fought and died heroically in the face of overwhelming odds. Many, the best of them, believed they were fighting the battle of the Lord against aggressive paganism. As the military situation deteriorated they prayed for a miracle. They were sincere and, in Jeremiah's eyes, wrong. What they thought of as obedience to God, he regarded as disobedience. He could see no future for his people except on the other side of disaster. It is typical of the man that, believing this to be "the word of the Lord" for his day, he said so openly and unambiguously . . . and faced the consequences.

THE HOUSE OF DAVID

Jeremiah 21:11–14

11"And to the house of the king of Judah say, 'Hear the word of the Lord, 12O house of David! Thus says the Lord:
"'Execute justice in the morning,
    and deliver from the hand of the oppressor
    him who has been robbed,
lest my wrath go forth like fire,
    and burn with none to quench it,
    because of your evil doings.'"

13"Behold, I am against you, O inhabitant of the valley,
    O rock of the plain,
                    says the Lord;
    you who say, 'Who shall come down against us,
        or who shall enter our habitations?'

14I will punish you according to the fruit of your doings,
>   says the Lord;
> I will kindle a fire in her forest,
> and it shall devour all that is round about her."

The story of Zedekiah's ill-fated delegation to Jeremiah leads into a section which gathers together a series of passages whose common theme is "the house of David". The opening words of verse 11 would be better translated as, "Concerning the house of the king of Judah", the title of the collection, just as the words, "Concerning the prophets" in 23:9, head a collection of sayings on prophecy.

The "house of David", however, can mean one of two things:

(1) the dynasty or royal family of David—this is its meaning in 21:12—or

(2) the palace of David, the royal residence—this is its meaning in 22:1.

We have already had occasion (see comment on 13:13) to talk about the central and important place which the Davidic royal family had in the religious life of Israel. Verse 12 draws our attention to an indispensible feature of responsible kingship in Israel and throughout the ancient Near East. Although royal power could be abused for personal aggrandizement—witness Jeremiah's savage attack on Jehoiakim in 22:13–19, or the story of Naboth's vineyard in 1 Kings 21—it was meant to be used responsibly to guarantee justice in society and, in particular, to protect those at risk: the poor, the alien, the orphan, the widow. In his famous code of laws, King Hammurabi of Babylon (circa 1700B.C.) claims to have been given royal power by the gods;

> to cause justice to prevail in the land,
> to destroy the wicked and the evil,
> that the strong might not oppress the weak.

Psalm 72, a coronation hymn, begins (verses 1–2)

> Give the king thy justice, O God,
>   and thy righteousness to the royal son!
> May he judge thy people with righteousness
>   and thy poor with justice!

That is a prayer which sadly falls on deaf ears in many parts of the world today, as people are sacrificed to political ideologies, and the interests of the state or the party or monetarism are invoked to deny people basic human rights. Jeremiah is in no doubt; failure to exercise power responsibly will lead to inevitable disaster, disaster here described in terms of an unstoppable, raging fire (cf.4:4).

From the royal family we turn in verses 13-14 to the city of David—the "you" at the beginning of verse 13 being feminine singular, referring to Jerusalem, the mother city. Yet verse 13 reads very oddly as a description of Jerusalem. The city was not in "the valley": it was built on a rocky promontory, surrounded by valleys on three sides. Nor, in the light of the surrounding countryside, would any modern tourist brochure invite you to visit Jerusalem, "the rock of the plain". "Enthroned over the valley", however, is probably a better translation than the RSV ("inhabitant of the valley") and "rock of the plain" should be translated "the rocky plateau"—both reasonable descriptions of Jerusalem.

Whatever its physical features or attractions, the royal city, as well as the royal family, is summoned to listen to the warning note. Not this time because of abuse of power or corruption—although there was plenty of that in Jerusalem, as Jeremiah frequently points out (eg 5:1-3)—but because of that soul-destroying complacency which says 'it can't happen to us'; a complacency never more dangerous than when it claims to be rooted in deeply held religious convictions (see the comment on the Temple Sermon in vol. 1, pp.70-74). Again the threat is of the coming fire of God's judgement, this time devouring "her forest", probably a reference to the lavish use made of cedar in some of the most important buildings in the city. Part of Solomon's palace complex had 45 cedar pillars, with cedar beams resting upon them and cedar panelled ceilings. It was called "the House of the Forest of Lebanon" (see 1 Kings 7:2).

A PALACE SERMON

Jeremiah 22:1-9

> [1]Thus says the Lord: "Go down to the house of the king of Judah, and speak there this word, [2]and say, 'Hear the word of the Lord, O King of Judah, who sit on the throne of David, you, and your servants, and your people who enter these gates. [3]Thus says the Lord: Do justice and righteousness, and deliver from the hand of the oppressor him who has been robbed. And do no wrong or violence to the alien, the fatherless, and the widow, nor shed innocent blood in this place. [4]For if you will indeed obey this word, then there shall enter the gates of this house kings who sit on the throne of David, riding in chariots and on horses, they, and their servants, and their people. [5]But if you will not heed these words, I swear by myself, says the Lord, that this house shall become a desolation. [6]For thus says the Lord concerning the house of the king of Judah:
>
> "'You are as Gilead to me,
>   as the summit of Lebanon,
> yet surely I will make you a desert,
>   an uninhabited city.
> [7]I will prepare destroyers against you,
>   each with his weapons;
> and they shall cut down your choicest cedars,
>   and cast them into the fire.
>
> [8]"'And many nations will pass by this city, and every man will say to his neighbour, "Why has the Lord dealt thus with this great city?" [9]And they will answer, "Because they forsook the covenant of the Lord their God, and worshipped other gods and served them."'"

Just as chapter 7 describes a sermon delivered at the entrance to "the house of the Lord", the Temple, so here we have a sermon delivered at "the house of the king of Judah", the royal palace in Jerusalem. It was not that Jeremiah had any right to be there. He was not preaching by royal command, nor as chaplain to the Royal Household or to the White House. He was an uninvited preacher; there only because he was under the compulsion of God to be there. What he had to say would hardly have put him on the guest preachers' list. The king in question is not identified. The sermon had an appropriate word for any king. It provides the general theological framework within which specific comments are later made on three kings.

The language and style of the sermon in verses 1-5 are very similar to those of the Temple Sermon. It picks up and develops the theme of 21:11-12; the need for royal power to be used responsibly to protect the defenceless in society, and to ensure that no-one uses the due processes of law to condemn the innocent. It promises a continuing greatness and a secure future to the Davidic dynasty (verse 4), but only *if* it lives in the light of its God-given responsibilities. It threatens disaster *if* such obedience is not forthcoming. That small and nagging word 'if' is never far from the centre of the true prophetic word.

The grim, ever-threatening reality of disaster is picked up in a brief poem in verses 6-7. Both Gilead and Lebanon were famed for their luxuriant forests. Indeed the part of Solomon's building complex which we described in the previous section was called "the House of the Forest of Lebanon". But this "House of the Forest of Lebanon" can easily become an uninhabited wilderness, its choice cedars hacked down and fed to the flames. Psalm 74:4-7 vividly describes that happening to the elaborate wooden panelling in the Temple as the Babylonian army sacked Jerusalem.

It can happen, says Jeremiah over and over again, to a disbelieving people. It did happen; and verses 8-9, very similar in language and thought to 1 Kings 9:8-9, claims that there is no mystery as to why it will happen. If God's own people cannot see why, then let them take a lesson from other peoples, outsiders who, viewing the ruins of Jerusalem, will say to one another, "that's what happens to a nation which turns its back on the one true living God, and seeks illusory security in the worship of other gods". It is a cutting comment designed to shock the people of God into facing the facts about themselves. But it is more than that. It is a salutary reminder that the outsider sometimes seems to have a clearer insight into what is happening in God's world than those who claim to belong to the people of God. We are often adept at providing answers to questions that nobody is asking; and blind to the questions we ought to be asking and answering.

SHALLUM AND JEHOIAKIM

Jeremiah 22:10-19

10Weep not for him who is dead,
  nor bemoan him;
but weep bitterly for him who goes
    away,
  for he shall return no more
  to see his native land.
11For thus says the Lord concerning Shallum the son of Josiah, king of Judah, who reigned instead of Josiah his father, and who went away from this place: "He shall return here no more, 12but in the place where they have carried him captive, there shall he die, and he shall never see this land again."

13"Woe to him who builds his house by unrighteousness,
    and his upper rooms by injustice;
  who makes his neighbour serve him for nothing,
    and does not give him his wages;
14who says, 'I will build myself a great house
    with spacious upper rooms,'
  and cuts out windows for it,
    panelling it with cedar,
    and painting it with vermillion.
15Do you think you are a king
    because you compete in cedar?
  Did not your father eat and drink
    and do justice and righteousness?
    Then it was well with him.
16He judged the cause of the poor and needy;
    then it was well.
  Is not this to know me?
    says the Lord.
17But you have eyes and heart
    only for your dishonest gain,
  for shedding innocent blood,
    and for practising oppression and violence."

¹⁸Therefore thus says the Lord concerning Jehoiakim the son of
Josiah, king of Judah:

"They shall not lament for him, saying,
  'Ah my brother!' or 'Ah sister!'
They shall not lament for him, saying,
  'Ah lord!' or 'Ah his majesty!'
¹⁹With the burial of an ass he shall be buried,
  dragged and cast forth beyond the gates of Jerusalem."

The rest of chapter 22 focusses upon the three kings who
occupied the throne in Jerusalem between the death of Josiah in
609 B.C. and the accession of the last king of Judah, Zedekiah, in
597 B.C. It was a period of increasing political and social
instability. Two of them reigned but a brief few months, the
third long enough to show only too clearly his true colours.

Shallum. As befits a man who held the reins of power for only
three months, the comment on Shallum is brief and regretful.
The fourth son of Josiah, he was put on the throne, according to
2 Kings 23:30, by "the people of the land", probably to continue
his father's popular, patriotic religious policy. On coming to the
throne he took the royal name Jehoahaz. Whatever popular
hopes may have centred on him, they were nipped in the bud as
the Egyptians deposed him to make way for a brother who
promised to be a more pliant puppet. His fate is referred to in a
short poem (verse 10) which, in very general terms and without
specifically naming Shallum, invites the people to stop
mourning for "him who is dead"—their national hero Josiah,
Shallum's father—and transfer their grief to the son doomed to
languish and die in exile. The following verses 11–12 interpret
the poem and point to its application by naming both Shallum
and Josiah. No comment is made on Shallum's character.

Jehoiakim. Things are very different when the prophet turns
to Shallum's brother Eliakim, who assumed power as Jehoiakim. There is no more savage indictment of a king in the entire
Old Testament than the scathing words with which Jeremiah
flays Jehoiakim (verses 13–19). King Jehoiakim seems to have
reciprocated Jeremiah's feelings, since he treats him with
studied contempt as a charlatan of a prophet (see 36:20–26).

The bitter attack in verses 13–17 dismisses Jehoiakim as the unworthy son of a worthy father. Josiah's life had been marked by a true relationship with God which expressed itself in that "justice" and "righteousness" which cares for the weak and those who are vulnerable in society. Jehoiakim was the opposite; a self-indulgent despot whose reign was based on "no justice" and "no righteousness" (verse 13). Keeping up with the royal "Joneses" of his day was his number one priority; the outward trappings of power all important—a well-lit, spacious royal residence, lavishly decorated with cedar panelling. Jeremiah sarcastically comments, "so that's what kingship means . . . competing in cedar!" (verse 15). And if his grandiose building projects meant inflicting forced labour upon his fellow countrymen, what of it? He could always appeal to the excellent example of another great royal builder, Solomon (1 Kings 5:13–14). Anyone who stood in his way was given short shrift (verse 17).

It is tempting to identify Jehoiakim with an oil-rich Arab sheikh; gilt Rolls Royce, Cadillacs, luxury residences at home and abroad, a fortune in some Swiss bank, while many of his own people still live on the verge of poverty. It stops us thinking more personally and painfully about how all of us in the affluent West tend to define life in terms of material possessions—poverty for us being the lack of a video—while our economic system condemns much of the rest of the world to continuing poverty, deprivation and malnutrition. Is this what living means—competing in automobiles and music centres?

The attack on Jehoiakim is capped by a stern word of judgement (verses 18–19): therefore! a sordid life will come to a sordid end, the customary royal mourning rites conspicuously absent. As translated in the RSV, the words "Ah my brother!" and "Ah sister!" refer to the way in which mourners at a funeral seek to comfort one another; and the words "Ah lord!" and "Ah his majesty!" refer to their common grief at the passing of a king. But it is possible, by a slight change in the text, to read the latter words as "Ah father!" and "Ah mother!", and to take "brother", "sister", "father" and "mother" as royal titles expressing the caring relationship in which the king stood in connection with his people. Either way *this* king is to die unlamented, his burial no better than "the burial of an ass", his body dumped unceremoniously like that of an unclean animal outside the city walls (see 36:30).

God's verdict on Jehoiakim is thus light years away from 'the guid conceit' which the king had of himself; and it is God's verdict which is the only relevant verdict in the eyes of the prophet, as it is the only relevant verdict on us.

JERUSALEM—FRIENDLESS AND DESOLATE

Jeremiah 22:20–23

> [20]"Go up to Lebanon, and cry out,
>   and lift up your voice in Bashan;
>   cry from Abarim, for all your lovers are destroyed.
> [21]I spoke to you in your prosperity,
>   but you said, 'I will not listen.'
>   This has been your way from your youth,
>   that you have not obeyed my voice.
> [22]The wind shall shepherd all your shepherds,
>   and your lovers shall go into captivity;
>   then you will be ashamed and confounded
>   because of all your wickedness. .
> [23]O inhabitant of Lebanon, nested among the cedars,
>   how you will groan when pangs come upon you,
>   pain as of a woman in travail!"

Before turning to the third king, there is a brief poem on the coming fate of Jerusalem. The reference to "the gates of Jerusalem" at the end of verse 19 leads naturally into this direct address to the royal metropolis. It may be that the poem is also placed here because it was thought to reflect the situation in Jerusalem just after the death of Jehoiakim in 597 B.C.

The poem begins by depicting Jerusalem bemoaning her fate and appealing in vain for help to the surrounding nations—to Lebanon in the north, to Bashan across the Jordan in the north-east, then south to Abarim, the mountains of Moab that look down over the north end of the Dead Sea. (It was from one of the Abarim mountains, Mt Nebo, that Moses had his dying glimpse of the Promised Land he was never to enter, according to Deut.32:48–50.) But if Jerusalem is looking for help she will look in vain. Her "lovers" (see Hos. 8:9), the political allies who had promised her support, cannot lift a finger to help her. They themselves are broken (see ch. 27 and the comments on pp. 53–55). Jerusalem was to discover only too late that she had no future in trying to make the right moves in the game of power politics in the ancient Near East. That merely blinded the people to their true calling as the people of God.

Notice the skilful play on words at the beginning of verse 22. The wind shall "shepherd", *ie* round up and drive away, your "shepherds", *ie* the king and others in positions of authority in the state. Sarcastically, Jerusalem is described in verse 23 as "inhabitant of Lebanon", so lavishly had the cedars of Lebanon been used in building projects in the city. If this suggested to the citizens power, wealth and security, they were in for a shock; the cold reality of sudden disaster gripping them like the pains of a woman in childbirth (see 4:31; 6:24).

Jerusalem can no more be exempt from the inevitable encounter with her day of reckoning than Jehoiakim was.

CONIAH

Jeremiah 22:24–30

24"As I live, says the Lord, though Coniah the son of Jehoiakim, king of Judah, were the signet ring on my right hand, yet I would tear you off 25and give you into the hand of those who seek your life, into the hand of those of whom you are afraid, even into the hand of Nebuchadrezzar king of Babylon and into the hand of the Chaldeans. 26I will hurl you and the mother who bore you into another country, where you were not born, and there you shall die. 27But to the land to which they will long to return, there they shall not return".

²⁸Is this man Coniah a despised, broken pot,
   a vessel no one cares for?
Why are he and his children hurled and cast
   into a land which they do not know?
²⁹O land, land, land, hear the word of the Lord!
³⁰Thus says the Lord:
   "Write this man down as childless,
      a man who shall not succeed in his days;
   for none of his offspring shall succeed
      in sitting on the throne of David,
      and ruling again in Judah."

Coniah's few months on the throne in 598 B.C. were in some ways a tragic re-run of Shallum's experience. You will find an account of his reign in 2 Kings 24:10-17. When Coniah succeeded to the throne he took the royal title Jehoiachin. He was quickly deposed by the Babylonians to whom he had surrendered the city, and then he was sent into exile with the Queen Mother (verse 26) and other leading citizens. No son of his ever sat on the throne of David.

In the ancient world, kings and other people in positions of authority used a personal "signet ring" to imprint their signature on the wax seal of documents. The "signet ring" was, therefore, a very valuable personal possession, almost like a banker's card today. Coniah's fate is graphically described by the Lord declaring that even if Coniah were the signet ring on his right hand, he would tear him off (verse 24). The same picture of "the signet ring on [the Lord's] hand" is used to describe the close relationship between God and a descendant of Coniah's some 70 years later in Haggai 2:23.

But in this passage Coniah has no future. In the poem in verses 28-30 he is compared to "a despised, broken pot, a vessel no one cares for . . . ". Since the word translated "pot" can indicate any kind of lifeless shape, it has also been translated as "a mere figurehead" or "a puppet" (NEB). However we translate, it describes an object nobody wants, fit only to be thrown out. He is to be entered in the official state records as "childless" (verse 30). Since we know that Coniah was not childless (see 1 Chron.3:16), the New English Bible translates it as "stripped of all honour". But "childless" is correct; childless in the sense that no child of his would ever follow him on the throne of David.

As in the case of Shallum, Jeremiah makes no personal attack on Coniah. He gives no reason for the tragic brevity of his reign. It is left to the narrator in 2 Kings to apply to both Shallum and Coniah the usual royal epitaph: "he did what was evil in the sight of the Lord, according to all that his father[s] had done" (2 Kings 23:32; 24:9). This is not a comment on their personal conduct. It only states that they did nothing to eliminate from Judah that continuing cancer of religious compromise and apostasy which sealed the fate of the nation. It is hard to see what Coniah could have done in the few brief months at his disposal.

If we turn to the end of the Book of Jeremiah, and the passage in 2 Kings 25:27ff. on which it draws, we find a rather different picture. It is some 50 years later; Jehoiachin is still in exile in Babylon, but he has been released from prison and is being treated with due courtesy and consideration. Perhaps this picture is intended to convey to the reader a glimmer of hope for the future; hope centred among the exiles in Babylon. As often in human experience the harsh verdict of the moment sometimes needs to be modified with the passing years. Certainly in the case of Jeremiah, as we shall see in the following chapter, and in particular in chapters 30-33, present judgement and hope for the future lie side by side in his message. Judgement without hope is merely soul-destroying: hope without judgement is merely wishful thinking.

A BRIGHTER FUTURE

Jeremiah 23:1-8

[1]"Woe to the shepherds who destroy and scatter the sheep of my pasture!" says the Lord. [2]Therefore thus says the Lord, the God of Israel, concerning the shepherds who care for my people: "You

have scattered my flock, and have driven them away, and you have not attended to them. Behold, I will attend to you for your evil doings, says the Lord. ³Then I will gather the remnant of my flock out of all the countries where I have driven them, and I will bring them back to their fold, and they shall be fruitful and multiply. ⁴I will set shepherds over them who will care for them, and they shall fear no more, nor be dismayed, neither shall any be missing, says the Lord.

⁵"Behold, the days are coming, says the Lord, when I will raise up for David a righteous Branch, and he shall reign as king and deal wisely, and shall execute justice and righteousness in the land. ⁶In his days Judah will be saved, and Israel will dwell securely. And this is the name by which he will be called: 'The Lord is our righteousness.'

⁷"Therefore, behold, the days are coming, says the Lord, when men shall no longer say, 'As the Lord lives who brought up the people of Israel out of the land of Egypt,' ⁸but 'As the Lord lives who brought up and led the descendants of the house of Israel out of the north country and out of all the countries where he had driven them.' Then they shall dwell in their own land."

Here we have a medley of three brief pieces which against the dark background of chapters 21 and 22 sound a note of hope.

The *first* piece (verses 1–4) is about "shepherds", bad and good; "shepherd" being used here, as elsewhere in the book (*eg* 2:8; 3:15), as one of the traditional titles for a king or ruler in the ancient world. The irresponsible rulers whose policies led, or were leading to, national disaster, are described as shepherds whose "shepherding" (RSV "care") has resulted in the scattering and destruction of the flock. Skilfully playing on different meanings of the Hebrew word *paqad*, the passage pronounces judgement upon such shepherds: "you have not *attended* to them . . . I will *attend* to you for your evil doings, says the Lord" (verse 2). The same Hebrew word occurs again in verse 4 in the phrase translated "neither shall any be *missing*". In contrast to such bad shepherds there is God himself, the shepherd who will gather his scattered sheep back into the safety of the fold where they will breed again (verse 3); and there are God-appointed shepherds, true kings who will one day fulfil all the hopes and expectations which surrounded the king; hopes so cruelly dashed by kings like Jehoiakim. If you wish to see a clear statement of such hopes, read Psalm 72. The same shepherd theme is developed at length in Ezekiel 34:1-24 as well. It lies behind the claim that Jesus makes: to be "the good shepherd" (see John 10:11).

The *second* piece (verses 5-6) is introduced by a phrase that occurs at the beginning of many visions of the future in the Old Testament, "Behold, the days are coming..." (cf.16:14). It speaks more directly of the place the royal family of David held in the life of Judah. It focusses upon the hope of a "righteous branch", or better "a true offshoot (cf. Zech.3:8; 6:12). This is the hope of the coming, one day, of a legitimate descendant of the family of David, who will rule ably, guaranteeing to his people peace and security and that right ordering of society summed up in the words "justice" and "righteousness". But the words contain a barbed dig at King Zedekiah, the last king of the independent Judean state. His own name was Mattaniah; the royal name he took, *Zedekiah*, means "Yahweh [the Lord] is my righteousness" or "Yahweh is my vindication". It is a name which expresses a confident faith in God, a faith Zedekiah denied in almost everything he did. If Zedekiah did not live up to the faith and expectations symbolized in his name, one day there would come such a king, a king rightly called "Yahweh is our righteousness" or our "vindication".

The *third* piece (verses 7-8) we have already met with elsewhere in the book at 16:14-15. See the comments in vol. 1, p.135.

There has been much discussion as to whether these three passages, or any of them, come from Jeremiah, or whether they are all later and presuppose that the exile to Babylon has already taken place. In a sense it hardly matters. They all speak of a faith which could not but look forward in hope. This faith was rooted in the past, in the God of the past, "the Lord who brought up the people of Israel out of the land of Egypt" (verse 7), the God who had given the people a king to rule over them. But this God of the past was no more than a pious memory unless he was also the God of the present and the future. Prophets like Jeremiah traced God's presence in judgement in the dark and threatening events of their own day, but they could not stop there. God's final word could never be merely judgement or woe; the future must again bring deliverance and hope. The picture of the Davidic king, who would truly shepherd his flock, could never end in a self-indulgent despot or in a weak vacillating monarch who hardly knew what to believe. There must in God's own time come a true king.

There is an unquenchable optimism in such a faith, an optimism well expressed in Christian terms in the words of a modern hymn:

> He's back in the land of the living,
> 　the man we decided to kill;
> he's standing among us, forgiving
> 　our guilt of Good Friday hill.
> He calls us to share in his rising,
> 　to abandon the grave of our past;
> he offers us present and future,
> 　a world that is open and vast.

The hymn then looks at the destruction, the evil, the hatred, the injustice in the world, yet dares to affirm:

> New life|shall arise from the ashes
> 　of hatred, and all shall be well.

(Frederik Herman Kaan)

A NOTE "CONCERNING THE PROPHETS"

The material in 23:9-40 is an excellent example of the way in which sayings, probably spoken on different occasions, have been gathered together by a later editor because they deal with a common theme. How many of the sayings go back to Jeremiah; how many reflect the views of later editors; how much of the material is poetry, how much of it prose, particularly from verse 23; how are we to account for significant differences between the Hebrew and the Greek texts: these are questions that can be endlessly discussed. However we answer them (the material is used to illustrate a problem which long perplexed people in Israel) the problem came to a head during the ministry of Jeremiah, and was never satisfactorily resolved. How do we know the difference between true and false prophecy (see vol.1,p.27)? If two prophets stand before you confidently saying "Thus says the Lord . . . " and delivering contradictory messages, whom do you believe? If like Jeremiah you are a prophet yourself, convinced that you have the relevant word to speak to the people, yet you find yourself in a minority of one, as other prophets demolish everything you are trying to say, how can you be sure that you have not got it wrong? As we have seen, Jeremiah himself found this a very difficult question to handle (see comment on 20:7ff.in vol.1, pp.161-162). It is no more easy to handle today as different groups within the Church passionately seek to convince us that they, and they alone, have God's answer to the problems of Church and society.

THE MEANING OF ADULTERY

Jeremiah 23:9-15

9Concerning the prophets:
   My heart is broken within me, all my bones shake;
   I am like a drunken man, like a man overcome by wine,
   because of the Lord and because of his holy words.
10For the land is full of adulterers;
       because of the curse the land mourns,
       and the pastures of the wilderness are dried up.
   Their course is evil, and their might is not right.
11"Both prophet and priest are ungodly;
       even in my house I have found their wickedness,
                   says the Lord.
12Therefore their way shall be to them
       like slippery paths in the darkness,
       into which they shall be driven and fall;
   for I will bring evil upon them in the year of their punishment,
                   says the Lord.
13In the prophets of Samaria
       I saw an unsavoury thing:
   they prophesied by Baal
       and led my people Israel astray.

14But in the prophets of Jerusalem I have seen a horrible thing:
   they commit adultery and walk in lies;
      they strengthen the hands of evildoers,
      so that no one turns from his wickedness;
      all of them have become like Sodom to me,
      and its inhabitants like Gomorrah."
15Therefore thus says the Lord of hosts
   concerning the prophets:
        "Behold, I will feed them with wormwood,
        and give them poisoned water to drink;
      for from the prophets of Jerusalem
   ungodliness has gone forth into all the land."

Two originally independent passages, (a) verses 9–12 and (b) verses 13–15, are here placed side by side. Each contains a charge, followed by a statement of coming judgement; each centres on the theme of adultery—"the land is full of adulterers" (verse 10), even the prophets "commit adultery" (verse 14).

(1) The *first* passage begins with one of these typical outbursts in which Jeremiah reveals his own inner feelings (cf.4:19): "my heart is broken within me". This does not mean that Jeremiah is heartbroken or that he is feeling sorry for himself. Rather he is shattered, almost out of his mind—like a man who has had too much to drink—as he struggles to square his belief in a holy God with what he sees going on all around him. The people have compromised their loyalty to the Lord by participating in the worship of the local gods of fertility (for this meaning of "adultery" see the comments on 3:6–11 in vol.1, pp.37–39). If they hoped thereby to guarantee a fertile, flourishing land, they were sadly mistaken. They look out instead upon a landscape parched and withered. Such is the inevitable result of a way of life which can only be characterized as "evil", with people putting their trust in what can only be regarded as "not right" (verse 10).

Into the prophet's troubled thoughts there breaks a word from the Lord, laying the blame for what has happened on the religious leaders, "both prophet and priest" (cf.2:8), who can only be described as godless, since they encourage pagan rites and practices even in the Temple at Jerusalem. It is evident that Josiah's attempt to purify and reform worship in Jerusalem had been short-lived. As the nation sank into an ever-deepening political crisis, it was prepared to opt for any port in a storm. You will find a similar picture drawn in Ezekiel 8. Such is the charge; now the judgement. This is a dark and slippery slope which can only lead to richly deserved tragedy.

(2) The *second* passage (verses 13–15) seeks, like 3:6–10, to burst the bubble of the 'it can't happen to us' mood in Judah, by insisting that what is going on in Jerusalem is worse than what had sealed the fate of the northern kingdom of Israel. The contrast this time is applied to "the prophets". The prophets of Samaria had been guilty of something "unsavoury" or offensive. They had undermined the nation's exclusive religious loyalty to the Lord and thus stood condemned as false prophets (see Deut.13:1–3). But there was a more dangerous, a more insidious stance being taken by the prophets of Jerusalem. They "commit adultery and walk in lies" (verse 14). What does this mean? It could be a charge of apostasy similar to the one hurled at the prophets of Samaria, since it "lies" (literally "the lie") might be another sarcastic way of referring to the god Baal. It is, however, more likely that we should give the word "adultery" in this context a strictly moral meaning.

Central to the true prophetic message as Jeremiah understood it was the call to "turn", *shuv* (for the meaning of this word see vol.1, pp.36–37). But here were prophets from whose message the call to "turn" was conspicuously absent. By the way they themselves lived and by preaching a word devoid of all moral challenge, they ensured that the inhabitants of Jerusalem were no better than the people of Sodom and Gomorrah, the cities which God destroyed (see the story in Gen.19). By default they were responsible for the nation's "ungodliness" (verse 15); they could not therefore be prophets of a God who never ceased to demand righteousness from his people. The messenger of God must reflect in his life and in his message the character of the God in whose name he claims to speak. There were many prophets in Jerusalem saying "Thus says the Lord ... Thus says the Lord", but Jeremiah was convinced their words were empty words, lies, for the same reason that Jesus was to underline in Matthew 7:21-23:

> Not every one who says to me "Lord, Lord," shall enter the kingdom of heaven, but he who does the will of my Father who is in heaven. On that day many will say to me, "Lord, Lord, did we not prophesy in your name, and cast out demons in your name, and do many mighty works in your name?" And then will I declare to them, "I never knew you; depart from me, you evildoers".

That is the charge; and the judgement upon these prophets is spelled out in terms of feeding them with "wormwood" and giving them poisoned water to drink (see the comment on 9:15 in vol.1, p.89).

PROPHETS GOD DID NOT SEND

Jeremiah 23:16-22

16Thus says the Lord of hosts: "Do not listen to the words of the prophets who prophesy to you, filling you with vain hopes; they speak visions of their own minds, not from the mouth of the Lord. 17They say continually to those who despise the word of the Lord, 'It shall be well with you'; and to every one who stubbornly follows his own heart, they say, 'No evil shall come upon you.'"

18For who among them has stood in the council of the Lord
    to perceive and to hear his word,
        or who has given heed to his word and listened?
19Behold, the storm of the Lord!
    Wrath has gone forth, a whirling tempest;
        it will burst upon the head of the wicked.
20The anger of the Lord will not turn back
        until he has executed and accomplished the intents of his mind.
    In the latter days you will understand it clearly.

21"I did not send the prophets, yet they ran;
    I did not speak to them yet they prophesied.

²²But if they had stood in my council,
  then they would have proclaimed my words to my people,
  and they would have turned them from their evil way,
  and from the evil of their doings."

This passage begins by returning to the charge which we have already come across in 6:14 and 8:11, that there are prophets who proclaim to the people a reassuring message, *shalom*, "peace" or "all is well", a message which encourages them to believe "no evil shall come upon you" (verse 17). Where do they get this message?

Not from God, claims Jeremiah; "they speak visions [Hebrew "a vision"] of their own minds". They have their own picture of God firmly embedded in their mind, one that is popular with their audience; that, and nothing else, is the source of their message (see the comment on 14:13ff. in vol.1, p.120). It is a vision that has never caused them an uneasy moment, never led them to that mind-shattering experience to which Jeremiah refers in verse 9. They trot out their happy-go-lucky trivialities because they have never "stood in the council of the Lord" (verse 18).

The word translated "council", *sod*, can refer to any group or gathering or the fellowship which a group provides. The same word is used in 15:17 where Jeremiah protests that he has not kept "company" with merrymakers. The "council of the Lord", however, is the Old Testament counterpart of the assembly of the gods in the surrounding polytheistic cultures; the assembly which, under the chairmanship of a divine president, met from time to time to discuss important issues and to take decisions. Even when Israel affirmed its belief in only one God, it still thought of him as presiding over a heavenly council (see *eg* Ps. 82; Job 1; 1 Kings 22:19ff.). Against this background, the true prophet is thought of as one who has access to what goes on in this divine privy council. To change the metaphor to a lovely Scottish expression, the true prophet is someone who has been 'far ben' with God.

That was where such prophets had never been, or their word

to the wicked would have been different, not one of basking in the sunshine of God's favour, but of being uprooted and destroyed by the whirlwind of God's anger (verses 19–20; these verses occur again at 30:23–24, but they are more appropriate here). Yet most people in Jerusalem, encouraged by such prophets, firmly believed that they were basking in the sunshine of God's favour. It was a view not easily shaken, as Jeremiah discovered to his cost. He had no illusions that there were going to be instant conversions. It would take time: "In the latter days you will understand it clearly" (verse 20). It was only after the destruction of Jerusalem by the Babylonians in 587 B.C. that the truth of what Jeremiah had been been saying firmly sank into the minds of some people; only then were the prophets of *shalom* discredited. Sometimes it takes shock treatment to open our eyes to what God has been trying to say to us for a long time.

The passage ends, verses 21–22, by categorically denying that there is any link between God and such prophets. They may be only too eager to prophesy—"they ran"; compare our expression "to rush into print"—but God did not send them. Otherwise their message would have been different, a challenging and corrective call to "turn" from evil. Let us not be too quick to blame either these prophets or the people who listened to them. There can be few of us who have not been tempted to confuse what we want to hear with the will of God.

LIES, DREAMS AND THE WORD OF GOD

Jeremiah 23:23–32

23"Am I a God at hand, says the Lord, and not a God afar off? 24Can a man hide himself in secret places so that I cannot see him? says the Lord. Do I not fill heaven and earth? says the Lord. 25I have heard what the prophets have said who prophesy lies in my name, saying, 'I have dreamed, I have dreamed!' 26How long shall there be lies in the heart of the prophets who prophesy lies, and who prophesy the deceit of their own heart, 27who think to make my people forget my name by their dreams which they tell one another, even as their fathers forgot my name for Baal? ²⁸Let the prophet who has a dream tell the dream, but let him who has my word speak my word faithfully. What has straw in common with wheat? says the Lord. ²⁹Is not my word like fire, says the Lord, and like a hammer which breaks the rock in pieces? ³⁰Therefore, behold, I am against the prophets, says the Lord, who steal my words from one another. ³¹Behold, I am against the prophets, says the Lord, who use their tongues and say, 'Says the Lord.' ³²Behold, I am against those who prophesy lying dreams, says the Lord, and who tell them and lead my people astray by their lies and their recklessness, when I did not send them or charge them; so they do not profit this people at all, says the Lord."

The opening two verses of this passage may be headed "A God on call?"—with a question mark! They seem to give an answer to the question people sometimes ask: Where is God? Everywhere, claims these verses, both near, "at hand" and "afar off"; a God from whom no-one can ever hide, since he is present in every corner of the universe (see Psalm 139). Perhaps this is meant to be a warning to the false prophets. You may deceive people by your smooth talk, but you will be called to account. There is no place to which you can run to escape from the God in whose name you wrongly claim to speak.

Yet there may be a deeper meaning. The emphasis in verse 23 seems to stress that God is not merely a God close at hand, but a God who is also afar off. Might not this be pointing us to part of the trouble with these prophets? They were on too familiar terms with God. They had God neatly folded up like a handkerchief in their pockets. They had cut God down to their own size, so that their relationship with him was untroubled, far too easy. Here was a God always available at their beck and call! They had lost the sense of the majesty, the greatness of God, everything that is conveyed to us by the word "awe".

Florence Nightingale, during a particularly difficult period in her life, when everything she touched seemed to go wrong, suddenly realised that in her prayers she had been telling God exactly what she expected him to do about it. She wrote in her diary, "I must remember that God is not my private secretary".

Was this part of the problem with these prophets? Were they too sure that they had a hotline to God, a God to whom they could dictate exactly what they expected him to do? Jeremiah's relationship with God was much more troubled, much more costly and therefore more authentic. He had never yielded to the temptation to turn the Lord who filled heaven and earth into his private secretary.

We now turn to look more closely at the message of these prophets and the claims they made for it. The charge here made against them centres on two words, "lies" (verses 25–26,32) and "dreams" (verses 25,27–28), and the words are linked when they are accused of prophesying "lying dreams" (verse 32). Their "lies" or falsehoods consist in the fact that they proclaim a message which is totally out of line with the character of the God in whose name they claim to speak. Such prophets are, therefore, no better than their predecessors who switched their loyalty from the God of Israel to the fertility gods of Canaan. But how do they justify their message? The authority they claim is that the message comes to them through what was traditionally one of the recognized ways in which God spoke to people in Israel and elsewhere; through "dreams"—see, for example, the story of Jacob at Bethel in Genesis 28:10–17. And when prophets had such dreams they shared them with their less fortunate non-dreaming companions (verse 27). What are we to make of this?

(1) No attack is made in this passage on dreams as such; but it does insist that the claim that a message comes through a dream does not guarantee the truth of that message, nor that it comes from God. The contents of dreams may reflect no more than what we would call the subconscious thoughts and desires of the dreamer. Thus the prophets who say "I have dreamed" may be doing no more than proclaiming "the deceit of their own heart" (verse 26); passing off their own thoughts as the word of God. There is no need to assume that when these prophets said, "I have dreamed", they were being anything other than sincere. They were probably recounting what to them had been a

genuine experience. But no particular type of experience, whether it is a dream or a highly emotional conversion experience, can *in itself* guarantee that the experience truly comes from God.

(2) There is nothing wrong in what we find some of these prophets doing—accepting their message from other prophets. That is how we all learn some of the most important things in life, *ie* from other people. We all accept certain things to be true on the basis of other people's experience. We would not go far in life if we did not, most of all in matters of faith. But the fact that other people teach us and claim that certain things are true in their experience, does not prove that they are true. We must be able to take what we learn from others and find out its truth for ourselves in our own experience. Only then do we discover what is "chaff", fit only to be thrown away, and what is "wheat", basic food for daily living, the word of God for us all (verse 28). But how do we know what the true word of God is for us? Two descriptions are given in verse 29 of the authentic word of God; it is "like fire", or as the New English Bible translates, "scorch[ing] like fire", and it is "like a hammer that splinters rock". Both descriptions are talking about what is threatening or challenging. If we find what God is saying to us easy to live with, purely comforting and reassuring, then we ought to be asking ourselves whether this is really God speaking to us, the God of the prophets, the God whose love led to a cross; or merely a god we want.

THE "LOAD" OF THE LORD

Jeremiah 23:33-40

33"When one of this people, or a prophet, or a priest asks you, 'What is the burden of the Lord?' you shall say to them, 'You are the burden, and I will cast you off, says the Lord.' 34And as for the prophet, priest, or one of the people who says, 'The burden of the Lord,' I will punish that man and his household. 35Thus shall you say, every one to his neighbour and every one to his brother, 'What has the Lord answered?' or 'What has the Lord spoken?' 36But 'the burden of the Lord' you shall mention no more, for the burden is every man's own word, and you pervert the words of the living God, the Lord of hosts, our God. 37Thus you shall say to the prophet, 'What has the Lord answered you?' or 'What has the Lord spoken?' 38But if you say, 'The burden of the Lord,' thus says the Lord, 'Because you have said these words, "The burden of the Lord," when I sent to you, saying, "You shall not say, 'The burden of the Lord,'" 39therefore, behold, I will surely lift you up and cast you away from my presence, you and the city which I gave to you and your fathers. 40And I will bring upon you everlasting reproach and perpetual shame, which shall not be forgotten.'"

You may have found this passage somewhat complicated to read. The trouble is that it is based upon a play on different meanings of the Hebrew word *massa*. It means literally "a load", something that you are forced to carry, or metaphorically it can mean a heavy responsibility. But it is also used for the "message" of a prophet, the message for which he is responsible to God. So in verse 33 the people who ask what is the message of the Lord, are bluntly told "you are"—you are "the load" which the Lord has to carry. And as for the prophets and other religious practitioners who piously proclaim the "message" of the Lord (a 'loaded' message if ever there was one!), they are going to be "unloaded" by the Lord—in verse 39, the words "I will surely lift you up" translate a verb which echoes the word *massa*.

The whole passage is a challenge, both to the people and the prophets, to take their responsibilities with the utmost seriousness or else face the consequences. It asks them—and us—to stop trotting out religious clichés and pious words that mean nothing. Yes, we should be asking, "What has the Lord to say to us today?", but the answers will not necessarily come from those who seem to use all the correct holy words; and those who find themselves naturally using such words should never forget the serious responsibility they carry.

G. WORDS OF HOPE AND JUDGEMENT (CHS. 24-25)

GOOD AND BAD FIGS

Jeremiah 24:1-10

[1]After Nebuchadrezzar king of Babylon had taken into exile from Jerusalem Jeconiah the son of Jehoiakim, king of Judah, together with the princes of Judah, the craftsmen, and the smiths, and had brought them to Babylon, the Lord showed me this vision: Behold, two baskets of figs placed before the temple of the Lord. [2]One basket had very good figs, like first-ripe figs, but the other basket had very bad figs, so bad that they could not be eaten. [3]And the Lord said to me, "What do you see, Jeremiah?" I said, "Figs, the good figs very good, and the bad figs very bad, so bad that they cannot be eaten."

[4]Then the word of the Lord came to me: [5]"Thus says the Lord, the God of Israel: Like these good figs, so I will regard as good the exiles from Judah, whom I have sent away from this place to the land of the Chaldeans. [6]I will set my eyes upon them for good, and I will bring them back to this land. I will build them up, and not tear them down; I will plant them, and not uproot them. [7]I will give them a heart to know that I am the Lord; and they shall be my people and I will be their God, for they shall return to me with their whole heart.

[8]"But thus says the Lord: Like the bad figs which are so bad they cannot be eaten, so will I treat Zedekiah the king of Judah, his princes, the remnant of Jerusalem who remain in this land, and those who dwell in the land of Egypt. [9]I will make them a horror to all the kingdoms of the earth, to be a reproach, a byword, a taunt, and a curse in all the places where I shall drive them. [10]And I will send sword, famine, and pestilence upon them, until they shall be utterly destroyed from the land which I gave to them and their fathers."

In the year 597 B.C., after a brief siege, King Jehoiachin surrendered the city of Jerusalem to the Babylonians (see the narrative in 2 Kings 24:8-17). The royal family, the cream of Jerusalemite society, and many of the skilled and able-bodied citizens, were deported to Babylon. A Babylonian puppet regime was established in Jerusalem, headed by Jehoiachin's uncle Zedekiah. Those who remained in Jerusalem seem to have regarded the deportees with mingled pity and scorn. After all, to be still in Jerusalem was to be in the city of God, to have access to the means of grace in the Temple and to be assured of God's continuing protection and favour. They had lost nothing essential to their faith; the exiles had lost everything. This passage presents us with a different verdict. In many ways it is similar to the "visions" we studied in 1:11-16 (see comment in vol. 1, pp. 15-18).

(1) It centres upon a common, everyday object that anyone might have seen; in this case two baskets of figs, probably brought by worshippers to the Temple as their gifts of first fruits (see Deut.26:5-11). The one basket is filled with choice, early ripening figs; the other basket is filled with poor quality figs hardly fit for human consumption. If this second basket contained first fruits offered to the Lord, then either the family from which they came was suffering from a bad harvest or it was palming off shoddy produce on God (verses 1-2).

(2) The baskets of figs trigger off a question in Jeremiah's mind: "What do you see, Jeremiah?" (verse 3).

(3) The prophet's reply, "Figs, the good figs very good, and the bad figs very bad", leads into an explanation of the meaning of the vision (verses 4ff.).

The good figs are identified with those people exiled to Babylon (verse 5), the bad figs with those who stayed in Jerusalem or in the surrounding countryside, or whose anti-Babylonian views had led them to seek refuge in Egypt (verses 8-10). This is not a verdict on the moral character or on the integrity of these different groups of people. It is a verdict on their current fate. It is a clear statement that the future under God lies not with those who remain in Jerusalem, congratulating themselves that they still have all their traditional privileges and still bask in God's favour. The future lies with the despised exiles, stripped of much that they had previously regarded as essential to their faith, thrown out into a cold, cruel world. Out there God is still with them, his purposes constructive; out there they will learn the lesson of tragedy, come to a true repentance and once again discover that they are God's people.

It was a lesson which Jeremiah repeatedly pressed home upon his people. In chapter 29 we shall find a letter Jeremiah wrote to the exiles making the same point. Often what we are tempted to regard as loss turns out to be gain. Sometimes the things we regard as essential to our faith, and fight desperately to retain—patterns of worship and congregational life—may, and indeed sometimes must, be taken from us if we are to rediscover the meaning of discipleship.

LOOKING BACK AND LOOKING FORWARD

Jeremiah 25:1-14

¹The word that came to Jeremiah concerning all the people of Judah, in the fourth year of Jehoiakim the son of Josiah, king of Judah (that was the first year of Nebuchadrezzar king of Babylon), ²which Jeremiah the prophet spoke to all the people of Judah and all the inhabitants of Jerusalem: ³"For twenty-three years, from the thirteenth year of Josiah the son of Amon, king of Judah, to this day, the word of the Lord has come to me, and I have spoken persistently to you, but you have not listened. ⁴You have neither listened nor inclined your ears to hear, although the Lord persistently sent to you all his servants the prophets, ⁵saying, 'Turn now, every one of you, from his evil way and wrong doings, and dwell upon the land which the Lord has given to you and your fathers from of old and for ever; ⁶do not go after other gods to serve and worship them, or provoke me to anger with the work of your hands. Then I will do you no harm'. ⁷Yet you have not listened to me, says the Lord, that you might provoke me to anger with the work of your hands to your own harm.

⁸"Therefore thus says the Lord of hosts: Because you have not obeyed my words, ⁹behold, I will send for all the tribes of the north, says the Lord, and for Nebuchadrezzar the king of Babylon, my servant, and I will bring them against this land and its inhabitants, and against all these nations round about; I will utterly destroy

them, and make them a horror, a hissing, and an everlasting reproach. [10]Moreover, I will banish from them the voice of mirth and the voice of gladness, the voice of the bridegroom and the voice of the bride, the grinding of the millstones and the light of the lamp. [11]This whole land shall become a ruin and a waste, and these nations shall serve the king of Babylon seventy years. [12]Then after seventy years are completed, I will punish the king of Babylon and that nation, the land of the Chaldeans, for their iniquity, says the Lord, making the land an everlasting waste. [13]I will bring upon that land all the words which I have uttered against it, everything written in this book, which Jeremiah prophesied against all the nations. [14]For many nations and great kings shall make slaves even of them; and I will recompense them according to their deeds and the work of their hands."

The Puzzle of the Book

Chapter 25:1–14 is a key passage for any conclusions we wish to reach about the Book of Jeremiah in its present form. It is one of the passages in which there is a considerable difference between the Hebrew text, translated in our English versions of the Bible, and the much shorter Greek (*Septuagint*) text. For example, the Greek text omits all the references to Nebuchadrezzar, the king of Babylon (in verses 1,9,11–12) and to the Chaldeans (*ie* the Babylonians) in verse 12. It then concludes verse 13 at the words "everything written in this book", and immediately follows this with the "oracles against the nations" which we find in chapters 46–51 in our English Bibles, although it gives these in a different order. How much of the passage, and in what form, goes back to Jeremiah, we do not know. Views have ranged all the way from those who regard the whole passage as a sermon written by later Deuteronomic editors (see Introduction, p.4) to those who, often with considerable hesitation, seek to unscramble the authentic words of Jeremiah within it. We can in this commentary only take it as it comes to us. The truth or otherwise of what it has to say hardly depends on it coming from Jeremiah.

Looking Back in Sorrow (verses 1-7)

This section looks back across the career of Jeremiah, and indeed across the witness of the prophets of Israel as a whole, those prophets who stood in the tradition of "his servants the prophets" (cf. 7:25), whom the Lord persistently sent to his people. It comes to the sad conclusion that this is a ministry that failed; the story of a people who repeatedly ignored the Lord's warnings and were deaf to the call to repent. Instead, by what they did, by their worship of other gods, they provoked the Lord's anger and sealed their own fate.

This, and many other passages, ought to destroy any romantic illusions we may have about the Bible. Sometimes people look back longingly and say, "If only we had been there when God spoke so clearly to the people of Israel, or if only we had been there when Jesus was teaching in Galilee, how much easier faith would have been!" Would it? It was not easier in ancient Israel; and how many of the people who met Jesus saw in him anything unusual or anything that made them say, "here is God in our midst". Israel was a living example of the truth that "there's none so blind as those who will not see". Israel's experience—and ours—is often a story of tragic blindness, as prophets in every age have found out to their frustration and their cost.

Looking Forward to Judgement—and Beyond (verses 8-14)

We may believe confidently that God's purposes will be fulfilled, but often be uncertain as to exactly how: then something happens, we look at it and say "that's it". In some of his early preaching, Jeremiah spoke about God's judgement coming upon his people in the form of a mysterious and threatening foe from the north (see 4:5ff. and comments in vol. 1, pp.45-48). As his ministry progressed, it became ever more clear that the threat to the very existence of Judah was coming from the neo-Babylonian empire. Here the foe from the north is clearly identified with Nebuchadrezzar, king of Babylon (verses 1,9,11-12), and it was the Babylonians who sacked Jerusalem in

587 B.C. and left behind a stunned and devastated land (verse 10). But was this not just a case of Satan casting out Satan? The Babylonians were little more than another ruthless military machine, pursuing their own imperialistic ambitions and trampling underfoot anyone who stood in their way.

The prophet Habakkuk, after describing the Babylonians as being like a fisherman trawling the nations into his net, asks the poignant question;

> Is he then to keep on emptying his net,
>   and mercilessly slaying nations for ever?

(Hab.1:17)

So this passage insists that Nebuchadrezzar is no more than "my servant" (verse 9), the agent God uses to bring judgement upon his people; but an agent who equally stands under God's judgement and who himself will be called to account for what he does, if not immediately, nevertheless certainly: "after seventy years are completed" (verse 12), 70 years being the normal life span and probably being used here as a good round number for an indefinite period of time. In fact, within 50 years of the destruction of Jerusalem, the Babylonian Empire had collapsed and another prophet was to hail Cyrus of Persia as God's agent, making possible the return of exiled Jews and the rebuilding of Jerusalem (see Isa. 44:28–45:1). The prophets of the Old Testament never retreat into their own private world of spirituality: they claim the whole world for God and believe that all nations, whether they know it or not, serve God's purposes and stand under the judgement of God. We shall return to this when we look at the oracles against the nations in chapters 46–51.

THE POTENT BREW OF GOD'S JUDGEMENT

Jeremiah 25:15–29

15Thus the Lord, the God of Israel, said to me: "Take from my hand this cup of the wine of wrath, and make all the nations to whom I

send you drink it. [16]They shall drink and stagger and be crazed because of the sword which I am sending among them."

[17]So I took the cup from the Lord's hand, and made all the nations to whom the Lord sent me drink it: [18]Jerusalem and the cities of Judah, its kings and princes, to make them a desolation and a waste, a hissing and a curse, as at this day; [19]Pharaoh king of Egypt, his servants, his princes, all his people, [20]and all the foreign folk among them; all the kings of the land of Uz and all the kings of the land of the Philistines (Ashkelon, Gaza, Ekron, and the remnant of Ashdod); [21]Edom, Moab, and the sons of Ammon; [22]all the kings of Tyre, all the kings of Sidon, and the kings of the coastland across the sea; [23]Dedan, Tema, Buz, and all who cut the corners of their hair; [24]all the kings of Arabia and all the kings of the mixed tribes that dwell in the desert; [25]all the kings of Zimri, all the kings of Elam, and all the kings of Media; [26]all the kings of the north, far and near, one after another, and all the kingdoms of the world which are on the face of the earth. And after them the king of Babylon shall drink.

[27]"Then you shall say to them, 'Thus says the Lord of hosts, the God of Israel: Drink, be drunk and vomit, fall and rise no more, because of the sword which I am sending among you.'

[28]"And if they refuse to accept the cup from your hand to drink, then you shall say to them, 'Thus says the Lord of hosts: You must drink! [29]For behold, I begin to work evil at the city which is called by my name, and shall you go unpunished? You shall not go unpunished, for I am summoning a sword against all the inhabitants of the earth, says the Lord of hosts.'"

The word that the Lord speaks to the prophet here centres upon "the cup of the wine of wrath", a cup from which not only Jerusalem and the cities of Judah must drink, but also all the other nations that made up the world known to Israel. The list in verses 19–26 covers most of the nations immediately surrounding Israel, from Egypt up the coastal plain to include the major Philistine cities, on to the people who occupied what is now the coast of Lebanon (Tyre and Sidon), across to the peoples who were Israel's eastern Transjordanian neighbours (Edom, Moab and Ammon), down to the desert peoples of the northern Arabian peninsula (Deda, Teman, Buz). It also includes nations much further to the east (Elam, Media and Babylon). Only Damascus of the nations mentioned in the oracles against the nations in chapters 46–51 is missing.

But what is this "cup of the wine" of the anger of the Lord, which is to make all these peoples drunk and incapable? It is a symbol of judgement that begins to feature frequently in prophecy round about the time of Jeremiah and later (*eg* Hab.2:16; Lam.4:21; Isa.51:17–23). It is often thought that the origin of the idea is to be found in the custom, well-known in Israel and among many peoples, of "trial by ordeal", in which someone under suspicion proves his innocence or guilt by drinking from a poisoned cup. You will see an example of this in Numbers 5:11ff. in the case of a woman whom her husband suspects of committing adultery. The disastrous effect of the nations drinking from this cup—they "fall and rise no more" (verse 27)—is therefore proof of the guilt of the nations in the eyes of God.

But there is another possibility. In Psalm 116 the worshipper, who has had a dramatic demonstration of the goodness of God in a situation of grave crisis in his life, brings to the Lord as part of his thanksgiving, "the cup of salvation" (Ps.116:13). Now we know that prophets often took what other people regarded as symbols of salvation and stood them on their head until they became symbols of judgement (see, for example, what Amos does to all the popular hopes that centred on the thought of a coming "day of the Lord" in chapter 5:18–20). So "the cup of salvation" becomes for a guilty people, "the cup of the wine" of the Lord's wrath. Paul was to do the same with the bread and wine of the Lord's supper, warning the Christians at Corinth that in certain circumstances when they eat the bread and drink from the cup, they are bringing judgement upon themselves (1 Cor.11:27–29). The God who loves is the God who judges; and only those who confuse God's love with a sloppy sentimentality are blind to this.

ON TRIAL—GUILTY AND CONDEMNED

Jeremiah 25:30-38

³⁰"You, therefore, shall prophesy against them all these words, and
say to them:
  'The Lord will roar from on high,
    and from his holy habitation utter his voice;
  he will roar mightily against his fold,
    and shout, like those who tread grapes,
    against all the inhabitants of the earth.
³¹The clamour will resound to the ends of the earth,
    for the Lord has an indictment against the nations;
  he is entering into judgment with all flesh,
    and the wicked he will put to the sword,
                      says the Lord.'

³²"Thus says the Lord of hosts:
  Behold, evil is going forth from nation to nation,
  and a great tempest is stirring
    from the farthest parts of the earth!
³³"And those slain by the Lord on that day shall extend from one
end of the earth to the other. They shall not be lamented, or
gathered, or buried; they shall be as dung on the surface of the
ground.
³⁴"Wail, you shepherds, and cry,
  and roll in ashes, you lords of the flock,
for the days of your slaughter and dispersion have come,
  and you shall fall like choice rams.
³⁵No refuge will remain for the shepherds,
  nor escape for the lords of the flock.
³⁶Hark, the cry of the shepherds,
  and the wail of the lords of the flock!
For the Lord is despoiling their pasture,
³⁷and the peaceful folds are devastated,
  because of the fierce anger of the Lord.
³⁸Like a lion he has left his covert,
  for their land has become a waste
    because of the sword of the oppressor.
  and because of his fierce anger."

The same message is now hammered home using a picture that we find frequently in Jeremiah and other prophets; that of a trial scene [(see comments in vol 1, pp.15 ff.). The Lord brings a case against the nations and, after due process of law, condemns the wicked to death (verse 31). It is one of those passages which by this time as you study the Book of Jeremiah you may be tempted to glance at quickly and say, "not again, haven't we heard this all before?" True, but it is worth looking at it a little more closely, if only to notice something which is typical of Hebrew poetry and of much of the language of the Bible; namely the way in which it jumps quickly from picture to picture, using each one to make one point. So at one moment the Lord is compared to a roaring lion, the next he is like a man treading grapes, shouting as he works; both pictures indicating that what God is about to say and do is going to come through loud and clear—as the Good News Bible translates at the end of verse 30 and the beginning of verse 31:

> Everyone on earth will hear him,
>   and the sound will echo to the ends of the earth.

The picture of God as a lion then reappears in verse 38 to make a different point: "like a lion he has left his covert" to stalk his prey with deadly effect. Likewise "the shepherds", "the lords of the flocks" in verses 34–36 are the rulers of the nations (see comment on 3:15).

It is very unwise, and indeed dangerous, to pick up the words "lion" and "shepherds" from this passage and read into them everything we want to say about lions or shepherds or indeed everything said about them elsewhere in the Bible. The Bible is a rich tapestry of pictures, but each must be seen in its context and each takes its meaning from its context.

H. A MARKED MAN (CHS. 26–29)

We have already looked at passages which show us very clearly the extent to which Jeremiah felt himself to be at odds with the religious establishment of his day. Now in chapters 26-29 we see the same issues dramatically illustrated in a series of incidents from Jeremiah's life, incidents recorded for us by a biographer, probably his secretary, Baruch. No longer are we listening to what Jeremiah has to say about "the prophets"; we now see him involved in a showdown at the Temple with one of them, Hananiah, a prophet from Gibeon (ch. 28), and using the diplomatic service to send a letter to the exiles in Babylon to counteract the advice being given to them by other prophets (ch. 29). A host of characters flit in and out of these chapters. Many of them must be turning in their grave at the thought that they are now remembered only because their paths crossed that of a man whom they dismissed as a traitor and a heretic. No doubt Pontius Pilate is equally surprised to find himself remembered as the man in whose governorship in Judah Jesus was crucified.

THAT UNPOPULAR SERMON AGAIN

Jeremiah 26:1-16

¹In the beginning of the reign of Jehoiakim the son of Josiah, king of Judah, this word came from the Lord, ²"Thus says the Lord: Stand in the court of the Lord's house, and speak to all the cities of Judah which come to worship in the house of the Lord all the words that I command you to speak to them; do not hold back a word. ³It may be they will listen, and every one turn from his evil way, that I may repent of the evil which I intend to do to them because of their evil doings. ⁴You shall say to them, 'Thus says the Lord: If you will not listen to me, to walk in my law which I have set before you, ⁵and to heed the words of my servants the prophets whom I send to you urgently, though you have not heeded, ⁶then I will make this house like Shiloh, and I will make this city a curse for all the nations of the earth.'"

⁷The priests and the prophets and all the people heard Jeremiah speaking these words in the house of the Lord. ⁸And when Jeremiah had finished speaking all that the Lord had commanded him to speak to all the people, then the priests and the prophets and all the people laid hold of him, saying, "You shall die! ⁹Why have you prophesied in the name of the Lord, saying, 'This house shall be like Shiloh, and this city shall be desolate, without inhabitant'?" And all the people gathered about Jeremiah in the house of the Lord.

¹⁰When the princes of Judah heard these things, they came up from the king's house to the house of the Lord and took their seat in the entry of the New Gate of the house of the Lord. ¹¹Then the priests and the prophets said to the princes and to all the people, "This man deserves the sentence of death, because he has prophesied against this city, as you have heard with your own ears."

¹²Then Jeremiah spoke to all the princes and all the people, saying, "The Lord sent me to prophesy against this house and this city all the words you have heard. ¹³Now therefore amend your ways and your doings, and obey the voice of the Lord your God, and the Lord will repent of the evil which he has pronounced against you. ¹⁴But as for me, behold, I am in your hands. Do with me as seems good and right to you. ¹⁵Only know for certain that if you put me to death, you will bring innocent blood upon yourselves and upon this city and its inhabitants, for in truth the Lord sent me to you to speak all these words in your ears."

¹⁶Then the princes and all the people said to the priests and the prophets, "This man does not deserve the sentence of death, for he has spoken to us in the name of the Lord our God."

In chapter 7:1-15 we had an account of an unpopular sermon which Jeremiah delivered at the Temple in Jerusalem (see comments in vol.1, pp.70-74). Chapter 26:1 gives the date of the sermon as "the beginning of the reign of Jehoiakim". This is a technical expression for the period between the accession of Jehoiakim in the autumn of 609 B.C. and the beginning of the new year in 608 B.C. There are many subtle points of difference between the two accounts, but the major difference is that this account switches attention from the content of the sermon to the reaction it provoked. To proclaim at the entrance to the Temple the destruction of temple and city was to invite a violent reaction. It came. Mob violence, instigated by the religious establishment of "priests and prophets" (verse 7), almost led to a lynching party. "You shall die!" they shouted at him, "Why have you prophesied in the name of the Lord, saying 'This house shall be like Shiloh, and this city shall be desolate, without inhabitant'?" (verse 9). They were not really asking "why?"; they were not interested in an answer. They had already made up their minds that Jeremiah was a public menace who had to be liquidated.

It is not an uncommon attitude, particularly in religious controversies. We come across people who hold what we regard as outrageous views. We ask them "why?", but we are not really interested in their answer. We already know that they are wrong and nothing is going to convince us otherwise. The closed mind is nowhere more evident than in religious circles, and in particular among those who most loudly protest that they are the followers of Him who is the truth. We are often afraid to listen to the truth.

But the reaction to Jeremiah's sermon was not unanimous. Jeremiah was saved from the lynching party by the intervention of "the princes" (verse 10), the court officers or the civil authorities who, having heard the riot, intervened to ensure a fair trial at the New Gate, where formal proceedings are instituted. Priests and prophets lead for the prosecution and demand the death penalty for what they clearly regard as false prophecy (see Deut.18:20). They concentrate upon his anti-Jerusalem sentiments, but carefully avoid any reference to the call to repentance which had been an essential element in his sermon (verse 11). Quoting out of context, or partially quoting, has been the stock-in-trade of religious and political demagogues in every age.

In his defence (verses 12–15) Jeremiah makes no attempt to deny what he said, but claims the authority of the Lord for saying it. He then submits himself to the jurisdiction of the court, with the warning that they are in danger of condemning an innocent man. The court acquits him, acknowledging his claim to be a genuine prophet (verse 16). It is a fascinating story.

At its centre, one man; around him various groups each with their own vested interests—the religious establishment out to silence a troublesome prophet, the civil authorities seeking to preserve law and order, the mob, fickle as always, one minute howling for blood, the next (see verse 16) defending the decision to acquit him. It is a story that was to be replayed in the experience of another man and the varying attitudes of others to him in the events that led to the crucifixion (see Mark chs. 14-15).

THREE PROPHETS—THREE RESPONSES

Jeremiah 26:17-24

¹⁷And certain of the elders of the land arose and spoke to all the assembled people, saying, ¹⁸"Micah of Moresheth prophesied in the days of Hezekiah king of Judah, and said to all the people of Judah: 'Thus says the Lord of hosts,

Zion shall be ploughed as a field;

Jerusalem shall become a heap of ruins,

and the mountain of the house a wooded height.'

¹⁹Did Hezekiah king of Judah and all Judah put him to death? Did he not fear the Lord and entreat the favour of the Lord, and did not the Lord repent of the evil which he had pronounced against them? But we are about to bring great evil upon ourselves."

²⁰There was another man who prophesied in the name of the Lord, Uriah the son of Shemaiah from Kiriath-jearim. He prophesied against this city and against this land in words like those of Jeremiah. ²¹And when King Jehoiakim, with all his warriors and all the princes, heard his words, the king sought to put him to death; but when Uriah heard of it, he was afraid and fled and escaped to Egypt. ²²Then King Jehoiakim sent to Egypt certain men, Elnathan the son of Achbor and others with him, ²³and they fetched Uriah from Egypt and brought him to King Jehoiakim, who slew him with the sword and cast his dead body into the burial place of the common people.

²⁴But the hand of Ahikam the son of Shaphan was with Jeremiah so that he was not given over to the people to be put to death.

As Jeremiah discovered to his cost, to be a prophet of the Lord was to be in the risk business, with no guarantee of success and no way of knowing what the audience reaction was going to be. Three different reactions are now illustrated.

(1) To justify the verdict of acquittal, some of the elders cite the case of Micah of Moresheth (verses 17–19), who was a contemporary of Isaiah some hundred years before Jeremiah. His message had in certain respects been just as stern and uncompromising as Jeremiah's—and Micah 3:12 is quoted in verse 18 to back this up. But no-one attempted to silence him. Indeed the response of the authorities, represented by King Hezekiah, was quite the opposite. It is a measure of how tantalizingly little we know of the history of the people of Israel, that the accounts of the reign of Hezekiah which we have in 2 Kings 18–20 and 2 Chronicles 29–32 are hard to reconcile. Although both accounts describe Hezekiah as a reforming king, neither attributes his reforms to the influence of prophets nor makes any mention of Micah. But Micah is here presented as a prophet whose harsh words about temple and city were heeded; and because they evoked a positive response, his message of coming disaster was averted. The Lord "repented of the evil" (verse 19), *ie* changed his mind. (For the way in which God's attitude to the people is thought to be dependent upon the people's response to him, see vol.1, pp.70–74).

(2) Another prophet Uriah, the son of Shemaiah, from Kiriath-jearim (some eight miles north-west of Jerusalem), was not so fortunate (verses 20–23). Nothing is known of Uriah apart from these verses. The incident recalled here has nothing to do with the Temple sermon. It probably took place somewhat later in the reign of Jehoiakim. After declaring the same prophetic home-truths as Jeremiah, Uriah fled to Egypt, from where he was extradited: extradition clauses are not uncommon in ancient Near Eastern treaty documents. He received summary justice and was publicly executed in Jerusalem. Elnathan, the son of Achbor, who is here mentioned as heading the extradition party (verse 22) appears in chapter 36 as one of the court officials who are sympathetic to Jeremiah,

warning him to go into hiding and urging the king not to destroy the scroll Jeremiah had dictated to Baruch (36:11-19,25). From the little we know of him, he seems, like many other politicians, prepared to follow his conscience in arguing a case and, indeed, in taking an unpopular line while an issue is still under discussion, but once authority has decided, he falls into line. He is the stuff of which excellent civil servants are made, but not martyrs. It takes a prophet unflinchingly and consistently to oppose a king, and the consequences for a prophet may be fatal.

(3) Why then did Jeremiah not suffer the same fate as Uriah at the hands of King Jehoiakim? He had friends in high places, in particular the family of Shaphan, one of whose sons, Ahikam, used his influence to protect him (verse 24). He may have been an influential voice in securing the verdict of acquittal, or he may have taken steps to ensure Jeremiah's personal safety after the verdict. Other members of the same family equally lent Jeremiah support in situations of personal difficulty (see 36:11ff.; 39:14; 40:5ff.).

So Jeremiah survived; neither heeded like Micah, nor martyred like Uriah—he survived to be ignored (a fate which has befallen many a prophetic figure), ignored until it was too late and the policies against which he had protested in vain had led to national disaster.

AN UNPOPULAR POLITICAL STANCE

Jeremiah 27:1-15

[1]In the beginning of the reign of Zedekiah the son of Josiah, king of Judah, this word came to Jeremiah from the Lord. [2]Thus the Lord said to me; "Make yourself thongs and yoke-bars, and put them on your neck. [3]Send word to the king of Edom, the king of Moab, the king of the sons of Ammon, the King of Tyre, and the king of Sidon by the hand of the envoys who have come to Jerusalem to Zedekiah king of Judah. [4]Give them this charge for their masters: 'Thus says

the Lord of hosts, the God of Israel: This is what you shall say to your masters: ⁵"It is I who by my great power and my outstretched arm have made the earth, with the men and animals that are on the earth, and I give it to whomever it seems right to me. ⁶Now I have given all these lands into the hand of Nebuchadrezzar, the king of Babylon, my servant, and I have given him also the beasts of the field to serve him. ⁷All the nations shall serve him and his son and his grandson, until the time of his own land comes; then many nations and great kings shall make him their slave.

⁸"'But if any nation or kingdom will not serve this Nebuchadrezzar king of Babylon, and put its neck under the yoke of the king of Babylon, I will punish that nation with the sword, with famine, and with pestilence, says the Lord, until I have consumed it by his hand. ⁹So do not listen to your prophets, your diviners, your dreamers, your soothsayers, or your sorcerers, who are saying to you, 'You shall not serve the king of Babylon.' ¹⁰For it is a lie which they are prophesying to you, with the result that you will be removed far from your land, and I will drive you out, and you will perish. ¹¹But any nation which will bring its neck under the yoke of the king of Babylon and serve him, I will leave on its own land, to till it and dwell there, says the Lord.'"

¹²To Zedekiah king of Judah I spoke in like manner: "Bring your necks under the yoke of the king of Babylon, and serve him and his people, and live. ¹³Why will you and your people die by the sword, by famine, and by pestilence, as the Lord has spoken concerning any nation which will not serve the king of Babylon? ¹⁴Do not listen to the words of your prophets who are saying to you, 'You shall not serve the king of Babylon,' for it is a lie which they are prophesying to you. ¹⁵I have not sent them, says the Lord, but they are prophesying falsely in my name, with the result that I will drive you out and you will perish, you and the prophets who are prophesying to you."

It is the year 594 B.C.; "the beginning of the reign of Zedekiah", to follow what must be the correct reading in verse 1 (many Hebrew manuscripts have Jehoiakim). Babylonian documents confirm that in the two previous years Nebuchadrezzar had to deal both with external enemies and with an attempted internal revolution. No wonder the small vassal states in the western Babylonian Empire thought that now was an appropriate time to make a bid for independence. Jerusalem was at the centre of a network of intrigue. Envoys came from several of the adjacent countries to consult with Zedekiah. The patriotic ticket in Jerusalem was no doubt firmly convinced that there would never be a more favourable time to throw off the yoke of Babylon.

Not so Jeremiah. At the Lord's command he takes a yoke, which would normally be attached to the neck of an ox by leather thongs, and ties it round his own neck. This is a typical example of a prophet using a "symbolic act" (see the comment on chapter 13 in vol.1, p.111). With dramatic simplicity it communicates and confirms what the prophet wishes to say. The yoke symbolizes the power of Babylon. Nebuchadrezzar, king of Babylon, is the agent of the Lord. The God who created the world and controls all that happens in it, has decreed that all nations must, for the present, submit to the Babylonians (verses 5-7). Never mind, claims Jeremiah, what is being said by the normal religious channels, be they prophets or anyone else who professes to foresee or to control the future; the choice God puts before you is simple. Revolt and you will be crushed by the Babylonians; remain loyal vassals of Babylon and you will enjoy security (verses 8-11).

That was the message Jeremiah told the envoys to take home with them. He then repeated it to King Zedekiah (verses 12-15), with a warning not to pay any attention to the prophets who were encouraging revolt. The Lord did not send them; they are lying (see comment on 14:15, vol.1, p.120).

Jeremiah's attitude in this situation would hardly increase his popularity. The appeal of freedom and patriotism has always been emotionally powerful, not least when it is backed by the religious establishment. Those who oppose it are liable to be dismissed as defeatist or hounded as traitors. It is a curious fact that, right down to the present day, no government ever objects to a Church which makes pronouncements which support government policies. But let voices be raised from within the Church challenging and criticizing the policies of the government, then this is attacked as illegitimate interference in politics. Like most of the great prophetic figures in the Old Testament, Jeremiah had no hesitation in interfering in the politics of his day. His sole justification—and he needed no other—was "Thus says the Lord . . . ".

MORE OF THE SAME

Jeremiah 27:16-22

16Then I spoke to the priests and to all this people, saying, "Thus says the Lord: Do not listen to the words of your prophets who are prophesying to you, saying, 'Behold, the vessels of the Lord's house will now shortly be brought back from Babylon,' for it is a lie which they are prophesying to you. 17Do not listen to them; serve the king of Babylon and live. Why should this city become a desolation? 18If they are prophets, and if the word of the Lord is with them, then let them intercede with the Lord of hosts, that the vessels which are left in the house of the Lord, in the house of the king of Judah, and in Jerusalem may not go to Babylon. 19For thus says the Lord of hosts concerning the pillars, the sea, the stands, and the rest of the vessels which are left in this city, 20which Nebuchadnezzar king of Babylon did not take away, when he took into exile from Jerusalem to Babylon Jeconiah the son of Jehoiakim, king of Judah, and all the nobles of Judah and Jerusalem—21thus says the Lord of hosts, the God of Israel, concerning the vessels which are left in the house of the Lord, in the house of the king of Judah, and in Jerusalem: 22They shall be carried to Babylon and remain there until the day when I give attention to them, says the Lord. Then I will bring them back and restore them to this place."

In a similar vein, Jeremiah now appeals to priests and people not to be misled by prophets who were confidently proclaiming that the furnishings, removed from the Temple and taken to Babylon in 597 B.C., would soon be returned. He regarded such a message, which must have had a large element of popular appeal in it, as a dangerous illusion which could only lead to further disaster. The same basic issue is to be portrayed powerfully and dramatically in the next two chapters, but before we turn to them it is perhaps worth pausing for a moment to look at another question raised by these verses, because it is a good example of the way in which the questions with which scholars wrestle are often questions that we all face and handle in our own way.

This passage is interesting because it is one of the places in the Book of Jeremiah where the Greek text is much shorter than the Hebrew text upon which our English Bibles are based. In particular, there is nothing in the Greek text corresponding to the closing words of verse 22 with its promise of the eventual restoration to Jerusalem of the furnishings taken from the Temple to Babylon. Any message of hope is totally lacking in the Greek text of this passage. We are left wondering whether the Hebrew text may not be the result of an updating of Jeremiah's original message sometime during or after the exile in Babylon.

To say this is not to deny that Jeremiah had a message of hope for his people. As we shall see in chapters 30-33, it has a central place in his thinking. But the message of a prophet in ancient Israel was never regarded as a fixed dead letter, written down once and unalterably for all time. The words of a great prophet were remembered and handed on by disciples, and they often adapted his words or even added to them to make his message more relevant to the changing circumstances of their own day. We still do this today as we take the words of Scripture and seek to apply them to our own lives and the problems of our day and generation. But this ongoing interpretation of Scripture is not something that begins only when we have the complete Bible in our hands. It is something that goes on all the time within the Bible, within the Old Testament and in, for example, the way in which the New Testament handles the Old Testament. If you want to see a good example of what we mean, turn to Hebrews chapter 7 and see what it does with the brief reference to Melchizedek in Genesis 14:18-20.

A CLASH IN THE TEMPLE—PROPHET
AGAINST PROPHET

Jeremiah 28:1-11

¹In that same year, at the beginning of the reign of Zedekiah king of Judah, in the fifth month of the fourth year, Hananiah the son of Azzur, the prophet from Gibeon, spoke to me in the house of the Lord, in the presence of the priests and all the people, saying, ²"Thus says the Lord of hosts, the God of Israel: I have broken the yoke of the king of Babylon. ³Within two years I will bring back to this place all the vessels of the Lord's house, which Nebuchadrezzar king of Babylon took away from this place and carried to Babylon. ⁴I will also bring back to this place Jeconiah the son of Jehoiakim, king of Judah, and all the exiles from Judah who went to Babylon, says the Lord, for I will break the yoke of the king of Babylon."

⁵Then the prophet Jeremiah spoke to Hananiah the prophet in the presence of the priests and all the people who were standing in the house of the Lord; ⁶and the prophet Jeremiah said, "Amen! May the Lord do so; may the Lord make the words which you have prophesied come true, and bring back to this place from Babylon the vessels of the house of the Lord, and all the exiles. ⁷Yet hear now this word which I speak in your hearing and in the hearing of all the people. ⁸The prophets who preceded you and me from ancient times prophesied war, famine, and pestilence against many countries and great kingdoms. ⁹As for the prophet who prophesies peace, when the word of that prophet comes to pass, then it will be known that the Lord has truly sent the prophet."

¹⁰Then the prophet Hananiah took the yoke-bars from the neck of Jeremiah the prophet, and broke them. ¹¹And Hananiah spoke in the presence of all the people, saying, "Thus says the Lord: Even so will I break the yoke of Nebuchadrezzar king of Babylon from the neck of all the nations within two years." But Jeremiah the prophet went his way.

This incident must have taken place about the same time as the events recorded in the previous chapter; at least in verse 10 Jeremiah is still wearing his yoke. Here we see clothed in flesh and blood some of the issues we have discussed earlier in the section dealing with "the prophets" (23:9ff.). Hananiah, the son of Azzur, the prophet from Gibeon, a small town some six miles north-west of Jerusalem, represents the religious establishment. We should probably think of him as the Grand Master of the prophetic Lodge attached to the Jerusalem Temple. His name means "the Lord is gracious", and the graciousness of God towards his people is the theme of his message (verses 2–4). Within a brief period, two years (verse 3), Judah's tribulations will be over, and the furnishing stolen from the Temple returned from Babylon along with the exiled king and his fellow countrymen.

Nothing could be further from what Jeremiah, yoke across his shoulders, had been saying. Yet outwardly there is no difference between Hananiah and Jeremiah. Each introduces his message with "Thus says the Lord . . . ". Who is to say that the one is sincere and the other is not? Each backs up his words by a symbolic act. Hananiah deliberately breaks the yoke Jeremiah has draped across his shoulders to indicate that, in a like manner, the yoke of Nebuchadrezzar, king of Babylon, would be broken (verses 10–11). His message is designed to encourage the envoys, who are in Jerusalem plotting rebellion, and to reassure the people.

In his reply (verses 6–9) Jeremiah begins by echoing Hananiah's words, just as an earlier prophet, Micaiah, son of Imlah, had done when he clashed with a group of 400 prophets (see 1 Kings 22:15): "Amen! May the Lord do so". "Amen" always indicates a very strong affirmation, as if in this case Jeremiah is saying to Hananiah, "Yes, I'll buy that". Was he being sarcastic? Or was he just saying, "Yes, that too would be my deepest wish, but it can't be true". It could not be true for two reasons:

(1) Such an uncritically optimistic word does not square with the message of previous prophets. They always had a stern word of judgement to say to Israel; they spoke of "war, famine, and pestilence . . ." (verse 8). You have only to read the books attributed to earlier prophets, such as Amos, Hosea and Micah, to be made aware that, whatever elements of hope for the future

there may be in their teaching, the notes of judgement and coming doom are never absent.

(2) In one of the tests of a false prophet in Deut.18:22 we read, "when a prophet speaks in the name of the Lord, if the word does not come to pass or come true, that is a word which the Lord has not spoken". Jeremiah here seems to be commenting on this test and suggesting that it really only applies to a prophet who proclaims *shalom*, "peace" or "all is well". This comes out of his unswerving conviction that a honey-tongued prophet, whose message is comfortingly reassuring and totally devoid of challenge, cannot be trusted. Only something dramatic happening could reverse that verdict. A religion devoid of challenge may be comforting, but at its heart there can be nothing other than a soppy, sentimental God. What is at stake here between Hananiah and Jeremiah—as it always is in religious controversy—is the question: in what kind of God do we believe?

Hananiah is totally unimpressed by Jeremiah's arguments. Deliberately he breaks the yoke which Jeremiah is carrying across his shoulders. This is his "symbolic act", declaring that the yoke of Babylon will be broken within two years. The confrontation ends with Jeremiah silently departing: he "went his way" (verse 11).

Would not those who witnessed the confrontation have come away with the impression that Jeremiah had retired defeated? Perhaps. But Jeremiah may have felt that nothing more needed to be said, nothing more could be said. The issues had been placed squarely before the people; they had to choose whom to believe. Certainly, Jeremiah had no further immediate word from the Lord. For that he had to wait. Since he had no further word to say, he did not say it! As the author of the Book of Ecclesiastes says, there is "a time to keep silence and a time to speak" (Eccles.3:7). There are occasions when further words only cloud the issues, however much they may act as a safety valve for our inner frustrations.

A DELAYED WORD

Jeremiah 28:12-17

> [12]Sometime after the prophet Hananiah had broken the yoke-bars from off the neck of Jeremiah the prophet, the word of the Lord came to Jeremiah: [13]"Go, tell Hananiah, 'Thus says the Lord: You have broken wooden bars, but I will make in their place bars of iron. [14]For thus says the Lord of hosts, the God of Israel: I have put upon the neck of all these nations an iron yoke of servitude to Nebuchadrezzar king of Babylon, and they shall serve him, for I have given to him even the beasts of the field.'" [15]And Jeremiah the prophet said to the prophet Hananiah, "Listen, Hananiah, the Lord has not sent you, and you have made this people trust in a lie. [16]Therefore thus says the Lord: 'Behold, I will remove you from the face of the earth. This very year you shall die, because you have uttered rebellion against the Lord.'"
>
> [17]In that same year, in the seventh month, the prophet Hananiah died.

It is some time later (verse 12)—we do not know how long— before Jeremiah has something else to say to Hananiah, and then he goes over to the attack. He has something to say both about Hananiah's message and his activities. Hananiah may have broken the wooden yoke bar Jeremiah carried, but all he had done was in effect to ensure that the wooden yoke would be replaced by an unbreakable iron one, symbolic of the unbreakable grip that the Babylonians currently held over the country. There is no need, by the way, to read verse 13 with the RSV "I" (*ie* God) instead of "you" (*ie* Hananiah). The passage is pointedly underlining that the symbolic act which Hananiah thought was liberating his people from oppression, was in fact increasing that oppression. Jeremiah then accuses Hananiah of trafficking in "a lie" (verse 15; see comment on 23:25) and indulging in "rebellion against God" (verse 16). He pronounces upon Hananiah the penalty laid down for a false prophet in Deut.18:20; "that same prophet shall die". Within two months the prophet who had prophesied that within two years his people would be freed from the yoke of Babylon, was dead. We do not know how he died; but there is no reason to doubt the fact. Jeremiah's solemn words, which were virtually a curse upon him, may have psychologically hastened his end.

It is tempting to think that this incident must have vindicated Jeremiah in the eyes of the people. But it did not; or if it did, it did so only momentarily. Within a few years, while the Babylonian forces were closing in on Jerusalem, Jeremiah found himself increasingly isolated, a prophet of national disaster to whom no-one was prepared to listen (see chs. 34ff.). It is hard to listen to someone who keeps on challenging our deepest prejudices, even if on occasion we discover that that person is right.

A SURPRISING LETTER (i)

Jeremiah 29:1–23

[1]These are the words of the letter which Jeremiah the prophet sent from Jerusalem to the elders of the exiles, and to the priests, the prophets, and all the people, whom Nebuchadrezzar had taken into exile from Jerusalem to Babylon. [2]This was after King Jeconiah, and the queen mother, the eunuchs, the princes of Judah and Jerusalem, the craftsmen, and the smiths had departed from Jerusalem. [3]The letter was sent by the hand of Elasah the son of Shaphan and Gemariah the son of Hilkiah, whom Zedekiah king of Judah sent to Babylon to Nebuchadrezzar king of Babylon. It said: [4]"Thus says the Lord of hosts, the God of Israel, to all the exiles whom I have sent into exile from Jerusalem to Babylon: [5]Build houses and live in them; plant gardens and eat their produce. [6]Take wives and have sons and daughters; take wives for your sons, and give your daughters in marriage, that they may bear sons and daughters; multiply there, and do not decrease. [7]But seek the welfare of the city where I have sent you into exile, and pray to the Lord on its behalf, for in its welfare you will find your welfare. [8]For thus says the Lord of hosts, the God of Israel: Do not let your prophets and your diviners who are among you deceive you, and do not listen to the dreams which they dream, [9]for it is a lie which they are prophesying to you in my name; I did not send them, says the Lord.

[10]"For thus says the Lord: When seventy years are completed for Babylon, I will visit you, and I will fulfil to you my promise and bring you back to this place. [11]For I know the plans I have for you, says the Lord, plans for welfare and not for evil, to give you a future and a hope. [12]Then you will call upon me and come and pray to me, and I will hear you. [13]You will seek me and find me; when you seek me with all your heart, [14]I will be found by you, says the Lord, and I will restore your fortunes and gather you from all the nations and all the places where I have driven you, says the Lord, and I will bring you back to the place from which I sent you into exile.

[15]"Because you have said, 'The Lord has raised up prophets for us in Babylon,'— [16]Thus says the Lord concerning the king who sits on the throne of David, and concerning all the people who dwell in this city, your kinsmen who did not go out with you into exile: [17]"Thus says the Lord of hosts, Behold, I am sending on them sword, famine, and pestilence, and I will make them like vile figs which are so bad they cannot be eaten. [18]I will pursue them with sword, famine, and pestilence, and will make them a horror to all the kingdoms of the earth, to be a curse, a terror, a hissing, and a reproach among all the nations where I have driven them, [19]because they did not heed my words, says the Lord, which I persistently sent to you by my servants the prophets, but you would not listen, says the Lord.'— [20]Hear the word of the Lord, all you exiles whom I sent away from Jerusalem to Babylon: [21]"Thus says the Lord of hosts, the God of Israel, concerning Ahab the son of Kolaiah and Zedekiah the son of Maaseiah, who are prophesying a lie to you in my name: Behold, I will deliver them into the hand of Nebuchadrezzar king of Babylon, and he shall slay them before your eyes. [22]Because of them this curse shall be used by all the exiles from Judah in Babylon: "The Lord make you like Zedekiah and Ahab, whom the king of Babylon roasted in the fire," [23]because they have committed folly in Israel, they have committed adultery with their neighbours' wives, and they have spoken in my name lying words which I did not command them. I am the one who knows, and I am witness, says the Lord.'"

If in Jerusalem there was diplomatic intrigue with many harbouring thoughts of rebellion against Babylon, there was also unrest among the Jews exiled in Babylon. This unrest was being fomented by prophets—two of them are named in verse 21—who were "prophesying a lie", almost certainly the same kind of lie that Hananiah was spreading in Jerusalem, that the days of the Babylonian Empire were numbered and that the exiles would soon be back home in Jerusalem. The uncertain political scene in Babylon (see p.53) may have encouraged the Jewish exiles to adopt a policy of non-cooperation with their Babylonian masters or even to begin planning a bid for freedom. To counteract the activities of such prophets Jeremiah wrote a letter to the exiles, probably shortly after the events described in the two previous chapters. An editor sketches in the background for us in verse 2 by summarizing the historical information you will find in 2 Kings 24:14-16. The letter was carried by official diplomatic couriers whom King Zedekiah had sent to Babylon, no doubt to reassure his imperial overlord that he was harbouring no thoughts of rebellion in his heart. We know nothing about the couriers beyond their names, although one of them, Elasah (verse 3), is another member of that family of Shaphan to whose good offices Jeremiah had reason to be grateful on more than one occasion (see 26:24; 36:11ff.).

The letter, which is to be found in verses 4-15 and 21-23, must have been as surprising to the exiles as anything that Jeremiah ever said to his compatriots in Jerusalem. There are several fascinating features in it.

(1) It tells the exiles to settle down to lead a normal life and to prepare for a lengthy stay in Babylon (verses 5-6). The exiles are in a novel situation, a situation not of their choosing, but they must come to terms with it. There is no use crying over spilled milk. They must learn to see their situation, not as tragedy, "evil" (verse 11), but as part of God's good purposes, designed for their *shalom*, "welfare", promising a new, hope-filled future. A return from exile is promised, but not yet—"when seventy years are completed for Babylon" (verse 10); seventy years probably intended to indicate a good round number and certainly to rule out any return within the lifetime of the present generation.

(2) The major surprise in the letter comes in verse 7 where the exiles are told to "seek the welfare of the city where I have sent you into exile, and pray to the Lord on its behalf, for in its welfare you will find your welfare". Although there is an element of self-interest in this—your *shalom* is bound up with its *shalom*—the command to pray to the Lord on behalf of Babylon, and to "seek" its *shalom,* is unexpected and startling. Jeremiah was writing to people who had been accustomed to gather in the Temple in Jerusalem to pray for the *shalom* of Israel and Jerusalem (see *eg* Pss. 122:8; 125:5; 128:6) and to react with bitter cries for vengeance against enemies who threatened their land. Not least among these enemies were the Babylonians who are savagely attacked for their treatment of Jerusalem in Psalm 137:7-8. To move from there to pray for Babylon, not for vengeance upon it, but for its welfare, is to take a big step. We are catching a glimpse here of a new spirituality which was to struggle against a narrow, nationalistic view of religion. In the fullness of time it led to Jesus' words, "Love your enemies and pray for those who persecute you" (Matt.5:44). We find that easy to say, but not so easy to practise. In Jeremiah's time it was not easy even to say.

(3) What lies behind this new spirituality is nothing other than a radically new understanding of what faith means. The author of Psalm 137, writing against the background of having been in exile in Babylon, protests that it was impossible to "sing the Lord's song in a foreign land" (Ps.137:4). Jeremiah insists that the exiles can, and must, find God out there in Babylon, just as surely as ever they claimed to find him back home in the Temple at Jerusalem. He challenges them to see that, having lost Jerusalem, the Temple, their homeland, everything that they had previously considered essential to their faith, they had in fact lost nothing. True faith consists in praying to a God who hears, in seeking "with all your heart" and finding (verse 13); and that can be done as surely by the waters of Babylon as in a temple in Jerusalem.

The word "Then", by the way, which appears at the beginning of verse 12 in the RSV translation is quite misleading. Jeremiah is not saying, you will seek me and find me "then", *ie* sometime in the future when you are back home; he is saying you will find me here and now. God has been set free from the confines of Jerusalem and its city in order to be found out there in what many of the exiles could only regard as a cold, tragic, God-forsaken situation. We must not assume from this that Jeremiah was against forms of worship or the Jerusalem Temple as such. These things could have been the means of grace for his people. They went wrong when they became instead a prison for God. The prison had to be smashed; God had to be set free to roam the world, there to be found by his people in unexpected places. The more we associate certain things and places with God, the more we need to be on our guard lest they narrow our vision of God and blind us to his presence everywhere.

A SURPRISING LETTER (ii)

Jeremiah 29:1–23 (*cont'd*), 24–32

24To Shemaiah of Nehelam you shall say: 25"Thus says the Lord of hosts, the God of Israel: You have sent letters in your name to all the people who are in Jerusalem, and to Zephaniah the son of Maaseiah the priest, and to all the priests, saying, 26"The Lord has made you priest instead of Jehoiada the priest, to have charge in the house of the Lord over every madman who prophesies, to put him in the stocks and collar. 27Now why have you not rebuked Jeremiah of Anathoth who is prophesying to you? 28For he has sent to us in Babylon, saying, "Your exile will be long; build houses and live in them, and plant gardens and eat their produce."

29Zephaniah the priest read this letter in the hearing of Jeremiah the prophet. 30Then the word of the Lord came to Jeremiah: 31"Send to all the exiles, saying, 'Thus says the Lord concerning Shemaiah of Nehelam: Because Shemaiah has prophesied to you when I did not send him, and has made you trust in a lie, 32therefore thus says the Lord: Behold, I will punish Shemaiah of Nehelam and his descendants; he shall not have any one living among this people to see the good that I will do to my people, says the Lord, for he has talked rebellion against the Lord.'"

Jeremiah also warns the exiles not to pay any attention to "the prophets and diviners" who come forward with dreams which are nothing other than "a lie" (verse 8). In verses 21ff., two such prophets, Ahab the son of Kolaiah and Zedekiah the son of Maaseiah, receive summary treatment at Jeremiah's hands. It is clear that the "lie" they were prophesying must have involved some kind of political activity against the Babylonian authorities, otherwise it is hardly likely that Nebuchadrezzar would have been involved in executing them. Roasting in fire (verse 22) was a well-authenticated form of capital punishment in ancient Babylon, vouched for a thousand years earlier than Jeremiah's day in the famous law code of Hammurabi. It retained its popularity for many years in Christendom as people were burned at the stake. The fate of these prophets was to be handed down as a horrible example of what you would wish upon your enemies in a curse. But if Nebuchadrezzar intervened to cut short the treasonable political activities of such prophets, in Jeremiah's eyes their crime was the two-fold religious one, with which he had repeatedly charged such prophets—immorality and speaking "lying words" in the name of the Lord, both springing inevitably out of a misunderstanding of the nature of Israel's God (verse 23). Beliefs, particularly false beliefs, are dangerous things. They can lead people to do horrifying things and to do them with an easy conscience in the firm conviction that they are doing the will of God.

We noted that Jeremiah's letter is contained in verses 4–15 and 21–23. There is little doubt that verse 21 follows on naturally from verse 15 where the people claim that the Lord has provided them with prophets in Babylon. The RSV indicates by dashes that verses 16–19 are an aside, interrupting the flow of the letter, although there is nothing in these verses that could not have come from Jeremiah. They stress that the nation is under judgement, doomed to total collapse for ignoring repeated warnings. If there is hope, it can only lie on the other side of national disaster. The nation has to be crucified before it can experience resurrection.

As always, what Jeremiah had to say provoked a hostile reaction. One of the exiles, Shemaiah of Nehelam, probably one of the prophets functioning in Babylon, writes to the religious authorities in Jerusalem complaining that they ought to have taken action against Jeremiah (verses 24-28). What the reaction of the authorities to this complaint was, we are not told. Perhaps like many other letters of complaint to the authorities it was left lying on the table. But the priest in charge of the Temple read the letter to Jeremiah; whether to invite his reply to the charges it contained or because he was sympathetic to Jeremiah, we do not know. Jeremiah's only response in the name of the Lord was to consign Shemaiah to the same fate that had befallen his Jerusalem counterpart, Hananiah.

Look back across these last few chapters and ponder anew the amazing courage of this man. He preaches an unpopular sermon in the Temple and is almost lynched (ch. 26); he seeks to influence the deliberations of a high-powered international conference (ch.27); he clashes with a rival prophet representing the religious establishment (ch. 28); and he writes a surprising, some would consider a treasonable, letter to his fellow countrymen in exile in Babylon (ch. 29). If you had asked him why, there would only have been one response: I am doing what the Lord has told me to do. He was being true to unshakeable convictions, which he could not prove to others, but to which he must witness, whatever the cost.

I. A FUTURE BRIGHT WITH HOPE
(CHS. 30-33)

Just as chapter 23:9-40 gathers together sayings "concerning the prophets", so chapters 30-33 form a little book within the book, gathering together sayings whose central theme is hope for the future. As we read them there are certain things we ought to keep in mind.

(1) It is likely that not all the sayings in these chapters come from Jeremiah himself. Here above all we must allow for the fact that later disciples of the prophet, or editors living during or after the exile in Babylon, will have taken Jeremiah's teaching and adapted or expanded it in the light of the needs of their own day (see comment on 27:16-22). When, however, we try to unscramble what goes back to Jeremiah from what is later, there is little agreement among scholars. I can only express my view that most of the material in these chapters goes back to Jeremiah himself, although some of it has been reshaped by other people before it reaches us.

(2) These chapters are an interesting illustration of the way in which Jeremiah, like all of us, was influenced by the past and helped to shape the future. Some of the passages in these chapters draw heavily upon the language and ideas of an earlier prophet, Hosea (see comment on 31:3,20); others use language with which we are familiar in the teaching of the later prophet of the exile, "Second" Isaiah (see comment on 30:10-11; 31:2,8-9). A prophet like Jeremiah stands on the shoulders of his prophetic predecessors, and it is part of his lasting greatness that he in turn was to influence those who came after him.

(3) To whom did Jeremiah address his words of hope? Repeatedly in chapters 30-31 we find passages addressed to "Jacob" and "Israel" (*eg* 30:10; 31:7) or "Ephraim" (31:6). Jacob, in the Old Testament, is the traditional ancestor of the northern group of tribes who made up the kingdom of Israel that collapsed before the Assyrian Empire in 721 B.C.. The kingdom of Israel is also referred to elsewhere in the Old Testament, particularly in Hosea, as Ephraim. It is clear from the references to Samaria, the capital of the kingdom of Israel, and to Ephraim in the poem in 31:5-6, that this poem originally held out a message of hope to the people of the northern

kingdom who had been scattered to the far corners of the Assyrian Empire. Jeremiah, at an early period in his ministry, may well have had a vision of the renewal and reunion of the whole people of God, north as well as south; but once Judah was on the verge of collapse, its fate sealed by the judgement of God, there had to be a message of hope that included Judah. So in some of the poems we find Judah linked with Israel (see 30:4; 31:31). It is quite likely that Jeremiah himself took some of his early messages of hope for Israel and adapted them to include Judah. That Jeremiah had a message of hope for his people is unquestionable. As we shall see it shines through the incident recorded in chapter 32. Without a word of hope in and beyond disaster, a religion has little to say to the world. At no time has this been more true than today. As I write these words it is the fortieth anniversary of the dropping of the first atomic bomb on Hiroshima.

PUNISHMENT DESERVED—A FUTURE PROMISED

Jeremiah 30:1–11

> [1]The word that came to Jeremiah from the Lord: [2]"Thus says the Lord, the God of Israel: Write in a book all the words that I have spoken to you. [3]For behold, days are coming, says the Lord, when I will restore the fortunes of my people Israel and Judah, says the Lord, and I will bring them back to the land which I gave to their fathers, and they shall take possession of it."
>
> [4]These are the words which the Lord spoke concerning Israel and Judah:
> [5]"Thus says the Lord:
>   We have heard a cry of panic,
>   of terror, and no peace.
> [6]Ask now, and see,
>   can a man bear a child?

Why then do I see every man
with his hands on his loins
like a woman in labour?
Why has every face turned pale?
⁷Alas! that day is so great there is none like it;
it is a time of distress for Jacob;
yet he shall be saved out of it.

⁸"And it shall come to pass in that day, says the Lord of hosts,
that I will break the yoke from off their neck, and I will burst their
bonds, and strangers shall no more make servants of them. ⁹But
they shall serve the Lord their God and David their king, whom I
will raise up for them.

¹⁰"Then fear not, O Jacob my servant,
says the Lord,
nor be dismayed, O Israel;
for lo, I will save you from afar,
and your offspring from the land of their captivity.
Jacob shall return and have quiet and ease,
and none shall make him afraid.
¹¹For I am with you to save you,
says the Lord;
I will make a full end of all the nations
among whom I scattered you,
but of you I will not make a full end.
I will chasten you in just measure,
and I will by no means leave you unpunished."

This passage clearly divides into several different sections.

(1) There is an introduction (verses 1–3) in which the prophet
is commanded by God to "write in a book all the words that I
have spoken to you" (verse 2). The words referred to are not the
whole range of the prophet's teaching, but the words of hope
which follow. For a general discussion of some of the problems
surrounding the Book of Jeremiah as a whole, see the
Introduction (pp. 1–5). Such a writing down may have
been intended to ensure that the message of hope would be
preserved for those who, in the desperate crisis of national
tragedy, needed to hear it over and over again. How often the
written word in the Bible has done just that when people have

been tempted to despair: in a lonely prison cell; in moments when people have felt that they are at the end of their tether; in the one experience common to us all, when our defences are down and we face the one certainty in life for all of us — the fact of death.

The message of hope is summed up in the phrase, "restoring the fortunes of my people" (verse 3). It is found here at the beginning of this little 'book of consolation', as it has been called; it occurs at its end in 3:26, and it beats like a persistent motif through the chapters (see 30:18; 31:23; 32:44; 33:7). It is a phrase found elsewhere in the Old Testament, *eg* Psalm 126:1 Traditionally, English versions of the Bible translate it as "bringing again—or causing to return, or turning again—the captivity" (AV). But this is a wrong and too narrow translation. The phrase points forward to a 'reversal of fortune', to the overcoming of difficult circumstances and the coming again of the fullness of life that God intends for his people. Of course, in the particular circumstances of exile in Babylon, such a 'reversal of fortune' would mean release from captivity and freedom to renew their life back home in their own land; but that in itself could never exhaust its meaning.

(2) A vivid poem in verses 5–7 describes the agony and the distress of "that day", the day of the Lord's judgement against his people. It depicts the men in the community, hands on thighs, as if they were experiencing the pangs of childbirth. There is no longer any *shalom* in the land, only terror, distress. It ends with a few words which all English translations render as a statement: "yet he [Jacob] shall be saved out of it", or as the New English Bible renders, "yet he shall come through it safely". The Hebrew might equally well be read as a question: "out of it, shall he be saved?" It would depend entirely on the tone of voice in which the words were originally spoken. But even if it is a question, it is a question which is answered in verses 8–9 which speak of a time coming when the yoke of oppression will be broken and the people reconstituted as the people of God, ruled over by their own king of the family of David.

(3) In words that are reminiscent of the teaching of the great prophet of the exile, "Second" Isaiah (note the words "fear not", the description of Jacob/Israel as "my servant", the picture of people returning from afar, all typical of passages like Isaiah 41:8-10) verses 10-11 proclaim a realistic word of hope. It is not a hope that side-steps disaster. The people will be justly punished for their sins, but there will be a return and a new life of security, free from fear, because of the character of Israel's God, a God who is "with you to save [deliver] you" in every circumstance. The writing is on the wall for Israel's oppressors, but Israel's history can never come to "a full end", or as we might say, to "a full stop". God's people can never be completely destroyed.

History ever since has been saying "yes" to this promise. Jews have faced extinction: persecuted by Christians, consigned to the ghetto, suffering in pogroms, dying by their millions in the holocaust—yet their history has never come to "a full end". Neither has the story of that other Israel, the new people of God, the Church. It has been written off as dead or irrelevant; it has been threatened with extinction by persecution. In our own day the communist regime in China closed churches and banned theological colleges; it was to be an irrelevance in the new China. Yet the Church became "the house church", and it is stronger in China today than when the communists took over. The secret of this ever new life is the God who said to Israel, "I am with you to save you", and repeated his promise in Jesus, "Lo, I am with you always, to the close of the age" (Matt.28:20).

CURING THE INCURABLE

Jeremiah 30:12-17

12"For thus says the Lord:
    Your hurt is incurable,
        and your wound is grievous.
13There is none to uphold your cause,
        no medicine for your wound, no healing for you.

¹⁴All your lovers have forgotten you;
    they care nothing for you;
for I have dealt you the blow of an enemy,
    the punishment of a merciless foe,
because your guilt is great,
    because your sins are flagrant.
¹⁵Why do you cry out over your hurt?
    Your pain is incurable.
Because your guilt is great,
    because your sins are flagrant,
    I have done these things to you.
¹⁶Therefore all who devour you shall be devoured,
    and all your foes, every one of them, shall go into captivity;
those who despoil you shall become a spoil,
    and all who prey on you I will make a prey.
¹⁷For I will restore health to you,
    and your wounds I will heal,
        says the Lord,
because they have called you an outcast:
    'It is Zion, for whom no one cares!'"

Suffering from a wound that could not be healed, was
Jeremiah's earlier despairing comment on the condition of his
people (8:22); it was also his bitter description of his own
spiritual agony (15:18). Now he uses the same picture to
describe the tragic plight of his people. This passage was
probably written soon after the destruction of Jerusalem by the
Babylonians in 587 B.C. What he sees is "an open wound upon
which no new skin will grow" (this is a better translation of the
second half of verse 13 than that which the RSV gives us). There
is no known human cure. "All your lovers", the political allies,
such as Egypt upon whom Judah depended for help, had
proved to be faithless. Faced with this situation, the people are
tempted to despair; the wound cannot be healed, the pain is
incurable. This is the human response and it is realistic since the
wound is inflicted by God. God has been forced to act against
his own people like "a merciless foe" (verse 14), because of their
guilt and sinfulness.

That is why, paradoxically, there is hope. What is humanly

incurable is curable by God. The God who wounds is the God who will heal and restore his people to full health (verse 17). The human agents God has used to further his destructive purposes, will themselves be destroyed (verse 16). They have contemptuously dismissed Zion as "an outcast . . . for whom no one cares" (verse 17). But that can never be God's verdict. God destroyed because he cared; he will heal because he still cares. This is a theme which is to be explored further in the poems in the Book of Lamentations written in the aftermath of the destruction of Jerusalem (Lam.3:31-33):

> For the Lord will not
>   cast off for ever,
> but, though he cause grief, he will have compassion
>   according to the abundance of his steadfast love;
> for he does not willingly afflict
>   or grieve the sons of men.

In Jeremiah's day, the people of Judah had to be led to the point where they were stripped of all human resources, before they were prepared to turn to the healing and renewing power which God alone could give. It is an experience that has been echoed across the centuries when people at the end of their tether, totally despairing, have found God and found healing and new life.

A NEW COMMUNITY

Jeremiah 30:18-24

> [18]"Thus says the Lord:
>   Behold, I will restore the fortunes of the tents of Jacob,
>   and have compassion on his dwellings;
>   the city shall be rebuilt upon its mound,
>   and the palace shall stand where it used to be.
> [19]Out of them shall come songs of thanksgiving,
>   and the voices of those who make merry.

I will multiply them, and they shall not be few;
    I will make them honoured, and they shall not be small.
20Their children shall be as they were of old,
    and their congregation shall be established before me;
    and I will punish all who oppress them.
21Their prince shall be one of themselves,
    their ruler shall come forth from their midst;
I will make him draw near, and he shall approach me,
    for who would dare of himself to approach me?

                                        says the Lord.

22And you shall be my people,
    and I will be your God."

23Behold the storm of the Lord!
    Wrath has gone forth, a whirling tempest;
    it will burst upon the head of the wicked.
24The fierce anger of the Lord will not turn back
    until he has executed and accomplished
        the intents of his mind.
In the latter days you will understand this.

If the previous section dealt with the great theological certainties that give hope of renewal, this passage comes down to earth to sketch out the picture of a restored community which owes its very existence to God's initiative and compassion:

the city rebuilt on its mound or 'tell', the royal palace restored (verse 18);

a teaming population, with all the bustle, joy and laughter in life, and children all around (verses 19-20);

the "congregation", probably the normal political or religious institutions, revived (verse 20);

a community governed by a native "prince" or ruler, who will be acceptable to God and will lead his people in the true worship of God (verse 21).

All this is in order to ensure that once again there will exist a people, bound to God in a covenant relationship: "You shall be my people, and I will be your God" (verse 22; for the meaning of "covenant" in the Old Testament see comments on chapter 11 in vol.1, pp.100–101).

In this picture we find that interesting blend of the human and the divine, the material and the spiritual, which is so characteristic of the Old Testament. These new people of God are assuredly to be in the world. The new city of God is an earthly city; the new Jerusalem is rebuilt on the ruins of the old. And in the fullness of time the God of Israel does not step out of the world; he comes into it himself in Jesus. He still calls his people to be fully in the world, even if they are not to conform to its standards (Rom.12:2).

Let us stop for a moment to take a closer look at what is said about this new "prince" or ruler in verse 21. He is not called "king". Why not? We do not really know, but perhaps the unfortunate character of most of the last kings of Judah, and the fact that the policies which they pursued were all out of step with the purposes of the Lord, made "king" a bad word and led to the hope of a new kind of ruler. Sometimes words do trigger off wrong associations in our minds—what do you immediately think of when you see the words "ecumenical" or "evangelical"?—and we need to use other words to communicate the truth these words ought to be conveying to us.

It is of the essence of this new ruler that he has a vital part to play in the religious life of the community, as indeed the king in Israel and in other parts of the ancient world had. They were priest kings (see Ps. 110). Since the Old Testament had a strong sense of the mystery and the awesomeness of God, the approach to God was hedged round with all kinds of restrictions; nothing and no-one unholy or unclean could come into his presence. Certain activities in worship were restricted to certain holy people—the priests. Into the innermost sanctuary in the Temple at Jerusalem, the holy of holies, only the High Priest could enter once a year. To violate such restrictions was to be struck down by the dangerous holiness of God—see the sad story of Uzzah (2 Sam.6) who with the best of intentions fatally touched the ark, the sacred symbol of God's presence in the midst of his people. So the new prince or ruler had to be a person specially authorized by God to exercise priestly functions on behalf of his people. It is against this background that the Letter to the Hebrews speaks of Jesus, King and great High Priest, through whom we may "with confidence draw near to the throne of grace, that we may receive mercy and find grace to help in time of need" (Heb.4:16).

Verses 23–24 are repeated from 23:19–20 and probably do not belong originally with the hopeful oracle we have just considered, although they remind us, not inappropriately, of the stern reality out of which Israel's future hopes were born.

LOVE UNCHANGING

Jeremiah 31:1–14

[1]"At that time, says the Lord, I will be the God of all the families of Israel, and they shall be my people."
[2]Thus says the Lord:
"The people who survived the sword
found grace in the wilderness;
when Israel sought for rest,
[3]the Lord appeared to him from afar.
I have loved you with an everlasting love;
therefore I have continued my faithfulness to you.
[4]Again I will build you, and you shall be built,
O virgin Israel!
Again you shall adorn yourself with timbrels,
and shall go forth in the dance of the merrymakers.
[5]Again you shall plant vineyards upon the mountains of Samaria;
the planters shall plant, and shall enjoy the fruit.
[6]For there shall be a day when watchmen will call
in the hill country of Ephraim:
'Arise, and let us go up to Zion, to the Lord our God.'"

[7]For thus says the Lord:
"Sing aloud with gladness for Jacob,
and raise shouts for the chief of the nations;
proclaim, give praise, and say,
'The Lord has saved his people, the remnant of Israel.'

⁸Behold, I will bring them from the north country,
  and gather them from the farthest parts of the earth,
among them the blind and the lame,
    the woman with child and her who is in travail, together;
  a great company, they shall return here.
⁹With weeping they shall come,
    and with consolations I will lead them back,
  I will make them walk by brooks of water,
    in a straight path in which they shall not stumble;
  for I am a father to Israel, and Ephraim is my first-born.

¹⁰"Hear the word of the Lord, O nations,
    and declare it in the coastlands afar off;
  say, 'He who scattered Israel will gather him,
    and will keep him as a shepherd keeps his flock.'
¹¹For the Lord has ransomed Jacob,
  and has redeemed him from hands too strong for him.
¹²They shall come and sing aloud on the height of Zion,
    and they shall be radiant over the goodness of the Lord,
  over the grain, the wine, and the oil,
    and over the young of the flock and the herd;
  their life shall be like a watered garden,
    and they shall languish no more.
¹³Then shall the maidens rejoice in the dance,
    and the young men and the old shall be merry.
  I will turn their mourning into joy,
    I will comfort them, and give them gladness for sorrow.
¹⁴I will feast the soul of the priests with abundance,
    and my people shall be satisfied with my goodness,
                                            says the Lord."

We find here three passages, (1) verses 2-6, (2) verses 7-9, (3) verses 10-14, each with its own introduction indicating that it is a word of the Lord, all of them originally holding out a message of hope for the survivors of the old northern kingdom of Israel. Verse 1 serves as a heading gathering them (and the passage that follows in verses 15-22) together.

(1) The *first* passage begins by reminding the people of their

past, a past which clearly witnessed the grace and the ever present love of God. Here was a God who brought his people out of slavery in Egypt, who protected them from a pursuing Egyptian army, who cared for them in the desert, who revealed himself to them at Mt Sinai "long ago" ("long ago" is better than the RSV's "from afar" in verse 3). This is a God who does not change, who is totally dependable, who maintains his *hesed*, his faithfulness or steadfast love. Therefore there must be hope for the future, hope that once again there will be a lively, joy–filled community, sustained by a thriving agriculture, in and around Samaria, the capital of the northern kingdom. North and south will be reunited in faith, in the worship of the Lord on Mt Zion, as pilgrimages from the north to Jerusalem are resumed.

The influence of Hosea is strong in these verses. It is Hosea who, against the background of his own tangled family life, talks about the love of God for his people:

> When Israel was a child, I loved him
> and out of Egypt I called my son.
>
> (Hos. 11:1)

It is Hosea who describes the people's faithfulness (*hesed*) as being "like the morning mist, like the dew that early vanishes" (Hos. 6:4), then speaks of a God who is not like that, who cannot stifle his compassion for his people. Here is hope based on nothing other than the known character of God, a hope well expressed in the opening lines of Joachim Neander's great hymn:

> All my hope on God is founded;
>   He doth still my trust renew;
> Me through chance and change he guideth,
>   only good and only true.

(2) The *second* passage (verses 7–9) describes the joyful homecoming of a people who had been scattered to the farthest

ends of the earth. But it is the return of a people very different from the once proud, self-confident northerners. The prophet Amos had sarcastically attacked the complacent aristocracy in Samaria who considered themselves to belong to "the first of the nations" (Amos 6:1): 'here's tae us, wha's like us!', had been their attitude. Now they are to come back as "the chief of the nations" (verse 7); but this is a new kind of greatness. It is the greatness of "the remnant of Israel", the few who survived national disaster and long years in exile, now to be delivered and gathered home again by God. Their new greatness lies in what God has done for them, and in nothing else. They come back, not like a triumphant army flaunting its power, but as "a great company", bringing with them those in need of care and protection, the blind and the lame, pregnant women, and women in labour (verse 8). They come back, not in arrogance or self-confidence, but "weeping" and "praying" (there is no need to read with the RSV "consolations" in verse 9), scarcely able to believe what is happening to them as God takes care of their needs and smoothes the way before them.

Much of the language here has close similarities to that of "Second" Isaiah who sees the return from exile as a new Exodus, a new journey through the wilderness (see *eg* Isa. 42:14-16; 43:5-6). But at the end, we return to Hosea's picture of father and son. Ephraim (Israel) is God's "first-born" son, stressing the close and special relationship between God and his people. The first-born son in the family traditionally belonged to God and had to be redeemed (see Exod. 13:1-2, 11-16); he also had a special status in the family and was heir to the family estate. But this special relationship is not Israel's right; it is God's gift.

(3) The *third* passage (verses 10-14) reminds us very strongly of "Second" Isaiah. There is the appeal to "the coastlands" and the nations (Isa. 41:1; 49:1); the picture of the Lord as the caring shepherd tending his flock (Isa. 40:11); and the use of the word "redeem" to describe what God does for his people (Isa. 41:14;

43:14). All combine to point to a renewed community experiencing and acknowledging "the goodness of the Lord" (verse 12); a goodness reflected in field and in flock, in a people from whose lives all grief and sorrow have been banished (verse 13), and among whom the true worship of God will once again flourish (verse 14). Running throughout the passage is the conviction that the whole of Israel's history—past, present and future—lies in the hands of God. The shepherd who now watches over his flock is the same shepherd who scattered Israel (verse 10). Nothing has happened to Israel which is not his doing.

Let us take a closer look at two words in verse 11 which are frequently used in the Bible to describe what God does for his people: "ransom" (*padah*) and "redeem" (*ga-al*). Both of them, like many other important theological words, have humble origins in the everyday life of the people. "Ransom" is a legal word; it describes what you pay in money or in kind to secure the release or return of something which has passed into someone else's possession (Exod. 13:13; Num. 18:15ff.). "Redeem" is more closely tied up with the life of the family. The "redeemer" (*go-el*) is the nearest next of kin who had, among other things, the responsibility to secure the release of a member of the family who had fallen into debt slavery, or to keep a piece of family property from being sold outwith the family (see chapter 32), or to marry the childless widow of a deceased brother to continue the family line (see the Book of Ruth). Both words are launched on a great theological future when they are used to describe what the Lord did for his people by bringing them out of captivity in Egypt (Deut. 9:26 *padah*; Exod. 6:6 *ga-al*; the RSV has "redeems" in both these passages). Here both words refer to another exodus, a new setting free of God's people to enable them to return to their homeland. Both were to be given yet profounder spiritual meaning, not least in the New Testament where they are used to describe what God in Christ has done for us.

WEEP NO MORE, EPHRAIM—AND JUDAH

Jeremiah 31:15-26

[15]Thus says the Lord:
"A voice is heard in Ramah, lamentation and bitter weeping.
Rachel is weeping for her children;
    she refuses to be comforted for her children,
    because they are not."
[16]Thus says the Lord:
"Keep your voice from weeping, and your eyes from tears;
for your work shall be rewarded,

                                        says the Lord,
    and they shall come back from the land of the enemy.
[17]There is hope for your future,

                                        says the Lord,
    and your children shall come back to their own country.
[18]I have heard Ephraim bemoaning,
    'Thou hast chastened me, and I was chastened,
    like an untrained calf;
    bring me back that I may be restored,
    for thou art the Lord my God.
[19]For after I had turned away I repented;
    and after I was instructed, I smote upon my thigh;
    I was ashamed, and I was confounded,
    because I bore the disgrace of my youth.'
[20]Is Ephraim my dear son?
    Is he my darling child?
For as often as I speak against him,
    I do remember him still.
Therefore my heart yearns for him;
    I will surely have mercy on him,

                                        says the Lord.
[21]"Set up waymarks for yourself, make yourself guideposts;
    consider well the highway, the road by which you went.
Return, O virgin Israel, return to these your cities.
[22]How long will you waver, O faithless daughter?
    For the Lord has created a new thing on the earth:
    a woman protects a man."

²³Thus says the Lord of hosts, the God of Israel: "Once more they shall use these words in the land of Judah and in its cities, when I restore their fortunes:

'The Lord bless you, O habitation of righteousness,
    O holy hill!'

²⁴And Judah and all its cities shall dwell there together, and the farmers and those who wander with their flocks. ²⁵For I will satisfy the weary soul, and every languishing soul I will replenish."

²⁶Thereupon I awoke and looked, and my sleep was pleasant to me.

Rachel in the Old Testament is regarded as the ancestress of the tribes which made up the northern kingdom of Israel; the mother of Joseph and Benjamin according to Genesis 35:24. Here she is depicted disconsolately weeping at Ramah, modern *el-Ram,* some five miles north of Jerusalem. Near Ramah, according to one Old Testament tradition, Rachel's tomb was to be found. She is weeping because she has lost her children. Into her weeping comes a word from God, telling her to dry her tears. Her children are not gone for ever; they will return home.

But it must not be merely a return to the past; so there is placed on the lips of Ephraim (verses 18-19) a liturgy outlining the essentials of true repentance. There is an acknowledgement of the rightness of God's past disciplining of a people described as an "untrained calf" (cf. the picture of Israel as a "stubborn heifer" in Hosea 4:16); there is an appeal for a new beginning rooted in God's acceptance of one who is penitent and filled with bitter remorse. These verses make skilful use, as Jeremiah does elsewhere (see comment on 3:1 ff. in vol.1, p.36) of the Hebrew word *shuv,*"to turn, to turn away, to turn back". Forms of it are to be found in the words translated, "bring me back" and "restored" in verse 18,"turned away" in verse 19, and also, a little later in verse 21, in the appeal "return . . . return", and in verse 22 in the description of Israel as "faithless".

The liturgy is capped by a moving statement (verse 20) of God's continuing concern for one who is still his "darling child"; one whom, in spite of everything, he can never blot out of his memory; one for whom his heart (literally "bowels"; see

comment on 4:19) yearns. It is a picture of God which Jesus was
to portray so vividly in the story of the loving father who can
never forget and who welcomes home his erring son (Luke
15:11–32).

The picture suddenly switches from Israel described as a
"son" in verse 20, to Israel as a "virgin" or a "daughter" in verses
21–22. She is bidden carefully to map out the way and to retrace
her steps back home. But as if to emphasize that the new life
cannot and must not be simply the old life all over again, Israel
is reminded that she is one who has "twisted and turned" (NEB)
or "dilly dallied" (John Bright, *Anchor Bible*)—RSV has
"waver"—and has been a wayward turncoat of a daughter.

But what are we to make of the second half of verse 22, of this
new thing "the Lord has created": "a woman protects a man"?
The New English Bible hardly helps by translating it as "a
woman turned into a man". It is a puzzling statement and no-
one is quite sure of its meaning. Certainly a woman protecting a
man would be a surprising reversal of the normal roles in
ancient Israel. Is this perhaps a popular saying to indicate
something totally unexpected and surprising, rather like our
saying, "never in a month of Sundays"? The Good News Bible
seems to be thinking along these lines when it translates, "I have
created something new and different, as different as a woman
protecting a man". But what is this new and surprising thing the
Lord creates? Is it the restoration of Israel or is it the change of
one who in the past was a "faithless daughter" into a responsible
community, or is it both? Isaiah 43:19 talks about a new thing
God is about to do, and there it means the surprising way in
which God is about to act to bring freedom and new life to his
people in exile. If the words "a woman protects a man" are
intended to convey the sense of something totally surprising,
then this is another of these places where we may need to rewrite
the Bible in order to get its meaning across, since the roles of
men and women in society today are very different from what
they were in Israel.

From these words of hope addressed to Israel, we turn (verses
23ff.) to similar encouraging words addressed to Judah: its

cities are to be rebuilt, its farmers and shepherds are to resume their daily work, and all in need will find their needs met. It is a sober enough vision, with no extravagant flights of fancy, but no doubt many people who lived through the destruction of Jerusalem and the ravaging of the countryside, would have asked for little more. At its heart there is a blessing, similar to the blessings we find upon Jerusalem in some of the Psalms (*eg* 128:5):

> May the Lord bless you from Zion!
> May you see the prosperity of Jerusalem
> all the days of your life!

Here the Lord's blessing is invoked upon Jerusalem and the Temple, described as "habitation of righteousness", that is to say God's rightful dwelling place, and the "holy hill", Mt Zion, the mountain set apart for God. No Old Testament writer could ever forget that at the centre of the life of God's people there must be worship, worship of the one true God whose presence in their midst could enrich and give direction to their lives. However scathing Jeremiah at times may have been in his attack on false ideas which had gathered round the Temple, there is no reason to believe that he would have contemplated a renewed community which did not have at its centre a place of worship.

If verse 22 was puzzling, what are we to make of verse 26: "Thereupon I awoke and looked, and my sleep was pleasant to me"? If these words are to be taken closely with the previous verse and their vision of the new community, then perhaps this is the comment of someone who, reading these words of hope, suddenly turns to look at the all too grim reality of the world around him and thinks, "well, it's a marvellous dream, but . . . ". And that is what we tend to say when we read some of the great promises and visions in the Bible. But what are visions for, if not to broaden our horizons, to leave us dissatisfied with ourselves and the world we know, and to encourage us to believe that under God there is a better world yet to be? Follow such visions through the Bible and you end up in the Book of Revelation with its magnificent vision of "a new heaven and a new earth", and at its centre a "new Jerusalem" (Rev. 21).

PERSONAL RESPONSIBILITY

Jeremiah 31:27-34

27"Behold, the days are coming, says the Lord, when I will sow the house of Israel and the house of Judah with the seed of man and the seed of beast. 28And it shall come to pass that as I have watched over them to pluck up and break down, to overthrow, destroy, and bring evil, so I will watch over them to build and to plant, says the Lord. 29In those days they shall no longer say:
'The fathers have eaten sour grapes,
and the children's teeth are set on edge.'
30But every one shall die for his own sin; each man who eats sour grapes, his teeth shall be set on edge.
31"Behold, the days are coming, says the Lord, when I will make a new covenant with the house of Israel and the house of Judah, 32not like the covenant which I made with their fathers when I took them by the hand to bring them out of the land of Egypt, my covenant which they broke, though I was their husband, says the Lord. 33But this is the covenant which I will make with the house of Israel after those days, says the Lord: I will put my law within them, and I will write it upon their hearts; and I will be their God, and they shall be my people. 34And no longer shall each man teach his neighbour and each his brother, saying, 'Know the Lord,' for they shall all know me, from the least of them to the greatest, says the Lord; for I will forgive their iniquity, and I will remember their sin no more."

Verses 27–30 make up the first of three passages introduced by the typical prophetic phrase heralding a future hope, "Behold, the days are coming, says the Lord . . . " (see also verses 31 and 38). It joins together "the house of Israel and the house of Judah" in its promise of reconstruction, using language taken from Jeremiah's call experience in 1:10 with its double-edged comment on Jeremiah's ministry, destructive and constructive.

Destruction has now taken place, the way is open for rebuilding. But first a problem has to be faced. Jeremiah here takes issue, as does the prophet Ezekiel (18:2), with a proverbial saying;

> The fathers have eaten sour grapes,
> and the children's teeth are set on edge.

It looks as if right to the end there were people in Jerusalem insisting that, if tragedy struck the nation, it was not their fault. They were but paying the penalty for the sins of their fathers. The idea of collective guilt spanning the generations plays a prominent part in the thinking of Israel. Israel's God, according to Exodus 20:5 is "a jealous God, visiting the iniquity of the fathers upon the children to the third and fourth generation of those who hate [him]". There is obviously truth in this. The decisions taken, the policies adopted by one generation can reap a bitter harvest in the next—witness, for example, the current social and political unrest in South Africa. Likewise *we* are passing on to the coming generation a legacy which will shape their lives; a legacy of uncertain moral values, of mass unemployment in the western industrialized nations, of a world increasingly divided between rich and poor, the "haves" and the "have nots". No nation, no generation, no family, no individual lives are uninfluenced, for better or for worse, by what has gone before.

But that does not mean that we can shuffle off responsibility and simply blame "them" or "the system" for everything that happens; or kid ourselves that the decisions we take don't matter. We can take choices, for better or for worse; we must accept personal responsibility for what we do. Passing the buck is a game as old as the Garden of Eden (remember? Adam blames Eve, Eve blames the serpent). It is a game which is no longer to be played in the future God plans. Then everyone will wear a badge which says "the buck stops here".

The passage supplies a salutary introduction to the more famous and more comforting passage which follows it, which is

why the two have been printed together at the head of this
section.

THE NEW COVENANT

Jeremiah 31:31-34 (*cont'd*)

It is somewhat ironic that for many people this is the only
passage from the Book of Jeremiah with which they are
familiar, and that is only because of the way in which it is taken
up in the New Testament and claimed to be fulfilled in and
through Jesus (see Luke 22:20; 1 Cor. 11:25; Heb. 8:8ff.). If, as
has been claimed, it is "one of the mountain peaks in the Old
Testament", we are unlikely to understand it unless we struggle
up its lower slopes and see it against the surrounding landscape
in the Book of Jeremiah.

Why the talk of a *new covenant*? "Covenant" (see comment
on chapter 11 in vol.1, pp. 100ff.) is one of the words used in the
Old Testament to describe the relationship between the Lord
and his people. It is a relationship rooted in God's initiative, in
what he has done *for* the people, but it looks for a response *from*
the people. Its meaning is summed up in the words "you shall be
my people and I shall be your God". It is Jeremiah's repeated
complaint that the obligations of the covenant were ignored by
the people. They were happy to bask in all that God had given
them, but unwilling to give the obedience for which he looked.
It is Jeremiah's bitter experience that no attempt at
reformation, however sincere, could remedy this situation. All
broke down on the sheer cussedness of human nature. Between
what God demanded and what the people could give, there was
an unbridgeable gulf. Jeremiah knew that this fact had to be
faced or all talk about a new future would end up under the
shadow of the same disobedience which had ruined the past.
The new covenant passage claims that the unbridgeable can be
bridged, but only from God's side.

This new covenant, which lies for Jeremiah in the unspecified future, is here compared and contrasted with the covenant at Mt Sinai, a covenant which was the Lord's gift to the people after he had delivered them from captivity in Egypt. In what sense is it new? It is new

(1) because instead of God's law or teaching (Hebrew, *torah*) facing the people as a demand written on tablets of stone (see Exod. 31:18; 34:28–29) or in any other kind of document, that teaching will be written within their hearts. In other words, instead of obedience being a question of response to external commandments, obedience is to become second nature to the people. Inner response will replace outward demand.

(2) because there will no longer be any need for instruction in what God requires. Every Tom, Dick and Harry will know what God requires, without any prompting.

(3) because this new relationship will be one where the tragic legacy of repeated past failure will be dealt with. Through forgiveness the past will become a closed book.

In other respects this new covenant is simply a re-run of the Sinai covenant: like it, it is based on God's initiative; like it, its object is that there should be in the world a "people of God" (verse 33). It is quite wrong to think that this new covenant is the point in the Old Testament where the focus of religion switches from the community to the individual. It does not. It is about a new kind of community. It is Jeremiah's way of throwing into the future for their solution all the problems and all the continuing wrong which he saw in the relationship between his people and God. Fundamental to everything, he says, is his conviction that the solution can only come from God.

Once we move beyond that central conviction, there are certain things in this passage that ought to raise questions in our minds. No Christian, for example, not even one who protests most loudly that he belongs to "the new covenant", ever claims that there is no longer any need for instruction in the faith by way of continuing teaching. Indeed such Christians are usually the most insistent on the need for sound teaching. Yet this passage seems to claim that under the new covenant such teaching will be unnecessary (verse 34). And there is a deeper problem. We can see why the New Testament—and "Testament" is simply the Latin word for "covenant"—claims that this hope of Jeremiah's has been fulfilled in Jesus. In him we see the unbridgeable bridged. In him we see a human life, which in all its glory and true humanity, gives that obedience which Israel was never able to give. But if we look at Christians, at the new people of God, at the Church, what are we to say? If Jeremiah were in our midst today might he not still be looking forward to a new covenant, for precisely the same reasons that led him to talk about the need for one in his own day? Is there any evidence that we in the Church today are any more obedient to God than Jeremiah was, or the people in his own day were? Perhaps instead of talking glibly as Christians, as we sometimes do, about the new covenant, we ought to take a long hard look at ourselves . . . and wonder.

AN UNBREAKABLE BOND

Jeremiah 31:35-40

[35]Thus says the Lord,
   who gives the sun for light by day and the fixed order of the moon
and the stars for light by night,
   who stirs up the sea so that its waves roar—
      the Lord of hosts is his name:
[36]"If this fixed order departs from before me, says the Lord,
   then shall the descendants of Israel cease
from being a nation before me for ever."
[37]Thus says the Lord:
   "If the heavens above can be measured,
      and the foundations of the earth below can be explored,
   then I will cast off all the descendants of Israel
      for all that they have done,

                                        says the Lord."

[38]"Behold, the days are coming, says the Lord, when the city shall be rebuilt for the Lord from the tower of Hananel to the Corner Gate. [39]And the measuring line shall go out farther, straight to the hill Gareb, and shall then turn to Goah. [40]The whole valley of the dead bodies and the ashes, and all the fields as far as the brook Kidron, to the corner of the Horse Gate toward the east, shall be sacred to the Lord. It shall not be uprooted or overthrown any more for ever."

We know that the destruction of Jerusalem by the Babylonians created a crisis of faith for many people. They thought it marked the end. God had either forgotten them, or was powerless to do anything to help them (see Isa. 40:27). This section draws on two pictures to affirm that nothing can ever finally sever the unbreakable bond that unites God to the people and guarantees that they shall have a future.

The *first*, in verses 35-36, draws upon the creation story in Genesis 1 and upon hymns that celebrated God's power over creation (see Amos 5:8; 9:6). The created world functions in accordance with a God-decreed "fixed order". Everything in the natural world has its place and its time. That fixed order would have to disintegrate before Israel would cease being a nation.

The *second*, verse 37, points to a universe, vast and mysterious, unfathomable by man. Only if the mystery of the universe could be unravelled, would Israel have no future. A crisis of faith is often rooted in a vision of God which lacks a grasp of the majesty, the mystery, the greatness of a God who is "the Lord of hosts", who has at his fingertips and under his control, all the forces that shape creation and human life. Your faith cannot be big, if your God is too small.

The chapter ends, verses 38-40, looking forward to the rebuilding of Jerusalem and takes us on a tour of the city, picking out various prominent features in its topography, from the tower of Hananel in the north-east corner (see Neh. 3:1) to the "Corner Gate" on the west side of the city (see 2 Chron. 26:9). According to the architect's plans (the measuring line) the city would extend as far as the hills of Gareb and Goath, both places otherwise unknown to us but probably on the south side of the city. The "whole valley" is probably a reference to the valley of Hinnom, a place with grim associations, including child sacrifice (see comment on 7:29 in vol.1, pp. 78-79). The grim associations are to be a thing of the past as the valley is set apart ("sacred") for the Lord. The tour ends in the Kidron valley and at the Horse Gate, both on the east side of the city.

Throughout chapters 30 and 31 we meet with a typical blend of great theological certainties and a sketch of the practical outworking of these certainties in the circumstances of Jeremiah's day. The challenge to us today is how to hold on to these certainties and work out their practical implications for our day.

AN ACT OF FAITH

Jeremiah 32:1-15

[1]The word that came to Jeremiah from the Lord in the tenth year of Zedekiah king of Judah, which was the eighteenth year of Nebuchadrezzar. [2]At that time the army of the king of Babylon was besieging Jerusalem, and Jeremiah the prophet was shut up in the court of the guard which was in the palace of the king of Judah. [3]For Zedekiah king of Judah had imprisoned him, saying, "Why do you prophesy and say, 'Thus says the Lord: Behold, I am giving this city into the hand of the king of Babylon, and he shall take it; [4]Zedekiah king of Judah shall not escape out of the hand of the Chaldeans, but shall surely be given into the hand of the king of Babylon, and shall speak with him face to face and see him eye to eye; [5]and he shall take Zedekiah to Babylon, and there he shall remain until I visit him, says the Lord; though you fight against the Chaldeans, you shall not succeed'?"

[6]Jeremiah said, "The word of the Lord came to me: [7]Behold, Hanamel the son of Shallum your uncle will come to you and say, 'Buy my field which is at Anathoth, for the right of redemption by purchase is yours.' [8]Then Hanamel my cousin came to me in the court of the guard, in accordance with the word of the Lord, and

said to me, 'Buy my field which is at Anathoth in the land of Benjamin, for the right of possession and redemption is yours; buy it for yourself.' Then I knew that this was the word of the Lord.

⁹"And I bought the field at Anathoth from Hanamel my cousin, and weighed out the money to him, seventeen shekels of silver. ¹⁰I signed the deed, sealed it, got witnesses, and weighed the money on scales. ¹¹Then I took the sealed deed of purchase, containing the terms and conditions, and the open copy; ¹²and I gave the deed of purchase to Baruch the son of Neriah son of Mahseiah, in the presence of Hanamel my cousin, in the presence of the witnesses who signed the deed of purchase, and in the presence of all the Jews who were sitting in the court of the guard. ¹³I charged Baruch in their presence, saying, ¹⁴"Thus says the Lord of hosts, the God of Israel: Take these deeds, both this sealed deed of purchase and this open deed, and put them in an earthenware vessel, that they may last for a long time. ¹⁵For thus says the Lord of hosts, the God of Israel: Houses and fields and vineyards shall again be bought in this land.'"

Nowhere is Jeremiah's conviction that there would be a future for his people beyond disaster more clearly demonstrated than in this incident. It occurred in the year 588/7 B.C. (verse 1). The Babylonian army is closing in for the kill. Jeremiah is in prison, accused of defecting to the enemy (see chapters 37–38) and of treasonable activities, as the narrator of the story explains in verses 2–5. We shall have occasion to look more closely at Jeremiah's attitude when we come to the interviews he had with King Zedekiah: 34:1–5; 37; 38:14–23. Whatever Jeremiah may be accused of, it can hardly be inconsistency. In all the interviews he tells the king that the city will fall to the Babylonians and that he himself will go into exile.

To his prison comes a cousin, Hanamel, asking him to exercise "the right of redemption" (verse 7), to fulfil his obligation as the next of kin (*go-el*; see comment on 31:11) to purchase a piece of the family estate in Anathoth, his native village. The account of the meeting between them in verses 6–8 is interesting because of the light it throws on how, in certain situations, the prophet reached assurance that what he was hearing was the word of God. It begins with a word from the Lord to Jeremiah, telling him that Hanamel is coming. But that in itself does not seem to have been fully convincing to Jeremiah. It is only after Hanamel comes that he declares that he "knew that this was the word of the Lord" (verse 8). Life still works out this way. We wonder sometimes what God's will for us is, or how we can know what it is, then something happens or we meet someone who, without knowing it, says or does something that confirms for us the way ahead.

We do not know why Hanamel was putting his plot of land on the market. Perhaps he had fallen into debt, or he had decided to sell and get out before the Babylonians overran the entire country. With due legal formality and in the presence of witnesses, Jeremiah purchased the field. There were two copies of the deed of purchase (verse 11): the one folded up and formally sealed, presumably with Jeremiah's personal seal; the other left open, unsealed, so that it could be easily consulted. This accords with Jewish practice vouched for elsewhere. The copies were then given to his scribe, Baruch (see ch. 36) to deposit in an earthenware jar so that "they may last for a long time" (verse 14). Such tall earthenware jars, with documents inside them, were found in the caves near the Dead Sea, as part of the library of the Qumran sect. They too had used earthenware jars to preserve their important documents.

In itself the incident is trivial; but think of the background. The Babylonian army is on the point of destroying Jerusalem. Normal business deals are at a standstill. The bottom had fallen out of the market. You probably could not give property away for nothing. There was no confidence in the future. In this situation, in a symbolic act, Jeremiah purchases that field to indicate his faith that "houses and fields and vineyards shall again be bought in this land" (verse 15). He is looking beyond disaster to the return of normal life. This is the theme which is developed in different ways in the rest of the chapter.

A PRAYER AND FURTHER WORDS OF HOPE

Jeremiah 32:16-44

16"After I had given the deed of purchase to Baruch the son of Neriah, I prayed to the Lord, saying: 17"Ah Lord God! It is thou who hast made the heavens and the earth by thy great power and by thy outstretched arm! Nothing is too hard for thee, 18who showest steadfast love to thousands, but dost requite the guilt of fathers to their children after them, O great and mighty God whose name is the Lord of hosts, 19great in counsel and mighty in deed; whose eyes are open to all the ways of men, rewarding every man according to his ways and according to the fruit of his doings; 20who hast shown signs and wonders in the land of Egypt, and to this day in Israel and among all mankind, and hast made thee a name, as at this day. 21Thou didst bring thy people Israel out of the land of Egypt with signs and wonders, with a strong hand and outstretched arm, and with great terror; 22 and thou gavest them this land, which thou didst swear to their fathers to give them, a land flowing with milk and honey; 23and they entered and took possession of it. But they did not obey thy voice or walk in thy law; they did nothing of all thou didst command them to do. Therefore thou hast made all this evil come upon them. 24Behold, the siege mounds have come up to the city to take it, and because of sword and famine and pestilence the city is given into the hands of the Chaldeans who are fighting against it. What thou didst speak has come to pass, and behold, thou seest it. 25Yet thou, O Lord God, hast said to me, "Buy the field for money and get witnesses"—though the city is given into the hands of the Chaldeans.'"

26The word of the Lord came to Jeremiah: 27"Behold, I am the Lord, the God of all flesh; is anything too hard for me? 28Therefore, thus says the Lord: Behold, I am giving this city into the hands of the Chaldeans and into the hand of Nebuchadrezzar king of Babylon, and he shall take it. 29The Chaldeans who are fighting against this city shall come and set this city on fire, and burn it, with the houses on whose roofs incense has been offered to Baal and drink offerings have been poured out to other gods, to provoke me to anger. 30For the sons of Israel and the sons of Judah have done nothing but evil in my sight from their youth; the sons of Israel have done nothing but provoke me to anger by the work of their hands, says the Lord. 31This city has aroused my anger and wrath, from the

day it was built to this day, so that I will remove it from my sight
[32]because of all the evil of the sons of Israel and the sons of Judah
which they did to provoke me to anger—their kings and their
princes, their priests and their prophets, the men of Judah and the
inhabitants of Jerusalem. [33]They have turned to me their back and
not their face; and though I have taught them persistently they have
not listened to receive instruction. [34]They set up their abominations
in the house which is called by my name, to defile it. [35]They built the
high places of Baal in the valley of the son of Hinnom, to offer up
their sons and daughters to Molech, though I did not command
them, nor did it enter into my mind, that they should do this
abomination, to cause Judah to sin.

[36]"Now therefore thus says the Lord, the God of Israel,
concerning this city of which you say, 'It is given into the hand of
the king of Babylon by sword, by famine, and by pestilence':
[37]Behold, I will gather them from all the countries to which I drove
them in my anger and my wrath and in great indignation; I will
bring them back to this place, and I will make them dwell in safety.
[38]And they shall be my people, and I will be their God. [39]I will give
them one heart and one way, that they may fear me for ever, for
their own good and the good of their children after them. [40]I will
make with them an everlasting covenant, that I will not turn away
from doing good to them; and I will put the fear of me in their
hearts, that they may not turn from me. [41]I will rejoice in doing
them good, and I will plant them in this land in faithfulness, with all
my heart and all my soul.

[42]"For thus says the Lord: Just as I have brought all this great evil
upon this people, so I will bring upon them all the good that I
promise them. [43]Fields shall be bought in this land of which you are
saying, It is a desolation, without man or beast; it is given into the
hands of the Chaldeans. [44]Fields shall be bought for money, and
deeds shall be signed and sealed and witnessed, in the land of
Benjamin, in the places about Jerusalem, and in the cities of Judah,
in the cities of the hill country, in the cities of the Shephelah, and in
the cities of the Negeb; for I will restore their fortunes, says the
Lord."

There are good reasons why many scholars have wondered how
much, if any, of the material in this section comes from
Jeremiah. What we have here is like a series of symphonic

variations written on the theme of Jeremiah's act of faith in purchasing the plot of land at Anathoth.

There is *first* (verses 16-25) a prayer attributed to Jeremiah. It begins and ends with the purchase of the field against the dark background of national disaster. Like some other prayers, attributed to specific occasions in the Old Testament (cf. Neh. 9:6-37), it is largely a general prayer of adoration and thanksgiving, praising God for all that he is and all that he has done for his people in the past. This surely tells us something about where our priorities in prayer ought to be. We are often tempted to rush into God's presence in prayer, to bring to him our immediate problems and concerns. But this is to try to use God for our own purposes, to use him as a kind of magician who, once he has done what we want him to do, may quietly go away. But prayer brings us into the presence of a God who is always there, to a God whose greatness and love are far beyond our feeble understanding, a God before whom we bow in adoration, knowing that we exist to serve his purposes. So the prayer that Jesus taught us begins not with "give us" or "forgive us" or "lead us not into temptation", but with "Father, hallowed be thy name. Thy kingdom come . . . " (Luke 11:2).

Second, in verses 26-35, there is a word of the Lord to Jeremiah, a word of unrelenting judgement, sealing the fate of the nation, cataloguing the sins of the people and their leaders in terms with which we should be familiar from earlier sections of the book.

Third, in verses 36-41, a further word looks beyond judgement to the renewal of God's covenant with his people. This is to be "an everlasting covenant" (verse 40), in which rebellion will be a thing of the past in a community which will truly worship God and experience his goodness and dependability.

Fourth, and finally, in verses 42-44, we return to Jeremiah and his purchase. The God who brought "evil" and disaster, is the God who will bring promised "good", with fields again being bought, and legal contracts being entered into, throughout the length and breadth of the country, from the land of Benjamin to the north of Jerusalem down south, to the rolling uplands of the Shephelah and the southern desert steppe of the Negeb.

As the echoing chords of this section die away, let us never forget that they have their origin in a simple, symbolic gesture, in an act of faith by a man in prison, a man detested and ignored by most of his contemporaries.

A BRIGHT FUTURE FOR JUDAH AND JERUSALEM

Jeremiah 33:1-13

[1]The word of the Lord came to Jeremiah a second time, while he was still shut up in the court of the guard: [2]"Thus says the Lord who made the earth, the Lord who formed it to establish it—the Lord is his name: [3]Call to me and I will answer you, and will tell you great and hidden things which you have not known. [4]For thus says the Lord, the God of Israel, concerning the houses of this city and the houses of the kings of Judah which were torn down to make a defence against the siege mounds and before the sword: [5]The Chaldeans are coming in to fight and to fill them with the dead bodies of men whom I shall smite in my anger and my wrath, for I have hidden my face from this city because of all their wickedness. [6]Behold, I will bring to it health and healing, and I will heal them and reveal to them abundance of prosperity and security. [7]I will restore the fortunes of Judah and the fortunes of Israel, and rebuild them as they were at first. [8]I will cleanse them from all the guilt of their sin against me, and I will forgive all the guilt of their sin and rebellion against me. [9]And this city shall be to me a name of joy, a praise and a glory before all the nations of the earth who shall hear of all the good that I do for them; they shall fear and tremble because of all the good and all the prosperity I provide for it.

[10]"Thus says the Lord: In this place of which you say, 'It is a waste without man or beast,' in the cities of Judah and the streets of Jerusalem that are desolate, without man or inhabitant or beast, there shall be heard again [11]the voice of mirth and the voice of gladness, the voice of the bridegroom and the voice of the bride, the voices of those who sing, as they bring thank offerings to the house of the Lord:

'Give thanks to the Lord of hosts,
    for the Lord is good,
    for his steadfast love endures for ever!'

For I will restore the fortunes of the land as at first, says the Lord.
    ¹²"Thus says the Lord of hosts: In this place which is waste,
without man or beast, and in all of its cities, there shall again be
habitations of shepherds resting their flocks. ¹³In the cities of the
hill country, in the cities of the Shephelah, and in the cities of the
Negeb, in the land of Benjamin, the places about Jerusalem, and in
the cities of Judah, flocks shall again pass under the hands of the
one who counts them, says the Lord."

It is natural enough that the incident recorded in chapter 32
should be followed by a series of passages looking forward to a
bright future for Judah and Jerusalem. The link with the
previous chapter is made in verse 1—the prophet is still in
prison. After an introduction celebrating the Lord as the God
of all creation, the God who alone shapes human history and
can reveal to man "hidden things" (verse 3) *ie* the things which
still lie in the future, there are three such passages each
introduced by "Thus says the Lord" (verses 4, 10 and 12).

The *first* passage, verses 4–9, begins by stressing the futility of
any attempt to defend the city against the Babylonians. The fate
of the city has been decided by God who has "hidden his face"
from the city because of the people's wickedness (verse 5). This
is an expression found frequently in the Old Testament to point
to something that has gone wrong in the relationship between
God and his people; he has turned away from them. So a
Psalmist in a crisis situation in his life cries out:

How long, O Lord? Wilt thou forget me for ever?
    How long wilt thou hide thy face from me?

                                                    (Ps. 13:1)

But even in destruction, God's purposes are creative. The same
God who destroys will bring "health and healing", *shalom* and
security (verse 6). Side by side with the physical renewal of the

city there will come a spiritual renewal based on God's forgiveness. But the object of this renewal is not simply the future of God's people; it is to be a witness to all the world of the great things that God can do. The joy and vitality of the new city will lead others to be filled with awe and wonder. The new people of God are not to live in isolation; their God is the God of all peoples (verse 9). Here surely we can see one of the most powerful continuing agents of evangelism; not merely preaching, nor an attack on other people for their sinfulness, but the vibrant life, the joy-filled character of the believing community. And of course it works the other way. Often the greatest question mark against the Gospel is the life of the Church, the gap between what we claim to be true and the reality of our lives. Those outside don't hear, or don't listen to what we say because of what we are.

The *second* passage, verses 10–11, uses a picture which Jeremiah has used several times to describe disaster: it is that of a community which no longer hears "the voice of mirth and the voice of gladness, the voice of the bridegroom and the voice of the bride" (7:34; 16:9; 25:10). But now these sounds of laughter and joy are to return, as well as the joyful voices of worshippers bringing their thank-offerings to God and singing words that closely echo what we find in some of the great Psalms of thanksgiving, notably Psalm 136. Turn for a moment to Psalm 136. It celebrates the "steadfast love" of God (his *hesed*), there in creation (verses 4–9), in Israel's past history (verses 10–22) and in the present experience of the worshippers (verses 23–25). This "steadfast love" is the essence of Israel's faith, reaching out to embrace the future as surely as it has marked the past and the present.

The *third* passage, verses 12–13, looks forward to the revival of the life of the countryside, with pastures to which shepherds can lead their flocks, and thriving communities to which shepherds can again bring their flocks, counting the sheep as they pass into the sheepfolds to see that not one is missing. It is a picture that you find Jesus using again and again to speak of God's care for all his children (Matt. 18:12–14; Luke 15:3–7; John 10:7–18).

TRUE KINGS AND TRUE PRIESTS

Jeremiah 33:14-26

[14]"Behold, the days are coming, says the Lord, when I will fulfil the promise I made to the house of Israel and the house of Judah. [15]In those days and at that time I will cause a righteous Branch to spring forth for David; and he shall execute justice and righteousness in the land. [16]In those days Judah will be saved and Jerusalem will dwell securely. And this is the name by which it will be called: 'The Lord is our righteousness.'

[17]"For thus says the Lord: David shall never lack a man to sit on the throne of the house of Israel, [18]and the Levitical priest shall never lack a man in my presence to offer burnt offerings, to burn cereal offerings, and to make sacrifices for ever."

[19]The word of the Lord came to Jeremiah: [20]"Thus says the Lord: If you can break my covenant with the day and my covenant with the night, so that day and night will not come at their appointed time, [21]then also my covenant with David my servant may be broken, so that he shall not have a son to reign on his throne, and my covenant with the Levitical priests my ministers. [22]As the host of heaven cannot be numbered and the sands of the sea cannot be measured, so I will multiply the descendants of David my servant, and the Levitical priests who minister to me."

[23]The word of the Lord came to Jeremiah: [24]"Have you not observed what these people are saying, 'The Lord has rejected the two families which he chose'? Thus they have despised my people so that they are no longer a nation in their sight. [25]Thus says the Lord: If I have not established my covenant with day and night and the ordinances of heaven and earth, [26]then I will reject the descendants of Jacob and David my servant and will not choose one of his descendants to rule over the seed of Abraham, Isaac, and Jacob. For I will restore their fortunes, and will have mercy upon them."

For centuries before Jeremiah's day, king and priest had played essential roles in the life of Israel; the one there to give them peace, security, justice and responsible leadership, the other to instruct the people in the ways of the Lord and to lead them in worship. We have seen how Jeremiah traced much of the tragedy of the people to the failure of those in positions of responsibility within the nation: to irresponsible, despotic kings, to priests who betrayed their teaching ministry. The new community would need to be better served. This hope is expressed here in a collection of four brief passages.

The *first* passage, verses 14–16, is a slight adaptation of a passage we have already looked at in 23:5–6 (see comment on p. 25). The main difference here is that the hopeful name, "The Lord is our righteousness", which in 23:6 is applied to the coming king, is now transferred to the city of Jerusalem. Since the true king to come was vital for the well-being of the entire community, it is hardly surprising that the name which symbolizes that king's confident faith in God should also be a name appropriate for the community over which he was to rule.

The *second* and *third* passages, verses 17–18 and 19–22, link with the king to come, "the Levitical priests", literally "the priests, the Levites"; a phrase typical of the Book of Deuteronomy, but not found elsewhere in the Book of Jeremiah. We must remember that there was a close link between the royal family of David and the Temple in Jerusalem. You will find it well expressed in Psalm 132, with the promises to David of a continuing dynasty (verses 11–12) side by side with the picture of Mt Zion as God's "resting place for ever" (verse 14). Come the Babylonian rape of Jerusalem, the Temple was a smouldering ruin and there was no longer a Davidic king. So the *second* passage looks forward to a future in which there will be both a man to sit on the throne and priests to serve in the Temple and lead the people in worship. (For the different kinds of sacrifices mentioned in verse 18, see comment on 6:20, vol.1, p. 67).

The *third* passage seeks to underpin this hope:

(1) by using an argument rather like that in 31:36, appealing to the "fixed order" of things in the natural world of God's creating. The regular succession of day and night is thought of as being rooted in a "covenant" God made with day and night. Just as that "covenant" can never be broken, since it is built into the very nature of things, neither can God's covenant, or special relationship, with David and the Levitical priests (verses 20–21);

(2) and by using the language of the promises made to Abraham of countless descendants (Gen. 15:5; 22:17) and applying it to the descendants of the royal family and the priesthood (verse 22).

The *fourth* passage, verses 23–26, begins with a despairing question on the lips of the people: has their relationship with God not come to an end? It then picks up the thought of the "covenant" which guarantees the fixed order of nature, and argues that only if this is a mirage, can the promises of God, both to the people and to the royal family, fail to be fulfilled.

In the second, as in the first half of the chapter, every hope for the future is again being staked upon the dependability of God.

The New Testament takes such hopes and promises and invites us to see them all coming together in Jesus, who is both true king and true priest. It picks up the promises made to Abraham of countless descendants and finds them being fulfilled in the new people of God—the Church—which, from an early period, began to gather into its fold many from all the nations of the world (see Gal. 3:6–9).

J. THE STORMY PETREL OF THE JERUSALEM SCENE (CHS.34–39)

As if to leave us in no doubt that the words of hope in chapters 30–33 are not an easy option, side-stepping the hard reality that faced Jerusalem, chapters 34–39 tell us of a series of incidents involving Jeremiah. Two of them, in chapters 35–36, take place in the reign of Jehoiakim; the others, in chapters 34 and 37–39, come from the last two years of the reign of Zedekiah, culminating in the destruction of Jerusalem, described in chapter 39. In all of them we find Jeremiah at the storm centre of the political and religious life in the capital, a man increasingly marked down as "Public Enemy Number One" . . . and paying the penalty.

NAUGHT FOR YOUR COMFORT—AN INTERVIEW WITH ZEDEKIAH

Jeremiah 34:1-7

> [1]The word which came to Jeremiah from the Lord, when Nebuchadrezzar king of Babylon and all his army and all the kingdoms of the earth under his dominion and all the peoples were fighting against Jerusalem and all of its cities: [2]"Thus says the Lord, the God of Israel: Go and speak to Zedekiah king of Judah and say to him, 'Thus says the Lord: Behold, I am giving this city into the hand of the king of Babylon, and he shall burn it with fire. [3]You shall not escape from his hand, but shall surely be captured and delivered into his hand; you shall see the king of Babylon eye to eye and speak with him face to face; and you shall go to Babylon.' [4]Yet hear the word of the Lord, O Zedekiah king of Judah! Thus says the Lord concerning you: 'You shall not die by the sword. [5]You shall die in peace. And as spices were burned for your fathers, the former kings who were before you, so men shall burn spices for you and lament for you, saying, "Alas, lord!"' For I have spoken the word, says the Lord."
>
> [6]Then Jeremiah the prophet spoke all these words to Zedekiah king of Judah, in Jerusalem, [7]when the army of the king of Babylon was fighting against Jerusalem and against all the cities of Judah that were left, Lachish and Azekah; for these were the only fortified cities of Judah that remained.

The general issues raised by Jeremiah's hard-line attitude in his interviews with the last king of Judah have already been touched upon in the comments on 21:1-10 (see pp. 8ff.). This interview takes place late in the year 588 B.C. as a Babylonian army, with contingents from many of the vassal states, closes in on Jerusalem. The situation is increasingly critical. Of the other Judean towns, only Lachish and Azekah, garrison towns southwest of Jerusalem, remain uncaptured (verse 7). From Lachish at this time there has come a collection of interesting letters written in Hebrew. In one of them, an urgent note comes to the military governor of Lachish from one of his field officers; "Let my lord know that we are watching for the signal of Lachish, according to all the indications which my lord has given, because we cannot see Azekah". It may be that this letter was written shortly after the interview in verses 2-5, when Azekah as well had fallen into Babylonian hands.

Jeremiah does not mince words. The city is doomed. Zedekiah himself will be taken to Babylon, there as a rebellious vassal to have the error of his ways forcibly brought home to him by his imperial overlord. But there is a glimmer of hope for Zedekiah personally, "You shall not die by the sword. You shall die in peace [*shalom*]", and be buried with honours appropriate to a king. Jeremiah seems to have regarded Zedekiah in a somewhat more favourable light than he did Jehoiakim (see 22:18-19). Whether "dying in peace [*shalom*]" is the right way to describe what happened to Zedekiah is another matter. According to 39:4-7 and 52:7-11, the Babylonians killed his sons before his eyes, then blinded him. His remaining years were spent in prison in Babylon. In another interview, Jeremiah makes no such unconditional promise to Zedekiah, but placed before him the choice with which he always confronted the people—if you surrender to the Babylonians your life will be spared, but if not . . . (see 38:17).

In sixteenth century Scotland, Andrew Melville stood before James VI to argue for the freedom of the Kirk: "there are two kings and two kingdoms in Scotland. There is Christ Jesus the King and his Kingdom, the Kirk, whose subject King James the Sixth is, and of whose Kingdom, not a king, nor a lord, nor a head, but a member". That gives classic expression to a view which recognizes the difference between Church and state. But a prophet like Jeremiah goes further. He works with no such distinction between Church and state. For him there are not two kingdoms, but only one—God's kingdom. There can, therefore, be no merely political decisions. There is only God to be obeyed or disobeyed. While Zedekiah no doubt received from his military and political aides no lack of advice based on what they saw as the realities of the situation, from Jeremiah he only received the uncompromising word of the Lord.

A BRUTALLY CYNICAL ACT

Jeremiah 34:8-22

[8]The word which came to Jeremiah from the Lord, after King Zedekiah had made a covenant with all the people in Jerusalem to make a proclamation of liberty to them, [9]that every one should set free his Hebrew slaves, male and female, so that no one should enslave a Jew, his brother. [10]And they obeyed, all the princes and all the people who had entered into the covenant that everyone would set free his slave, male or female, so that they would not be enslaved again; they obeyed and set them free. [11]But afterward they turned around and took back the male and female slaves they had set free, and brought them into subjection as slaves. [12]The word of the Lord came to Jeremiah from the Lord: [13]"Thus says the Lord, the God of Israel: I made a covenant with your fathers when I brought them out of the land of Egypt, out of the house of bondage, saying, [14]'At the end of six years each of you must set free the fellow Hebrew who has been sold to you and has served you six years; you must set him free from your service.' But your fathers did not listen to me or incline their ears to me. [15]You recently repented and did what was right in my eyes by proclaiming liberty, each to his neighbour, and you made a covenant before me in the house which is called by my name; [16]but then you turned around and profaned my name when each of you took back his male and female slaves, whom you had set free according to their desire, and you brought them into subjection to be your slaves. [17]Therefore, thus says the Lord: You have not obeyed me by proclaiming liberty, every one to his brother and to his neighbour; behold, I proclaim to you liberty to the sword, to pestilence, and to famine, says the Lord. I will make you a horror to all the kingdoms of the earth. [18]And the men who transgressed my covenant and did not keep the terms of the covenant which they made before me, I will make like the calf which they cut in two and passed between its parts— [19]the princes of Judah, the princes of Jerusalem, the eunuchs, the priests, and all the people of the land who passed between the parts of the calf; [20]and I will give them into the hand of their enemies and into the hand of those who seek their lives. Their dead bodies shall be food for the birds of the air and the beasts of the earth. [21]And Zedekiah king of Judah, and his princes I will give into the hand of their enemies and into the hand of those who seek their lives, into the hand of the

army of the king of Babylon which has withdrawn from you. 22Behold, I will command, says the Lord, and will bring them back to this city; and they will fight against it, and take it, and burn it with fire. I will make the cities of Judah a desolation without inhabitant."

Early in the year 588 B.C. the Babylonians temporarily lifted the siege of Jerusalem to settle scores with an Egyptian force threatening their rear (verse 21). In this setting, in Jerusalem, there took place an act of cold and calculating cynicism.

Some time earlier, the community, led by King Zedekiah, had "made a covenant" (verse 8), had entered into a solemn agreement in the presence of God in the Temple, to emancipate all their fellow Hebrew slaves. No doubt, as ever, the motives for this action were mixed. Slaves in a beleaguered city would be regarded by some as a liability, just extra mouths to be fed: let them fend for themselves. But there were other reasons. The slaves were to be released in accordance with the provisions of the laws in Exodus 21:1ff. and Deuteronomy 15:1,12, which stated that debtor slaves should be set free "every seven years". (Similar laws governing the release of slaves are to be found in other law codes from the ancient Near East; the code of Hammurabi, for example, legislates for the release of the wife and children of a debtor sold into slavery at the end of three years.) These laws, like many other laws, had been flagrantly disregarded in Judah in Jeremiah's day. The "covenant" to emancipate such slaves was perhaps part of a last ditch effort to persuade God to work a miracle to secure the future of the city. If so, as has been well said, it was "a death-bed repentance with the usual sequence on recovery". As soon as the Babylonians began to pull back from Jerusalem and the miracle seemed to be happening, the people thought that they had acted with undue haste in releasing the slaves, and went back on their solemn pledge. After all, if life was going to return to normal, slaves would again be needed.

Jeremiah's reaction was swift and predictable. He had no doubt what the word of the Lord was in this situation. He reminded the people of the "covenant" the Lord had made with them when he had released them from slavery in Egypt. Included in that covenant was the obligation upon the people to free their slaves. By their brutally cynical act they had slapped God in the face (verse 16). They had pretended to set others free; they themselves would be set free—to fall victim to sword, pestilence and famine.

In verse 18 we are given an interesting glimpse into part of a ritual involved in entering into a covenant. A calf was cut in half and the contracting parties to the covenant walked together between the severed halves laid out on the ground (see Gen. 15:7ff.). In doing so they were invoking a curse upon themselves: if ever we violate the terms of this covenant, may the fate of the animal be our fate. Similar rites, involving the slaughter of an animal, are known to us from other parts of the ancient world. Such, said Jeremiah, would be the fate of the people who had shamelessly gone back on this covenant— death, with their leaders handed over to the Babylonians who would soon return (verse 22) to sack Jerusalem and every other city throughout the land.

It is easy to sit in judgement on Zedekiah and the people. We would perhaps do better to ponder the words of Jesus, "Judge not, that you be not judged" (Matt.7:1). Have we never been in situations, particularly tight situations, in which we have made promises to other people and to God, promises which have too easily and conveniently been forgotten when things have changed?

A SHINING EXAMPLE OF FAITHFULNESS

Jeremiah 35:1–19

[1]The word which came to Jeremiah from the Lord in the days of Jehoiakim the son of Josiah, king of Judah: [2]"Go to the house of the Rechabites, and speak with them, and bring them to the house of the Lord, into one of the chambers; then offer them wine to drink." [3]So I took Ja-azaniah the son of Jeremiah, son of

Habazziniah, and his brothers, and all his sons, and the whole house of the Rechabites. ⁴I brought them to the house of the Lord into the chamber of the sons of Hanan the son of Igdaliah, the man of God, which was near the chamber of the princes, above the chamber of Maaseiah the son of Shallum, keeper of the threshold. ⁵Then I set before the Rechabites pitchers full of wine, and cups; and I said to them, "Drink wine." ⁶But they answered, "We will drink no wine, for Jonadab, the son of Rechab, our father, commanded us, 'You shall not drink wine, neither you nor your sons for ever; ⁷you shall not build a house; you shall not sow seed; you shall not plant or have a vineyard; but you shall live in tents all your days, that you may live many days in the land where you sojourn.' ⁸We have obeyed the voice of Jonadab the son of Rechab, our father, in all that he commanded us, to drink no wine all our days, ourselves, our wives, our sons, or our daughters, ⁹and not to build houses to dwell in. We have no vineyard or field or seed; ¹⁰but we have lived in tents, and have obeyed and done all that Jonadab our father commanded us. ¹¹But when Nebuchadrezzar king of Babylon came up against the land, we said, 'Come, and let us go to Jerusalem for fear of the army of the Chaldeans and the army of the Syrians.' So we are living in Jerusalem."

¹²Then the word of the Lord came to Jeremiah: ¹³"Thus says the Lord of hosts, the God of Israel: Go and say to the men of Judah and the inhabitants of Jerusalem, Will you not receive instruction and listen to my words? says the Lord. ¹⁴The command which Jonadab the son of Rechab gave to his sons, to drink no wine, has been kept; and they drink none to this day, for they have obeyed their father's command. I have spoken to you persistently, but you have not listened to me. ¹⁵I have sent to you all my servants the prophets, sending them persistently, saying, 'Turn now every one of you from his evil way, and amend your doings, and do not go after other gods to serve them, and then you shall dwell in the land which I gave to you and your fathers.' But you did not incline your ear or listen to me. ¹⁶The sons of Jonadab the son of Rechab have kept the command which their father gave them, but this people has not obeyed me. ¹⁷Therefore, thus says the Lord, the God of hosts, the God of Israel: Behold, I am bringing on Judah and all the inhabitants of Jerusalem all the evil that I have pronounced against them; because I have spoken to them and they have not listened, I have called to them and they have not answered."

¹⁸But to the house of the Rechabites Jeremiah said, "Thus says the Lord of hosts, the God of Israel: Because you have obeyed the command of Jonadab your father, and kept all his precepts, and done all that he commanded you, ¹⁹therefore thus says the Lord of hosts, the God of Israel: Jonadab the son of Rechab shall never lack a man to stand before me."

The previous chapter described a blatant act of disobedience to God. In contrast, this chapter records a shining example of faithfulness. We go back some ten years. King Jehoiakim has rebelled against his Babylonian overlord. Marauding bands of Babylonian troops, with contingents from some of the surrounding vassal states, are creating havoc in the Judean countryside (see 2 Kings 24:2). Refugees pour into Jerusalem, among them the "house of the Rechabites", the Rechabite community or group (verses 2, 11). The founder of this group, Jehonadab son of Rechab, appears in 2 Kings 10:15 aiding and abetting Jehu's bloody revolt which liquidated the dynasty of Ahab.

The Rechabite community was founded in protest against the corrupting influence of Canaanite life and religion. Israel's settlement in Canaan was regarded as a tragic mistake. The desert was their ideal. They lived in tents. The settled agricultural life, and all its ways, was abhorrent; so they drank no wine. The very fact that such a Rechabite group was in Jerusalem may have led Jeremiah to wonder whether they were compromising their conscience. He takes them to one of the many small rooms in the Temple complex, the room assigned to "the sons of Hanan" (verse 4). If the description of Hanan as "the man of God" means that he is a prophet—that is what it means in some other Old Testament stories—then "the sons of Hanan" are probably a group of prophets attached to the Temple. And Jeremiah did not think much of the faithfulness of such prophets (see 23:9ff.). Some of the Temple officials were in all likelihood present when Jeremiah placed before the Rechabites bowls of wine, and goblets, and said to them "drink". They refused, citing their Rechabite principles, and claiming that only dire necessity had driven them temporarily to seek safety in Jerusalem. In Jeremiah's eyes their attitude shone like a beacon of sanity in a corrupt society.

Out of the incident came two words from the Lord:

(1) a word to the people of Judah and Jerusalem (verses 13–17). It is a word sharply contrasting their behaviour with that of the Rechabites. The Rechabites have remained faithful to the principles of their founding father, but the people of Judah and Jerusalem have been faithless to God, persistently ignoring the prophets sent to call them to repentance. Therefore they face disaster;

(2) a word to the Rechabites (verses 18–19). It is a word that commends their faithfulness and promises their continued existence as a group with a place in God's purposes.

At no point in the incident does Jeremiah commend the Rechabite *principles*. The Rechabites seem to have made the fundamental mistake of assuming that you can stop the clock and opt out of a changing society and culture. There are many communes and groups today, some of them religious, who are saying the same thing. They believe that the only answer to the problems of our complex, western technological society is to opt out and return to a simple, more or less self-sufficient, agrarian life. But prophets like Jeremiah never said "back to the desert". That would have been the easy way out, when faced with the problems of an increasingly urban and commercial society. Instead they called on their people to live in a changing society, but to put into practice the same concern for social brotherhood, the same commitment to righteousness and justice, the same loyalty to the Lord, which had all been part of Israel's heritage before the settlement in Canaan. For better or for worse we now live in the nuclear and space age, in the era of advanced and advancing technology. There is no way back. We can only go forward, wrestling with what obedience to God means for us in the world in which God has put us, not yearning for a past which we often so misleadingly call "the good old days".

It was not the principles of the Rechabites, but their

faithfulness, Jeremiah commended. It is such faithfulness that God looks for from all of us. There is no higher accolade than "Well done, good and faithful servant . . . enter into the joy of your master" (Matt. 25:21).

BANNED, BUT NOT SILENCED

Jeremiah 36:1-26

[1]In the fourth year of Jehoiakim the son of Josiah, king of Judah, this word came to Jeremiah from the Lord: [2]"Take a scroll and write on it all the words that I have spoken to you against Israel and Judah and all the nations, from the day I spoke to you, from the days of Josiah until today. [3]It may be that the house of Judah will hear all the evil which I intend to do to them, so that every one may turn from his evil way, and that I may forgive their iniquity and their sin."

[4]Then Jeremiah called Baruch the son of Neriah, and Baruch wrote upon a scroll at the dictation of Jeremiah all the words of the Lord which he had spoken to him. [5]And Jeremiah ordered Baruch, saying, "I am debarred from going to the house of the Lord; [6]so you are to go, and on a fast day in the hearing of all the people in the Lord's house you shall read the words of the Lord from the scroll which you have written at my dictation. You shall read them also in the hearing of all the men of Judah who come out of their cities. [7]It may be that their supplication will come before the Lord, and that every one will turn from his evil way, for great is the anger and wrath that the Lord has pronounced against this people." [8]And Baruch the son of Neriah did all that Jeremiah the prophet ordered him about reading from the scroll the words of the Lord in the Lord's house.

[9]In the fifth year of Jehoiakim the son of Josiah, king of Judah, in the ninth month, all the people in Jerusalem and all the people who came from the cities of Judah to Jerusalem proclaimed a fast before the Lord. [10]Then, in the hearing of all the people, Baruch read the words of Jeremiah from the scroll, in the house of the Lord, in the chamber of Gemariah the son of Shaphan the secretary, which was in the upper court, at the entry of the New Gate of the Lord's house.

¹¹When Micaiah the son of Gemariah, son of Shaphan, heard all the words of the Lord from the scroll, ¹²he went down to the king's house, into the secretary's chamber; and all the princes were sitting there: Elishama the secretary, Delaiah the son of Shemaiah, Elnathan the son of Achbor, Gemariah the son of Shaphan, Zedekiah the son of Hananiah, and all the princes. ¹³And Micaiah told them all the words that he had heard, when Baruch read the scroll in the hearing of the people. ¹⁴Then all the princes sent Jehudi the son of Nethaniah, son of Shelemiah, son of Cushi, to say to Baruch, "Take in your hand the scroll that you read in the hearing of the people, and come." So Baruch the son of Neriah took the scroll in his hand and came to them. ¹⁵And they said to him, "Sit down and read it," So Baruch read it to them. ¹⁶When they heard all the words, they turned one to another in fear; and they said to Baruch, "We must report all these words to the king." ¹⁷Then they asked Baruch, "Tell us, how did you write all these words? Was it at his dictation?" ¹⁸Baruch answered them, "He dictated all these words to me, while I wrote them with ink on the scroll." ¹⁹Then the princes said to Baruch, "Go and hide, you and Jeremiah, and let no one know where you are."

²⁰So they went into the court to the king, having put the scroll in the chamber of Elishama the secretary; and they reported all the words to the king. ²¹Then the king sent Jehudi to get the scroll, and he took it from the chamber of Elishama the secretary; and Jehudi read it to the king and all the princes who stood beside the king. ²²It was the ninth month, and the king was sitting in the winter house and there was a fire burning in the brazier before him. ²³As Jehudi read three or four columns, the king would cut them off with a penknife and throw them into the fire in the brazier, until the entire scroll was consumed in the fire that was in the brazier. ²⁴Yet neither the king, nor any of his servants who heard all these words, was afraid, nor did they rend their garments. ²⁵Even when Elnathan and Delaiah and Gemariah urged the king not to burn the scroll, he would not listen to them. ²⁶And the king commanded Jerahmeel the king's son and Seraiah the son of Azriel and Shelemiah the son of Abdeel to seize Baruch the secretary and Jeremiah the prophet, but the Lord hid them.

In the Introduction, pp. 1–3, we look at what chapter 36 has to tell us about the *Book* of Jeremiah; let us turn now to some of the other issues it raises. The date is given in verse 9 as "the fifth year of Jehoiakim the son of Josiah, king of Judah, in the ninth month" *ie* December 604 B.C. The occasion was a "fast day" when people from all over the country had crowded into the Temple precincts at Jerusalem. A "fast day" was always a sign of some crisis in the community, a crisis in which an appeal was made to God for help. This particular fast day was probably caused by the deteriorating military situation. In the previous year the Babylonians had soundly defeated Jehoiakim's Egyptian allies at the battle of Carchemish in Syria, and news had probably reached Jerusalem that Ashkelon in the coastal plain had just fallen to the Babylonians. Into the Temple courtyards came people anxious about their future, eager for any word of reassurance from the Lord.

Jeremiah at this time is *persona non grata* to King Jehoiakim, banned from going to the Temple—not surprisingly, in the light of his unwelcome Temple sermon (chs. 7 and 26) or his brush with the Temple authorities described in 20:1–6. Unable to speak the word of the Lord to the assembled people, at God's command he dictates to *Baruch the son of Nereiah* his call for repentance, a call which had been central to his message for many years. This is the earliest incident in the Book of Jeremiah in which Baruch features. By this time, however, he was obviously already a trusted friend of Jeremiah, his personal secretary or scribe who wrote down the words he dictated. He seems to have been with Jeremiah for the last twenty years of his life, and from his pen may have come some of the accounts of the prophet's activities during these years. How large the dictated scroll was we do not know, but it cannot have been too large since it was to be read three times in the course of that day (see verses 6, 15, 21). Baruch duly read the scroll from a secretary's room in the upper court overlooking the outer courtyard in which the people had assembled. What the reaction of the people was, we do not know. The interest of the story switches elsewhere.

The contents of the scroll must have been sufficiently disturbing, or the action of the banned prophet in having his words read on a public occasion sufficiently questionable, for a report of the incident to be communicated to the palace; to "the princes" (verse 12), the state officials who were meeting in the private room of the secretary of state, Elishama. We have a fascinating glimpse here into what is perhaps the nearest equivalent in the Old Testament to a cabinet meeting. Knowing the right people, belonging to the right family, have always been important factors in public life. Among those present were Elnathan (whose father, Achbor, had held high office under Jehoiakim's predecessor, Josiah) and Gemeriah (whose father, Shaphan, had been a state secretary under Josiah). On hearing the report of the incident, the officials sent for Baruch. They treated him with respect and invited him to sit down and read the scroll (verse 15). They were deeply disturbed by what they heard. Since the scroll must have contained material which could be construed as inflammatory, anti-government statements, a report had to be sent to the king. Anxiety round the table was probably further heightened when they ascertained from Baruch that it was indeed the words of Jeremiah that he had spoken. Yet the officials were not hostile. They knew the king well enough to realise that his immediate reaction was likely to be "off with their heads"; so they advised Baruch to go underground and to take Jeremiah with him. On more than one occasion Jeremiah was to be grateful that he had friends or sympathizers in high places.

The king's reaction is graphically described (verses 22ff.). It is winter. Surrounded by courtiers, the king is sitting in his winter quarters near a blazing open fire (brazier). As the scroll is read to him, with studied contempt he cuts it into strips with a knife and drops it column by column into the fire. Ignoring pleas from officials to preserve the scroll, he remains totally indifferent to what is written on the scroll. The words of the prophet go up in smoke: king and courtiers can sleep easily in their beds. Orders go out for the arrest of Baruch and Jeremiah, "but the Lord hid them" (verse 26), which is another way of saying, what the Greek text in fact says here, that they had gone into hiding. Providence for the Old Testament is not something which works apart from human decisions and actions. God works in and through us and other people, in the situations we face and in the way we cope with them.

REPEATING THE MESSAGE—AND MORE

Jeremiah 36:27–32

²⁷ Now, after the king had burned the scroll with the words which Baruch wrote at Jeremiah's dictation, the word of the Lord came to Jeremiah: ²⁸"Take another scroll and write on it all the former words that were in the first scroll, which Jehoiakim the king of Judah has burned. ²⁹And concerning Jehoiakim king of Judah you shall say, 'Thus says the Lord, You have burned this scroll, saying, "Why have you written in it that the king of Babylon will certainly come and destroy this land, and will cut off from it man and beast?" ³⁰Therefore thus says the Lord concerning Jehoiakim king of Judah, He shall have none to sit upon the throne of David, and his dead body shall be cast out to the heat by day and the frost by night. ³¹And I will punish him and his offspring and his servants for their iniquity; I will bring upon them, and upon the inhabitants of Jerusalem, and upon the men of Judah, all the evil that I have pronounced against them, but they would not hear.'"

³²Then Jeremiah took another scroll and gave it to Baruch the scribe, the son of Neriah, who wrote on it at the dictation of Jeremiah all the words of the scroll which Jehoiakim king of Judah had burned in the fire; and many similar words were added to them.

This incident is one of the earliest we have of an attempt to apply official censorship to unpopular views. Whether it is done by religious or political authorities, the attempt to silence opposition by banning or destroying the written word is an exercise in futility. Alexander Solzhenitsyn, who more than most suffered from state censorship in his native Russia, said in his Nobel Lecture on Literature:

"Literature, together with language, protects the soul of the nation . . . But woe to the nation whose literature is disturbed by the intervention of power. Because this is not just a violation of 'the freedom of the press', it is a closing down of the heart of the nation, a slashing to pieces of the memory".

But just as Solzhenitsyn could not be effectively silenced even in his native Russia, no more could Jehoiakim's knife slash to pieces or close down what the prophet had to say to the heart of his people.

Jeremiah's response, no doubt from his underground hiding place, is two-fold:

(1) At God's command he redictates the words of the offensive scroll to Baruch, and for good measure "many similar words were added to them" (verse 32). The response to the attempt to silence him is more of the same.

(2) Focussing upon the fact that Jehoiakim's objection to the scroll centred upon its words concerning the coming destruction of the nation at the hands of the Babylonians, Jeremiah adds a further word of judgement upon king and people. No descendant of Jehoiakim is ever to sit upon the throne—a statement not strictly fulfilled, since Jehoiakim's son did reign if only for a few months. Jehoiakim himself is to come to an ignominious end (cf. 22:18–19). There is perhaps conscious irony in the words of the second half of verse 30. We have seen the king sitting by a blazing fire in his winter quarters, "casting" Jeremiah's scroll into the flames; now his dead body is to be "cast out", unburied, exposed "to the heat by day and the frost by night".

In chapter 22:13–17 we have Jeremiah's savage attack upon Jehoiakim as the corrupt, unworthy son of a godly father, Josiah. Perhaps the story of the scroll that Jehoiakim destroyed is intended to underline the contrast. Both have dealings with a scroll in the Temple. Josiah, according to 2 Kings 22, has a scroll read to him; he listens . . . it leads to national reformation. Jehoiakim has a scroll read to him; he does not listen, he consigns it to the flames . . . it leads to national disaster. So the different choices we take, when faced with similar situations, are fraught with consequences for good or for evil.

AN URGENT REQUEST—AN UNCOMPROMISING REPLY

Jeremiah 37:1-10

¹Zedekiah the son of Josiah, whom Nebuchadrezzar king of Babylon made king in the land of Judah, reigned instead of Coniah the son of Jehoiakim. ²But neither he nor his servants nor the people of the land listened to the words of the Lord which he spoke through Jeremiah the prophet.

³King Zedekiah sent Jehucal the son of Shelemiah, and Zephaniah the priest, the son of Maaseiah, to Jeremiah the prophet, saying, "Pray for us to the Lord our God." ⁴Now Jeremiah was still going in and out among the people, for he had not yet been put in prison. ⁵The army of Pharaoh had come out of Egypt; and when the Chaldeans who were besieging Jerusalem heard news of them, they withdrew from Jerusalem.

⁶Then the word of the Lord came to Jeremiah the prophet: ⁷"Thus says the Lord, God of Israel: Thus shall you say to the king of Judah who sent you to me to inquire of me, 'Behold, Pharaoh's army which came to help you is about to return to Egypt, to its own land. ⁸And the Chaldeans shall come back and fight against this city; they shall take it and burn it with fire. ⁹Thus says the Lord, Do not deceive yourselves, saying, "The Chaldeans will surely stay away from us," for they will not stay away. ¹⁰For even if you should defeat the whole army of Chaldeans who are fighting against you, and there remained of them only wounded men, every man in his tent, they would rise up and burn this city with fire.'"

With chapters 37 and 38 we move the clock forward again to the reign of Zedekiah; to the last fateful years of his reign. The events in these chapters are crowded into a brief period between the summer of 588 B.C., when the Babylonians temporarily slackened their grip on Jerusalem to deal with the Egyptians, and July 587 B.C., when the city was sacked. From 37:11 to the end of chapter 38, we are faced with a puzzle that you must unravel for yourself. It is this: twice Jeremiah is arrested (37:11-14 and 38:4-5); twice he appears before the "princes" and ends up in a cistern (37:15 and 38:6); twice he is taken from there to be interviewed by King Zedekiah (37:16-20 and

38:14-26); and twice he pleads with Zedekiah not to send him back to "the house of Jonathan the secretary" (37:20 and 38:26). Although there are differences between the accounts, they are no greater than those we find in the two accounts of the Temple sermon in chapters 7 and 26, and no greater than the differences we find in the Gospels concerning the life of Jesus or the resurrection. Unless we hold to certain rigid views about the inspiration of the Bible, we lose little by seeing in these chapters two accounts of one and the same event. Both paint the same picture of the prophet in his relationship with the king, his uncompromising message, and his harsh treatment at the hands of the civil authorities. The stories are vivid and speak for themselves with little needed by way of comment.

The same is true of the story that precedes them. After the opening verses 1-2, which switch the scene from the reign of Jehoiakim to that of Zedekiah, we have an account, similar to the one which we have already come across in 21:1-10, of a delegation sent by King Zedekiah to Jeremiah with the request, "Pray for us to the Lord"; pray, in other words, that by a miracle we may yet be delivered from the Babylonians. This incident takes place slightly earlier than the events recounted later in the chapter, since Jeremiah is not yet under arrest (verse 4). The word that Jeremiah sends back is clear and uncompromising: don't deceive yourselves, the Babylonians have only temporarily withdrawn. They shall return. The city is doomed, doomed not by the Babylonians, but by God.

Verse 10 shows us, beyond any shadow of doubt, that political and military considerations did not influence Jeremiah's views. Suppose, he says to Zedekiah, you win a great victory and there are left of the Babylonian army only wounded men lying in their tents, they would still "rise up and burn this city with fire." There is a bleak and awesome certainty about Jeremiah's words. They are not open to argument. They can have done little to increase his popularity in the eyes of the king or of his officials; one of whom, Jehucal son of Shelemiah, is later named as being among those who took active steps to have Jeremiah silenced (see 38:1). It is hard to see what the

E

politicians of the day could have made of Jeremiah. They were concerned to take responsible decisions in the light of what seemed to them to be the political realities of the day. Jeremiah was concerned to proclaim the word of the Lord. It is a classic confrontation that we find again in the Gospel story; Pilate weighing up the political realities in the turbulent province in which he was responsible for law and order and the *Pax Romana,* against Jesus whose kingdom is "not of this world" (John 18:36).

Yet it is unwise to dismiss Jeremiah as a starry-eyed religious fanatic. He had consistently advocated, as the word of the Lord, a political stance—surrender to Babylon—a stance which was a live option if only those in power had had the courage to take it. No more is the costly, self-sacrificing kingship of love which took Jesus to the cross irrelevant to the problems of our world—if only we have the courage to live it.

ARREST, IMPRISONMENT AND A SECRET INTERVIEW

Jeremiah 37:11–21

[11]Now when the Chaldean army had withdrawn from Jerusalem at the approach of Pharaoh's army, [12]Jeremiah set out from Jerusalem to go to the land of Benjamin to receive his portion there among the people. [13]When he was at the Benjamin Gate, a sentry there named Irijah the son of shelemiah, son of Hananaih, seized Jeremiah the prophet, saying, "You are deserting to the Chaldeans." [14]And Jeremiah said, "It is false; I am not deserting to the Chaldeans." But Irijah would not listen to him, and seized Jeremiah and brought him to the princes. [15]And the princes were enraged at Jeremiah, and they beat him and imprisoned him in the house of Jonathan the secretary, for it had been made a prison.

[16]When Jeremiah had come to the dungeon cells, and remained there many days, [17]King Zedekiah sent for him, and received him. The king questioned him secretly in his house, and said, "Is there any word from the Lord?" Jeremiah said, "There is." Then he said,

"You shall be delivered into the hand of the king of Babylon."
¹⁸Jeremiah also said to King Zedekiah, "What wrong have I done to you or your servants or this people, that you have put me in prison? ¹⁹Where are your prophets who prophesied to you, saying, 'The king of Babylon will not come against you and against this land'? ²⁰Now hear, I pray you, O my lord the king: let my humble plea come before you, and do not send me back to the house of Jonathan the secretary, lest I die there." ²¹So King Zedekiah gave orders, and they committed Jeremiah to the court of the guard; and a loaf of bread was given him daily from the bakers' street, until all the bread of the city was gone. So Jeremiah remained in the court of the guard.

During the lull in the siege, Jeremiah tries to leave the city "to go to the land of Benjamin to receive his portion there among the people" (verse 12). It is not entirely clear what this means. The incident must have happened before Jeremiah redeemed the piece of family property in chapter 32, since in chapter 32 Jeremiah is already in prison. It may be that in view of the critical political situation, Jeremiah had been invited to return to his native village of Anathoth to discuss with other members of the family what to do with the family estate. The sentry, on duty at the Benjamin Gate on the north side of the city, can hardly be blamed for arresting him and charging him with deserting to the enemy. After all Jeremiah had been urging everyone else in Jerusalem to do just that, and we know that some of them had done it (38:19). What could be more natural than that he should be following his own advice? No doubt instructions had gone out from the military authorities to keep a close watch on Jeremiah.

Vehemently, but in vain, Jeremiah denies that he is deserting. He is handed over to the state officials—"the princes"—who flog him and imprison him "in the house of Jonathan the secretary" (verse 15). Why he was taken to the house of Jonathan, rather than to the state prison, called "the court of the guard" (verse 21), we do not know. Perhaps he was considered too dangerous, too much of a security risk to mix with common criminals; perhaps in the isolation of Jonathan's house he could more easily be subjected to "third degree" treatment. The house of Jonathan is soon to have for Jeremiah the horrific associations that Gestapo headquarters had for many Jews in the 1930s in Germany.

In the house of Jonathan, Jeremiah ends up in "the dungeon cells" (verse 16), literally the cistern house. Such cisterns were usually hewn out of limestone rock. Narrow at the top, they opened out into a bottle-shaped cavity in which water was stored. They were rather like the bottle dungeons that you find in old castles, such as the castle at St Andrews in Scotland; and they could serve the same purpose. There prisoners could be left to rot, to go mad or to die. Jeremiah was saved from such a fate by the intervention of Zedekiah, still pathetically anxious to know, "Is there any word from the Lord?" (verse 17). Yes, there is, says Jeremiah, but it is no different from what it has been all along (see 21:7).

There is no way in which Jeremiah would attempt to bribe his way out of his desperate plight by telling Zedekiah what he wanted to hear. He protests to the king about the injustice of his treatment, contrasting his plight with that of "the prophets" who had always prophesied that all would be well, and whom events were now showing to be false prophets. Such prophets, according to Deuteronomy 18:20, ought to be put to death, but they are still at liberty; while Jeremiah who had persistently proclaimed a word that nobody wished to hear, but a word that events were justifying, was in prison. It is true, is it not, that we have a continuing capacity to close our ears to the truth about ourselves when it hurts, and to go on listening to what we want to hear, even when we know that it is not true.

King Zedekiah obviously cannot get Jeremiah out of his system. He seems to have had a shrewd suspicion that what Jeremiah was saying might be the truth, however unpalatable. His interview with the prophet takes place "secretly" (verse 17), Zedekiah being unable or unwilling to cross the state officials and his political advisers who had taken action against Jeremiah. He shows his sympathy for Jeremiah to the extent of granting the prophet's request not to be sent back to his private hell in the house of Jonathan. He has him transferred to the state prison, "the court of the guard", near to the palace, where he was at least guaranteed food and a certain degree of freedom. It is to this "court of the guard" that his cousin Hanamel came on family business (see ch. 32). It is there that Jeremiah remained during the final Babylonian attack on Jerusalem (see 38:28).

He survived on rations brought to him daily from "the street of the bakers" (verse 21), an interesting glimpse into the way in which, in the ancient world, people who followed the same craft or trade would live in the same quarter of the town. The system long remained, and the memory of it is still preserved in our street names, like Baker Street or Petticoat Lane.

ARREST AND IMPRISONMENT—ANOTHER VERSION

Jeremiah 38:1-13

¹Now Shephatiah the son of Mattan, Gedaliah the son of Pashhur, Jucal the son of Shelemiah, and Pashhur the son of Malchiah heard the words that Jeremiah was saying to all the people, ²"Thus says the Lord, He who stays in this city shall die by the sword, by famine, and by pestilence; but he who goes out to the Chaldeans shall live; he shall have his life as a prize of war, and live. ³Thus says the Lord, This city shall surely be given into the hand of the army of the king of Babylon and be taken." ⁴Then the princes said to the king, "Let this man be put to death, for he is weakening the hands of the soldiers who are left in this city, and the hands of all the people, by speaking such words to them. For this man is not seeking the welfare of this people, but their harm." ⁵King Zedekiah said, "Behold, he is in your hands; for the king can do nothing against you." ⁶So they took Jeremiah and cast him into the cistern of Malchiah, the king's son, which was in the court of the guard, letting Jeremiah down by ropes. And there was no water in the cistern, but only mire, and Jeremiah sank in the mire.

⁷When Ebedmelech the Ethiopian, a eunuch, who was in the

king's house, heard that they had put Jeremiah into the cistern—
the king was sitting in the Benjamin Gate—⁸Ebedmelech went
from the king's house and said to the king, ⁹"My lord the king, these
men have done evil in all that they did to Jeremiah the prophet by
casting him into the cistern; and he will die there of hunger, for
there is no bread left in the city." ¹⁰Then the king commanded
Ebedmelech, the Ethiopian, "Take three men with you from here,
and lift Jeremiah the prophet out of the cistern before he dies." ¹¹So
Ebedmelech took the men with him and went to the house of the
king, to a wardrobe of the storehouse, and took from there old rags
and worn-out clothes, which he let down to Jeremiah in the cistern
by ropes. ¹²Then Ebedmelech the Ethiopian said to Jeremiah, "Put
the rags and clothes between your armpits and the ropes." Jeremiah
did so. ¹³Then they drew Jeremiah up with ropes and lifted him out
of the cistern. And Jeremiah remained in the court of the guard.

In this version of Jeremiah's arrest, the state officials openly
accuse Jeremiah of treason. They condemn him out of his own
mouth, quoting his own words against him; verses 2–3 being
virtually a quotation of what Jeremiah said in 21:9–10. They
rightly demand from the king the death penalty for a man who
was undermining the morale of soldiers and civilians; a man
who, instead of working for the *shalom* of his country, was
doing his best to destroy it. Their attitude is perfectly
understandable; Jeremiah did no more and no less than any
other person who has been shot for high treason in time of war.
Zedekiah reveals the weakness of his own position and where
true power in fact lay in Jerusalem, by handing Jeremiah over
to his accusers (verse 5). Again we are reminded of Pilate,
washing his hands before the crowd and handing Jesus over to
those who were howling for his blood (Matt.27:24). This time
Jeremiah is dragged off to be lowered by rope into a cistern
belonging to "Malchiah, the king's son", there no doubt to be
left to die a slow and lingering death, sinking into the mud in the
otherwise empty cistern. We know nothing more about
Malchiah nor whether he had any relationship with Jonathan
the state secretary who featured in the previous arrest story. It is
clear, however, that Malchiah was working hand in hand with

the powerful political lobby out to silence the prophet.

Once again it is claimed that Jeremiah owed his life to the king. Ebedmelech—his name means "servant of the king"—an Ethiopian eunuch, one of the palace staff, reports the prophet's plight to the king and is told to take a small rescue party with him to get Jeremiah out of the cistern before he dies. Ebedmelech seems to have been one of those thoughtful, practical people who do the little things to make life that bit easier for others. He not only takes a rope to pull Jeremiah out of the cistern, but realising that the rescue operation may be difficult, with the rope liable to cut into Jeremiah's flesh as they try to pull him out of the mud, he collects old rags and worn out clothing from a palace store room and lowers them, together with the rope, to Jeremiah, so that he may put them under his arms to cushion himself and prevent unnecessary pain. It is often such thoughtfulness in little things that leaves the most lasting impression in our memories. Mission accomplished, Jeremiah is transferred to "the court of the guard".

A SECRET INTERVIEW—ANOTHER VERSION

Jeremiah 38:14–28

14King Zedekiah sent for Jeremiah the prophet and received him at the third entrance of the temple of the Lord. The king said to Jeremiah, "I will ask you a question; hide nothing from me." 15Jeremiah said to Zedekiah, "If I tell you, will you not be sure to put me to death? And if I give you counsel, you will not listen to me." 16Then King Zedekiah swore secretly to Jeremiah, "As the Lord lives, who made our souls, I will not put you to death or deliver you into the hand of these men who seek your life."

17Then Jeremiah said to Zedekiah, "Thus says the Lord, the God of hosts, the God of Israel, If you will surrender to the princes of the king of Babylon, then your life shall be spared, and this city shall not be burned with fire, and you and your house shall live. 18But if you do not surrender to the princes of the king of Babylon, then this city shall be given into the hand of the Chaldeans, and they shall burn it with fire, and you shall not escape from their hand." [19]King Zedekiah said to Jeremiah, "I am afraid of the Jews who have deserted to the Chaldeans, lest I be handed over to them and they abuse me." [20]Jeremiah said, "You shall not be given to them. Obey now the voice of the Lord in what I say to you, and it shall be well with you, and your life shall be spared. [21]But if you refuse to surrender, this is the vision which the Lord has shown to me: [22]Behold, all the women left in the house of the king of Judah were being led out to the princes of the king of Babylon and were saying,

'Your trusted friends have deceived you
　　and prevailed against you;
now that your feet are sunk in the mire,
　　they turn away from you.'

[23]All your wives and your sons shall be led out to the Chaldeans, and you yourself shall not escape from their hand, but shall be seized by the king of Babylon; and this city shall be burned with fire."

[24]Then Zedekiah said to Jeremiah, "Let no one know of these words and you shall not die. [25]If the princes hear that I have spoken with you and come to you and say to you, 'Tell us what you said to the king and what the king said to you; hide nothing from us and we will not put you to death,' [26]then you shall say to them, 'I made a humble plea to the king that he would not send me back to the house of Jonathan to die there.'" [27]Then all the princes came to Jeremiah and asked him, and he answered them as the king had instructed him. So they left off speaking with him, for the conversation had not been overheard. [28]And Jeremiah remained in the court of the guard until the day that Jerusalem was taken.

This account of an interview between king and prophet is revealing for the light it throws on the character both of Zedekiah and Jeremiah.

Let us look first at Zedekiah. His sense of insecurity runs through the interview from beginning to end. The interview has to take place once more in secret; this time "at the third entrance of the temple of the Lord" (verse 14). Where this "third entrance" was, we do not know; it may have been a royal, private passage-way leading from the palace to the Temple. It was obviously considered suitable for an interview, away from the public gaze or the prying eye of certain officials. The king is desperately anxious that the interview should be entirely 'off the record'. He makes Jeremiah promise at the end (verses 25-27) not to divulge what has transpired between them to the state officials, even under threat of death. All that Jeremiah is permitted to divulge is that he has petitioned the king not to be sent back to face death in "the house of Jonathan"; a curious statement which fits in better with the arrest story in chapter 37 than the one we have just read in chapter 38, unless we assume that the cistern of Malchiah and the cistern in the house of Jonathan are one and the same place.

Zedekiah is still unwilling or unable to surrender the city to the Babylonians, and one of the reasons he gives is that he is afraid of the Jews who had already deserted to the Babylonians—presumably some of them in response to the prophet's words—and who would hold Zedekiah personally responsible for the continuing, long drawn-out agony of their people (verse 19). A man like Zedekiah, riddled with fears, is a man who can never take firm decisions. "What will other people think or do?" has never been a satisfactory guide for responsible living. Zedekiah dithered until Jerusalem burned.

What of Jeremiah? He seems to be very much on edge. Before he will speak, he wants reassurance that what he says will not simply be taken down and used in evidence against him. He is afraid that if he speaks the unpalatable truth to the king he will be signing his own death warrant; he knows, on the basis of past experience, that any advice he offers to the king is liable to be ignored (verse 15). It is only after the king guarantees his safety that he speaks. There is, however, no comfort for Zedekiah in the word Jeremiah has to proclaim; no compromise in his message. The only safety lies, even at the eleventh hour, in surrendering the city to the Babylonians.

The consequences of refusing to do so are spelled out to the king in the form of a "vision which the Lord has shown to me" (verse 21). It is a vision of the womenfolk in the palace being led out to be handed over to the king of Babylon, and chanting as they go, a lament:

They misled you, overruled you,
  These good "friends" of yours;
 Now your feet are sunk in the bog,
  They have left you and gone.

(verse 22; John Bright's translation, Anchor Bible)

If this is a traditional lament we have no knowledge of it elsewhere in the Old Testament, although echoes of its language are to be found in several Psalms. Psalm 41:9 speaks about being betrayed by one who was trusted as a "bosom friend", who now exults in the psalmist's misfortune; while in Psalm 69:13, the psalmist pleads with God to rescue him from "sinking in the mire". The words translated by the RSV, "your trusted friends", at the beginning of the lament, are literally, in Hebrew, "the men of your *shalom*", the people who claim to be interested in your welfare. The reference could be either to Zedekiah's political and religious advisers, or to his erstwhile allies, the Egyptians, in whom he had placed great hopes.

At the end of the interview Jeremiah agrees with Zedekiah not to divulge to the state officials what had taken place between them. Even when the officials promise him, under interrogation, immunity from execution, he calmly lies to them. It is almost as if he were sheltering behind his own personal 'Official Secrets Act'. He lies primarily to protect the king, as many others have lied to protect sources of information or, for example, to protect, in time of war, refugees or soldiers they were sheltering. We can argue back and forward as to whether Jeremiah's lie was justified. It is an issue that probably never occurred to the narrator of the story. He was primarily concerned to show us how, to the very end, Jeremiah, in spite of the personal pressures upon him, remained true to his prophetic calling, refusing to compromise on his message about the necessary destruction of Jerusalem. Strangely and providentially he survived, living on daily prison rations.

THE FALL OF JERUSALEM

Jeremiah 39:1–18

[1]In the ninth year of Zedekiah king of Judah, in the tenth month, Nebuchadrezzar king of Babylon and all his army came against Jerusalem and besieged it; [2]in the eleventh year of Zedekiah, in the fourth month, on the ninth day of the month, a breach was made in the city. [3]When Jerusalem was taken, all the princes of the king of Babylon came and sat in the middle gate: Nergal-sharezer, Samgar-nebo, Sarsechim the Rabsaris, Nergal-sharezer the Rabmag, with all the rest of the officers of the king of Babylon. [4]When Zedekiah king of Judah and all the soldiers saw them, they fled, going out of the city at night by way of the king's garden through the gate between the two walls; and they went toward the Arabah. [5]But the army of the Chaldeans pursued them, and overtook Zedekiah in the plains of Jericho; and when they had taken him, they brought him up to Nebuchadrezzar king of Babylon, at Riblah, in the land of Hamath; and he passed sentence upon him. [6]The king of Babylon slew the sons of Zedekiah at Riblah before his eyes; and the king of Babylon slew all the nobles of Judah. [7]He put out the eyes of Zedekiah, and bound him in fetters to take him to Babylon. [8]The Chaldeans burned the king's house and the house of the people, and broke down the walls of Jerusalem. [9]Then Nebuzaradan, the captain of the guard, carried into exile to Babylon the rest of the people who were left in the city, those who had deserted to him, and the people who remained. [10]Nebuzaradan, the captain of the guard, left in the land of Judah some of the poor people who owned nothing, and gave them vineyards and fields at the same time.

[11]Nebuchadrezzar king of Babylon gave command concerning Jeremiah through Nebuzaradan, the captain of the guard, saying, [12]"Take him, look after him well and do him no harm, but deal with him as he tells you." [13]So Nebuzaradan the captain of the guard, Nebushazban the Rabsaris, Nergal-sharezer the Rabmag, and all the chief officers of the king of Babylon [14]sent and took Jeremiah from the court of the guard. They entrusted him to Gedaliah the son of Ahikam, son of Shaphan, that he should take him home. So he dwelt among the people.

[15]The word of the Lord came to Jeremiah while he was shut up in the court of the guard: [16]"Go, and say to Ebed-melech the Ethiopian, 'Thus says the Lord of hosts, the God of Israel: Behold, I

will fulfil my words against this city for evil and not for good, and they shall be accomplished before you on that day. ¹⁷But I will deliver you on that day, says the Lord, and you shall not be given into the hand of the men of whom you are afraid. ¹⁸For I will surely save you, and you shall not fall by the sword; but you shall have your life as a prize of·war, because you have put your trust in me, says the Lord.'"

This chapter in many ways sets the seal on Jeremiah's prophetic ministry. It describes briefly in verses 1–10 the event which vindicated Jeremiah's message; the capture of Jerusalem by the Babylonians in July 587 B.C. Had it not happened, we would in all probability be reading in our Bible today not the Book of Jeremiah but the Book of Hananiah (see ch. 28). A fuller account, of which these verses seem to be an abridgement, is to be found in chapter 52. Certain features in this account seem to be somewhat garbled. In particular, verse 3 seems to mix up the personal names and titles of some high-ranking Babylonian officials. It probably should contain the names of only three officials—as in the New English Bible—and is best read in the light of the information in verse 13. But the identity of certain Babylonian officials is of minor interest. We are more concerned with the fate of the two people central to the previous chapters—King Zedekiah and Jeremiah.

Like many other rulers, when the situation gets out of control—most recently Milton Obote in Uganda—the king seeks safety in flight. Under cover of darkness and with his personal bodyguard, he slips out of the city "by way of the king's garden through the gate between the two walls" (verse 4). (If that was a secret escape route, its secret remains down to the present day.) Out of the city he makes his way down to the "Arabah", the southern end of the Jordan valley. Near Jericho, however, he is captured by Babylonian troops, taken to Nebuchadrezzar's head-quarters at Riblah in Syria, and there he is dealt with summarily as befits a rebellious vassal. After being forced to witness the execution of his sons and his entourage, he himself is blinded and sent in chains to Babylon.

Chapter 52:11 tells us that he died in prison in Babylon, but gives us no indication as to how long his imprisonment lasted. Meanwhile looting continued in Jerusalem, where Nebuzaradan, the emperor's personal envoy, organized a mass deportation of the surviving population, leaving only the poorest peasants to cultivate the land. Neither king nor people could escape the judgement of God that Jeremiah had consistently predicted. We may ignore God, or disobey him, or seek to escape from him, but sooner or later he catches up.

What of Jeremiah? Verses 11–14 give us one account of what happened to the prophet when the city fell (you will find another account in 40:1–6). The Babylonian authorities were obviously well informed about Jeremiah's apparently favourable attitude. The information probably came from Jewish deserters. He was on their list of trusted collaborators. A Babylonian military tribunal authorized his release from "the court of the guard", and he was handed over for safe-keeping to "Gedaliah the son of Ahikam, son of Shaphan" (verse 14). Once again the family of Shaphan plays its part in Jeremiah's life (see at 26:24). Gedaliah had, in fact, been appointed by the Babylonians as governor of the reorganized province of Judah.

Verses 15–18, which go more naturally with the previous chapter, contain a word of hope for Ebedmelech, the Ethiopian eunuch who had rescued Jeremiah from the cistern (38:7–13). When the city falls he is to be protected and to escape with his life (for the language of verse 18 see the comment on 21:9), "because you have put your trust in me, says the Lord". This phrase, in its context, does not need to have any deep religious significance. It may simply mean that Ebedmelech had been sympathetic to, and had done something to help, Jeremiah, the prophet of the Lord. Perhaps he would have been as surprised by this verdict on his life as were those who gathered round the throne of judgement to be told, "Truly I say to you, as you did it to one of the least of these my brethren, you did it to me" (Matt. 25:40).

K. AFTER THE HOLOCAUST (CHS.40–45)

Chapters 40–44 describe a series of incidents, set in the days, the months and perhaps the years, immediately after the destruction of Jerusalem. For Jeremiah and for the people, the period ought to have marked a watershed in their lives. The city was in ruins, the countryside ravaged. But if external circumstances had changed, much else, including the people's attitude to God and the prophet's uphill ministry, remained unchanged. (On chapter 45 see the relevant commentary, below.)

FREEDOM FOR JEREMIAH

Jeremiah 40:1–6

[1]The word that came to Jeremiah from the Lord after Nebuzaradan the captain of the guard had let him go from Ramah, when he took him bound in chains along with all the captives of Jerusalem and Judah who were being exiled to Babylon. [2]The captain of the guard took Jeremiah and said to him, "The Lord your God pronounced this evil against this place; [3]the Lord has brought it about, and has done as he said. Because you sinned against the Lord, and did not obey his voice, this thing has come upon you. [4]Now, behold, I release you today from the chains on your hands. If it seems good to you to come with me to Babylon, come, and I will look after you well; but if it seems wrong to you to come with me to Babylon, do not come. See, the whole land is before you; go wherever you think it good and right to go. [5]If you remain, then return to Gedaliah the son of Ahikam, son of Shaphan, whom the king of Babylon appointed governor of the cities of Judah, and dwell with him among the people; or go wherever you think it right to go." So the captain of the guard gave him an allowance of food and a present, and let him go. [6]Then Jeremiah went to Gedaliah the son of Ahikam, at Mizpah, and dwelt with him among the people who were left in the land.

This passage presents us with a rather different account of how Jeremiah was set free by the Babylonians and entrusted to Gedaliah, son of Ahikam. We find Jeremiah, among a group of deportees from Jerusalem, in a transit camp at Ramah, some five miles north of the capital. No doubt in the process of screening the deportees, Nebuzaradan comes across Jeremiah. He is obviously aware of the prophet's message predicting the disaster that had overtaken Jerusalem—the "you" in verse 3 is plural, and refers to the people, not to the prophet. He releases Jeremiah and offers him the choice of a safe conduct to Babylon and a prosperous new life, or of staying among his own people.

What Jeremiah's reply to this generous offer was we do not know, since the opening words of verse 5 do not make sense in the Hebrew text. English Bibles present us with a variety of guesses. As good as any is the New English Bible: "Jeremiah had not yet answered when Nebuzaradan went on, 'Go back ... '" (cf.GNB). This suggests that Jeremiah had at least shown no enthusiasm for a free passage to Babylon. The upshot is that Jeremiah, generously treated by Nebuzaradan, joins Gedaliah at Mizpah (modern Tell en-Nasbeh) some eight miles north of Jerusalem, where Gedaliah had established his administrative head-quarters for the province.

(If you wish to reconcile this story with that in 39:11–14, then you have to assume that, after his initial release from imprisonment by the Babylonian authorities, Jeremiah was picked up by Babylonian troops somewhere in Jerusalem, and rounded up with the other intended deportees. The authorities then discovered their mistake as the deportees were being screened at Ramah. That is not impossible, given that the situation in Jerusalem immediately after the capture of the city must have been somewhat chaotic. But just as we have seen various accounts of the prophet's arrest and imprisonment, so more than one story may have been told as to how Jeremiah was treated by the Babylonians, and how he came to join Gedaliah at Mizpah.)

If the people and the politicians in Jerusalem misunderstood Jeremiah, it is equally likely that the Babylonians made the same mistake. To them he must have seemed pro-Babylonian, a trustworthy collaborator. But Jeremiah was no more merely pro-Babylonian, than he was merely a traitor to his own country. The explanation of his whole life and of all his activities lay in that "word of the Lord" which gripped, which tore him apart, and to which he could not be false. He refused what Babylon had to offer him; he chose to stay among his own people, because he believed he had unfinished business among them. There could be hope beyond disaster. There could be continuing faith in the Lord even in a ravaged countryside and among a people deprived of much that they had hitherto considered essential to their faith. Perhaps he now expected that they would be more prepared to listen to him; if so, he was to be sadly disillusioned.

FIRST STEPS IN RECONSTRUCTION—FOILED

Jeremiah 40:7–41:3

7When all the captains of the forces in the open country and their men heard that the king of Babylon had appointed Gedaliah the son of Ahikam governor in the land, and had committed to him men, women, and children, those of the poorest of the land who had not been taken into exile to Babylon, 8they went to Gedaliah at Mizpah—Ishmael the son of Nethaniah, Johanan the son of Kareah, Seraiah the son of Tanhumeth, the sons of Ephai the Netophathite, Jezaniah the son of the Maacathite, they and their men. 9Gedaliah the son of Ahikam, son of Shaphan, swore to them and their men, saying, "Do not be afraid to serve the Chaldeans. Dwell in the land, and serve the king of Babylon, and it shall be well with you. 10As for me, I will dwell at Mizpah, to stand for you before the Chaldeans who will come to us; but as for you, gather wine and summer fruits and oil, and store them in your vessels, and dwell in your cities that you have taken." 11Likewise, when all the Jews who were in Moab and among the Ammonites and in Edom and in other lands heard that the king of Babylon had left a remnant in Judah and had appointed Gedaliah the son of Ahikam, son of

Shaphan, as governor over them, [12]then all the Jews returned from all the places to which they had been driven and came to the land of Judah, to Gedaliah at Mizpah; and they gathered wine and summer fruits in great abundance.

[13]Now Johanan the son of Kareah and all the leaders of the forces in the open country came to Gedaliah at Mizpath [14]and said to him, "Do you know that Baalis the king of the Ammonites has sent Ishmael the son of Nethaniah to take your life?" But Gedaliah the son of Ahikam would not believe them. [15]Then Johanan the son of Kareah spoke secretly to Gedaliah at Mizpah, "Let me go and slay Ishmael the son of Nethaniah, and no one will know it. Why should he take your life, so that all the Jews who are gathered about you would be scattered, and the remnant of Judah would perish?" [16]But Gedaliah the son of Ahikam said to Johanan the son of Kareah, "You shall not do this thing, for you are speaking falsely of Ishmael."

[1]In the seventh month, Ishmael the son of Nethaniah, son of Elishama, of the royal family, one of the chief officers of the king, came with ten men to Gedaliah the son of Ahikam, at Mizpah. As they ate bread together there at Mizpah, [2]Ishmael the son of Nethaniah and the ten men with him rose up and struck down Gedaliah the son of Ahikam, son of Shaphan, with the sword, and killed him, whom the king of Babylon had appointed governor in the land. [3]Ishmael also slew all the Jews who were with Gedaliah at Mizpah, and the Chaldean soldiers who happened to be there.

At Mizpah Gedaliah, the Babylonian nominee, set up his provisional government of reconstruction (cf. 2 Kings 25:22–24). His policy was to accept the *fait accompli* of Babylonian rule and to resume, as far as possible, normal life. The harvest of the soil had to be gathered and settlements rebuilt (verse 10). Round him there gathered three distinct groups of people:

(1) the economically underprivileged peasants who had not been deported (verse 7);

(2) "the captains of the forces in the open country and their men" (verse 7), that is, units of the Judean army who had probably been carrying on guerrilla warfare against the Babylonians and had not yet been mopped up. They seem to

have realized that further resistance to the occupation troops was, for the time being at least, futile;

(3) and Jewish refugees who came back from across the Jordan, where they had fled to escape the Babylonian invasion (verses 11–12).

It was always going to be a rather uneasy coalition of people with different loyalties and different hopes. In return for their submission to Babylonian rule, Gedaliah promised to represent their interests to the Babylonian authorities.

At first the signs were promising. Harvest came and was well up to expectations (verse 12). But Gedaliah's administration was fragile. As many countries in central Africa today have discovered to their cost, it is never easy to integrate guerrilla groups into the life of a people seeking peace and reconciliation. Nor are those who have fled the country always welcomed back with open arms by those who have stayed to live through armed struggle and national tragedy. Gedaliah's own position was far from easy. In the eyes of many people he must have seemed little more than a Babylonian stooge, a quisling. Whatever hopes there may have been for this community were shattered by the assassination of Gedaliah.

When a group of guerrilla commanders, led by Johanan the son of Kareah (verse 13), came to inform Gedaliah that one of their number, Ishmael the son of Nethaniah, was involved in a plot against his life, instigated by a foreign power, "Gedaliah would not believe them" (verse 14). He may have dismissed it as inter-group animosity or he may have been the kind of person who genuinely refused to believe that one of his own associates would plot against him. History is strewn with examples of those who have trusted others implicitly, only to discover too late that their trust was misplaced: none more dramatic than Caesar's dying words, *Et tu, Brute*. So when Johanan, well aware of the catastrophic effect the death of Gedaliah would have upon the community, offers quietly to liquidate Ishmael, Gedaliah says "no".

What the interests of the conspirators in the plot were is hard to say. Since the Ammonites had been deeply involved in previous anti-Babylonian movements (27:3), perhaps Baalis, the king of the Ammonites, was trying to create continuing unrest in Judah. Ishmael, who in 41:1 is described as the grandson of a member of the royal family, may have been hoping to gain power for himself in Judah. If so, his plan badly misfired, and in the aftermath of the assassination he was forced to flee to Ammon.

Johanan's suspicions were more than justified. As Gedaliah provided hospitality for Ishmael and ten companions at Mizpah, he was assassinated. It was a brutal act done in violation of all the normally accepted conventions of hospitality in the east, where a host guarantees his guests the protection of his house, and a guest does not lift a finger against his host. It was not only brutal, it was senseless. Ishmael must have known that to assassinate the Babylonian-appointed governor at Mizpah, and his entourage, and then to eliminate the no doubt token Babylonian military unit in the town, was to invite reprisals from the occupation regime. Perhaps he had dreams of leading a successful Jewish revolt against a foreign overlord, as Judas Maccabeus was to do some four centuries later (see 1 and 2 Maccabees in the Apocrypha). If that were his plan, he had seriously misjudged the situation. The time for such a move was not yet.

The assassination of Gedaliah took place, according to 41:1, "in the seventh month". Since no year is mentioned, the implication seems to be that this is the October of the same year as the fall of Jerusalem. If so, events had moved very swiftly. Gedaliah's attempt at reconstruction had been short-lived. It is often easier to destroy than to rebuild. The knife that plunged into Gedaliah destroyed in a moment the dreams that he, and no doubt others, had of a reviving and prospering Jewish community in Judah in the years immediately after the Babylonian sack of Jerusalem.

FURTHER BLOODSHED

Jeremiah 41:4-18

⁴On the day after the murder of Gedaliah, before any one knew of it, ⁵eighty men arrived from Shechem and Shiloh and Samaria, with their beards shaved and their clothes torn, and their bodies gashed, bringing cereal offerings and incense to present at the temple of the Lord. ⁶And Ishmael the son of Nethaniah came out from Mizpah to meet them, weeping as he came. As he met them, he said to them, "Come in to Gedaliah the son of Ahikam." ⁷When they came into the city, Ishmael the son of Nethaniah and the men with him slew them, and cast them into a cistern. ⁸But there were ten men among them who said to Ishmael, "Do not kill us, for we have stores of wheat, barley, oil, and honey hidden in the fields." So he refrained and did not kill them with their companions.

⁹Now the cistern into which Ishmael cast all the bodies of the men whom he had slain was the large cistern which King Asa had made for defence against Baasha king of Israel; Ishmael the son of Nethaniah filled it with the slain. ¹⁰Then Ishmael took captive all the rest of the people who were in Mizpah, the king's daughters and all the people who were left at Mizpah, whom Nebuzaradan, the captain of the guard, had committed to Gedaliah the son of Ahikam. Ishmael the son of Nethaniah took them captive and set out to cross over to the Ammonites.

¹¹But when Johanan the son of Kareah and all the leaders of the forces with him heard of all the evil which Ishmael the son of Nethaniah had done, ¹²they took all their men and went to fight against Ishmael the son of Nethaniah. They came upon him at the great pool which is in Gibeon. ¹³And when all the people who were with Ishmael saw Johanan the son of Kareah and all the leaders of the forces with him, they rejoiced. ¹⁴So all the people whom Ishmael had carried away captive from Mizpah turned about and came back, and went to Johanan the son of Kareah. ¹⁵But Ishmael the son of Nethaniah escaped from Johanan with eight men, and went to the Ammonites. ¹⁶Then Johanan the son of Kareah and all the leaders of the forces with him took all the rest of the people whom Ishmael the son of Nethaniah had carried away captive from Mizpah after he had slain Gedaliah the son of Ahikam—soldiers, women, children, and eunuchs, whom Johanan brought back from Gibeon. ¹⁷And they went and stayed at Geruth Chimham near

Bethlehem, intending to go to Egypt [18]because of the Chaldeans; for they were afraid of them, because Ishmael the son of Nethaniah had slain Gedaliah the son of Ahikam, whom the king of Babylon had made governor over the land.

Ishmael's next act, on the day after the murder of Gedaliah, is hard to understand. A group of eighty pilgrims from the north—from Shiloh, Shechem and Samaria—reach Mizpah on their way to Jerusalem. They obviously know of the destruction of Jerusalem and the Temple. They come in mourning. The typical outward signs of mourning are there for all to see—shaven beards, torn clothes, lacerated bodies. The site of the Temple at Jerusalem, however much a ruin, is still to them a sacred site, the one legitimate place for the worship of the Lord, according to the reformation King Josiah carried out in 621 B.C., a reformation designed to reunite north and south. They come bringing offerings and they come at the traditional time for the celebration of the New Year festival in the Jerusalem Temple. If the reconstruction that some scholars have made of that festival is right, it celebrates the victory of the Lord over all the forces in the world that threaten his kingship. Psalms 93, 96–99 are thought by many to belong to this festival. Read them and assimilate their lively faith that "the Lord reigns". But does he? The pilgrims come in mourning, because of the forces in the world that seem to deny that the Lord reigns. They come doubtless in hope that their faith in God's kingship may be renewed.

Ishmael, pretending to share their mourning, invites them into the city in the name of Gedaliah, then proceeds to massacre seventy of them, throwing their bodies into a cistern, "the large cistern" which King Asa of Judah had constructed some three hundred years earlier to increase the defence potential of Mizpah (1 Kings 15:22). The other ten, who claimed to have hidden stores of food, he spared, probably to hold them for ransom. Why Ishmael committed this atrocity we can only guess. Perhaps he was trying to ensure that no news of what had happened at Mizpah the previous day should reach the outside world, until he had consolidated his position. If so, it was simply the misfortune of these people that they found themselves in the wrong place at the wrong time. They were the innocent victims of another's political ambitions. The seventy who died are then symbolic of the tragedy of so many people in our world today, whose only crime is that they are in the wrong place at the wrong time. You find their blood in the streets of , Beirut, of San Salvador, of the black townships of South Africa, in Northern Ireland and Nicaragua; and the distraught faces of relatives fill our TV screens.

Apart from Gedaliah, his immediate entourage, a Babylonian platoon and the unfortunate seventy, others in Mizpah escaped the massacre, only to be forced to join Ishmael as he returned to his base in Ammon. Who "the king's daughters" mentioned in verse 10 are, is hard to say. They need not be strictly daughters of King Zedekiah; this could be a general term indicating any of the womenfolk connected with the royal family. The people leave; the hopes centred in Mizpah are gone.

It is clear that the assassination of Gedaliah and the subsequent blood-bath took place while other military commanders, including Johanan, were absent from the town. On hearing of the tragedy, however, they immediately set out in pursuit of Ishmael. They caught up with him "at the great pool which is in Gibeon", some three miles south-west of Mizpah (verse 12). At the site of ancient Gibeon, (modern el-Jib) there has been uncovered a huge round reservoir, hewn out of rock, with steps leading down some eighty-two feet to the water supply at the bottom. This may be what is meant by "the great pool". There Ishmael finds himself deserted by the people whom he had forced to leave Mizpah: he himself, however, makes good his escape, with eight companions, to Ammon. He leaves behind him a bitter legacy. Johanan and the others realise only too well that the events at Mizpah are bound to provoke reprisals from the Babylonians. There is only one place, not controlled by Babylon, that seems to offer long term security. The survivors from Mizpah take the road south—to

Egypt. They camp (verse 17) at "Geruth Chimham" near Bethlehem, a place not otherwise mentioned in the Old Testament (for "Chimham" as the name of a person, see 2 Sam.19:37–40).

It is noteworthy that in all the events described in 40:7–41:18, there is no mention of Jeremiah. We last heard of him in 40:6, having taken up residence with Gedaliah at Mizpah. How did he escape Ishmael's blood-bath? Was he absent from Mizpah when it happened? Had he nothing to say about the murder of Gedaliah and the massacre of the pilgrims? At this point we are totally in the dark. Jeremiah now resurfaces at the point where the decision has already been taken to go to Egypt. It is as if, as far as Jeremiah the prophet is concerned, the events at Mizpah do little more than set the scene for his next prophetic word; and it is one no more acceptable to his listeners than his previous words had been.

IS THERE A WORD FROM THE LORD?

Jeremiah 42:1–22

¹Then all the commanders of the forces, and Johanan the son of Kareah and Azariah the son of Hoshaiah, and all the people from the least to the greatest, came near ²and said to Jeremiah the prophet, "Let our supplication come before you, and pray to the Lord your God for us, for all this remnant (for we are left but a few of many, as your eyes see us), ³that the Lord your God may show us the way we should go, and the thing that we should do." ⁴Jeremiah the prophet said to them, "I have heard you; behold, I will pray to the Lord your God according to your request, and whatever the Lord answers you I will tell you; I will keep nothing back from you." ⁵Then they said to Jeremiah, "May the Lord be a true and faithful witness against us if we do not act according to all the word with which the Lord your God sends you to us. ⁶Whether it is good or evil, we will obey the voice of the Lord our God to whom we are sending you, that it may be well with us when we obey the voice of the Lord our God."

⁷At the end of ten days the word of the Lord came to Jeremiah. ⁸Then he summoned Johanan the son of Kareah and all the commanders of the forces who were with him, and all the people from the least to the greatest, ⁹and said to them, "Thus says the Lord, the God of Israel, to whom you sent me to present your supplication before him: ¹⁰If you will remain in this land, then I will build you up and not pull you down; I will plant you, and not pluck you up; for I repent of the evil which I did to you. ¹¹Do not fear the king of Babylon, of whom you are afraid; do not fear him, says the Lord, for I am with you, to save you and to deliver you from his hand. ¹²I will grant you mercy, that he may have mercy on you and let you remain in your own land. ¹³But if you say, 'We will not remain in this land,' disobeying the voice of the Lord your God ¹⁴and saying, 'No, we will go to the land of Egypt, where we shall not see war, or hear the sound of the trumpet, or be hungry for bread, and we will dwell there,' ¹⁵then hear the word of the Lord, O remnant of Judah. Thus says the Lord of hosts, the God of Israel: If you set your faces to enter Egypt and go to live there, ¹⁶then the sword which you fear shall overtake you there in the land of Egypt; and the famine of which you are afraid shall follow hard after you to Egypt; and there you shall die. ¹⁷All the men who have set their faces to go to Egypt to live there shall die by the sword, by famine, and by pestilence; they shall have no remnant or survivor from the evil which I will bring upon them.

¹⁸"For thus says the Lord of hosts, the God of Israel: As my anger and my wrath were poured out on the inhabitants of Jerusalem, so my wrath will be poured out on you when you go to Egypt. You shall become an execration, a horror, a curse, and a taunt. You shall see this place no more. ¹⁹The Lord has said to you, O remnant of Judah, 'Do not go to Egypt.' Know for a certainty that I have warned you this day ²⁰that you have gone astray at the cost of your lives. For you sent me to the Lord your God saying, 'Pray for us to the Lord our God, and whatever the Lord our God says declare to us and we will do it.' ²¹And I have this day declared it to you, but you have not obeyed the voice of the Lord your God in anything that he sent me to tell you. ²²Now therefore know for a certainty that you shall die by the sword, by famine, and by pestilence in the place where you desire to go to live."

For the refugees from Mizpah the decision to go to Egypt was a big step to take. They were turning their backs on their homeland for fear of Babylonian reprisals; they were moving to an uncertain future in a foreign land. The military leaders and the community as a whole, now reduced to a comparatively small group, wish to be reassured that they have taken the right decision. They wish to be sure of God's will, so they approach Jeremiah asking him to "pray to the Lord your God for us", to pray for guidance as to what they ought to do. Jeremiah agrees to their request, but warns them that if it is the Lord's answer that they want, it is the Lord's answer they will get; that and nothing else. The people protest that that *is* what they want. They solemnly and emphatically promise that they will obey the "voice of the Lord our God", "whether it is good or evil" (verse 6); a Hebrew idiom equivalent to our expression, 'whatever it may be'.

We have noticed before that the way people talk about God can be very revealing (see comment on 2:14-19 in vol.1,pp.29-30). Is this true in this passage? When the people first approach Jeremiah, they ask him to pray for us to "the Lord your God" (verses 2-3), as if they believed that, as a prophet, Jeremiah had some special hot-line to God, which ensured that God was more his than theirs. As if to emphasize that this is not so, Jeremiah replies that he will pray for them to "the Lord your [*ie* the people's] God" (verse 4), the God who is not his private possession, but the God of everyone present. When it comes to their loud protestations that they will accept God's answer whatever it is, the people are talking about "the Lord our God" (verse 6), as if they had accepted the point Jeremiah had made. But perhaps they are already on the way to drawing the wrong conclusions from it. As becomes clear in 43:1-4, however much the people claim that they are truly seeking God's guidance, they are really only wanting God to confirm and to give his blessing to what they have already decided for themselves. They already know what they want to hear from this God and their minds are closed to anything else. Perhaps they are unconsciously using God—"*our* God"—as we are so often in danger of doing, not least in our prayers.

If the people knew what they wanted God to say, Jeremiah did not. He has no immediate word to give them (cf.28:11–12). It was ten days before he could come to the people and say, "Thus says the Lord . . . " (verse 9). What was he doing during these ten days? We are not told, but it is reasonable to assume that through prayer and meditation, he was wrestling with the issues that faced him and his people, using his mind, his God-given common sense, and seeking guidance. He did not speak until he was convinced that he knew the will of God.

Then he spoke in a way that left the people in no doubt. This is God's word: stay where you are; here is where God means you to rebuild your lives. Don't be afraid of Babylonian reprisals. Trust in the Lord's presence; trust in his power and compassion. God has sent disaster upon the land, but not willingly. He had sent it "with great sorrow" (GNB—this is better than the RSV's "repent" in verse 10). God's purpose is that you should "remain in your own land" (verse 12). To go to Egypt in search of security is to court disaster. It is disobedience to the will of God. Everything that you fear may happen to you here in Judah, that and more will be your fate in Egypt. To go to Egypt is once again to lay yourselves open to "the anger and the wrath of God", and to experience the harsh reality of his judgement. Go to Egypt and you will never again see your native land (verses 13–18).

The closing section of the chapter, verses 19–22, anticipates that the response of the people will be to reject the word of the Lord. It spells out the dire consequences of so doing. That is why many scholars think that 43:1–4, which describe the people's response, ought to come before these verses. Certainly to our way of thinking the story is more dramatic if verses 19–22 come after 43:1–4. On the other hand, Jeremiah's word had so often been rejected in the past that he must have known that what he was now saying was not what the people wanted to hear. He may therefore have thrown down the gauntlet to them, by anticipating their rejection of the word.

DOWN TO EGYPT

Jeremiah 43:1-13

¹When Jeremiah finished speaking to all the people all these words of the Lord their God, with which the Lord their God had sent him to them, ²Azariah the son of Hoshaiah and Johanan the son of Kareah and all the insolent men said to Jeremiah, "You are telling a lie. The Lord our God did not send you to say, 'Do not go to Egypt to live there'; ³but Baruch the son of Neriah has set you against us, to deliver us into the hand of the Chaldeans, that they may kill us or take us into exile in Babylon." ⁴So Johanan the son of Kareah and all the commanders of the forces and all the people did not obey the voice of the Lord, to remain in the land of Judah. ⁵But Johanan the son of Kareah and all the commanders of the forces took all the remnant of Judah who had returned to live in the land of Judah from all the nations to which they had been driven— ⁶the men, the women, the children, the princesses, and every person whom Nebuzaradan the captain of the guard had left with Gedaliah the son of Ahikam, son of Shaphan; also Jeremiah the prophet and Baruch the son of Neriah. ⁷And they came into the land of Egypt, for they did not obey the voice of the Lord. And they arrived at Tahpanhes.

⁸Then the word of the Lord came to Jeremiah in Tahpanhes: ⁹"Take in your hands large stones, and hide them in the mortar in the pavement which is at the entrance to Pharaoh's palace in Tahpanhes, in the sight of the men of Judah, ¹⁰and say to them, 'Thus says the Lord of hosts, the God of Israel: Behold, I will send and take Nebuchadrezzar the king of Babylon, my servant, and he will set his throne above these stones which I have hid, and he will spread his royal canopy over them. ¹¹He shall come and smite the land of Egypt, giving to the pestilence those who are doomed to the pestilence, to captivity those who are doomed to captivity, and to the sword those who are doomed to the sword. ¹²He shall kindle a fire in the temples of the gods of Egypt; and he shall burn them and carry them away captive; and he shall clean the land of Egypt, as a shepherd cleans his cloak of vermin; and he shall go away from there in peace. ¹³He shall break the obelisks of Heliopolis which is in the land of Egypt; and the temples of the gods of Egypt he shall burn with fire.'"

Predictable or not, the response Jeremiah gets is blunt, angry and insolent: "You are telling a lie" (verse 2). They are accusing him of being a false prophet (see 23:9ff.); and not only that, but of being unduly influenced in his message by Baruch, whom they seem to suspect of having strong pro-Babylonian leanings. This is the first indication we have had that Baruch, along with Jeremiah, had survived the destruction of Jerusalem.

That Baruch had any influence over what Jeremiah had to say is not suggested by any of the previous incidents in which Baruch has appeared. His relationship to Jeremiah has been very much that of a scribe, taking down what Jeremiah dictates to him and reading the prophet's script. Nevertheless there may be a reason for the charge made here. It may well be that during the days in which Jeremiah waited for the word of the Lord, he discussed the situation with Baruch. There is no particular virtue in claiming to be alone with God to the exclusion of other people. One of the ways in which guidance still comes to us is through seeking the advice of fellow Christians. But if Baruch was there to listen and to advise, it was not the word of Baruch that Jeremiah proclaimed to the people, it was the word of the Lord.

Having rejected the word of the Lord that came to them on the lips of Jeremiah, the refugee group set out for Egypt and reached Tahpanhes, a frontier town in the eastern Delta of the Nile (verse 7;cf.2:16). With them went Jeremiah and Baruch. Did Jeremiah go willingly or did those in charge of the group give him no option? He was a prophet. He had been known to be right in the past. Although the people were convinced that he was wrong in his most recent word, they may have thought that he would be a useful person to have around at some future date. On the other hand, it would have been quite in character for Jeremiah willingly to go along with the people who had rejected the word of the Lord. He did so by staying in Jerusalem to share the self-inflicted agony of his people, even when he counselled them to desert to the Babylonians. He may have believed that God wanted him to stay with his people in their continuing disobedience. That is always a more difficult and costly thing to do than to spend all your time in the company of like-minded believers.

The last words of Jeremiah that we have, come to us from Egypt. How long he survived in Egypt we do not know. But however long or short his stay in Egypt, one thing is clear. If we define the success of a prophet in terms of his ability to communicate effectively with other people so that they come to accept the truth of what he is saying in the name of God, then Jeremiah was no more successful among his compatriots in Egypt than he had been back home in Jerusalem. The only 'success' that came his way was that from beginning to end, in spite of pressure from those around him, in spite of inner turmoil, he remained faithful to the word that God gave him.

Jeremiah had warned the refugees that there would be no lasting security for them in Egypt. He now underlines this message to those in Tahpanhes by means of a symbolic act (verse 9) and an accompanying word (verses 10-13). For the meaning of such symbolic acts and their place in the prophet's life and ministry, see comment on 13:1-14, vol.1, p.111. Although the exact meaning of some of the words in verse 9 is not clear—for example, the words translated, "mortar" and "pavement"—what the prophet did and why he did it are hardly in doubt.

In the presence of his fellow refugees—"the men of Judah"— he took some large stones and embedded them in some kind of cement or mortar, near the entrance to one of the local "government buildings" (GNB—this is probably the meaning of the words that the RSV translates as "Pharaoh's palace" in verse 9). As the accompanying word makes clear, these large stones were to be the pedestal upon which the Babylonian emperor, Nebuchadrezzar, would place his throne, and over which he would pitch his royal tent, when he crushed the power of Egypt. He would descend upon the land, devastate it, and set fire to the Egyptian temples, including the famous temple of Re, the sun god, at Heliopolis (Sun city), near Memphis (verse 13). The extent of the Babylonian "clean out" of Egypt is portrayed in a homely and vivid illustration, familiar to many who have travelled in the east, and neatly translated in GNB: "As a shepherd picks his clothes clean of lice, so the king of Babylon will pick the land of Egypt clean, and then leave victorious" (verse 12).

Some ten years later Nebuchadrezzar did march against Egypt. He did not, however, "clean out" the land as this passage suggests. He did not seem to have had in mind any permanent conquest of Egypt. It was more by way of a warning expedition, letting the Egyptians know that any interference by them in what were considered to be the internal affairs of the Babylonian Empire would not be tolerated.

These words of Jeremiah's, therefore, were, in certain respects, not fulfilled to the letter. It is doubtful whether he would have lost any sleep over that. He was not in the game of setting himself up as an expert political analyst or pundit. The details of a coming Babylonian invasion of Egypt were hardly his concern. His purpose was to drive home to his fellow countrymen that, having rejected the word of the Lord by seeking refuge in Egypt, the new life they hoped to build there would come crashing down about their ears. If they had left Judah because of their fear of Babylonian reprisals, in Egypt the Babylonians would catch up with them. For those who deliberately "did not obey the voice of the Lord" (verse 4), there could be no future.

SOME PEOPLE NEVER LEARN

Jeremiah 44:1-14

[1]The word that came to Jeremiah concerning all the Jews that dwelt in the land of Egypt, at Migdol, at Tahpanhes, at Memphis, and in the land of Pathros, [2]"Thus says the Lord of hosts, the God of Israel: You have seen all the evil that I brought upon Jerusalem and upon all the cities of Judah. Behold, this day they are a desolation, and no one dwells in them, [3]because of the wickedness which they committed, provoking me to anger, in that they went to burn

incense and serve other gods that they knew not, neither they, nor you, nor your fathers. ⁴Yet I persistently sent to you all my servants the prophets, saying, 'Oh, do not do this abominable thing that I hate!' ⁵But they did not listen or incline their ear, to turn from their wickedness and burn no incense to other gods. ⁶Therefore my wrath and my anger were poured forth and kindled in the cities of Judah and in the streets of Jerusalem; and they became a waste and a desolation, as at this day. ⁷And now thus says the Lord God of hosts, the God of Israel: Why do you commit this great evil against yourselves, to cut off from you man and woman, infant and child, from the midst of Judah, leaving you no remnant? ⁸Why do you provoke me to anger with the works of your hands, burning incense to other gods in the land of Egypt where you have come to live, that you may be cut off and become a curse and a taunt among all the nations of the earth? ⁹Have you forgotten the wickedness of your fathers, the wickedness of the kings of Judah, the wickedness of their wives, your own wickedness, and the wickedness of your wives, which they committed in the land of Judah and in the streets of Jerusalem? ¹⁰They have not humbled themselves even to this day, nor have they feared, nor walked in my law and my statutes which I set before you and before your fathers.

¹¹"Therefore thus says the Lord of hosts, the God of Israel: Behold, I will set my face against you for evil, to cut off all Judah. ¹²I will take the remnant of Judah who have set their faces to come to the land of Egypt to live, and they shall all be consumed; in the land of Egypt they shall fall; by the sword and by famine they shall be consumed; from the least to the greatest, they shall die by the sword and by famine; and they shall become an execration, a horror, a curse, and a taunt. ¹³I will punish those who dwell in the land of Egypt, as I have punished Jerusalem, with the sword, with famine, and with pestilence, ¹⁴so that none of the remnant of Judah who have come to live in the land of Egypt shall escape or survive or return to the land of Judah, to which they desire to return to dwell there; for they shall not return, except some fugitives."

We come now to the final act as far as Jeremiah's relationship with his own people is concerned. It is an attack on Jewish settlers in Egypt for having apparently learned nothing from bitter past experience. A wide range of Jewish settlements are listed in this passage: from Migdol, a town like Tahpanhes in the eastern Nile Delta region, through Memphis some thirteen miles south of modern Cairo, to Pathros, a word which means "the land of the south", a region which would include the Jewish settlement which we know existed at Elephantine, near Assuan, and from which there have survived a series of documents in Aramaic, spanning the fifth century B.C. For centuries there had been a good deal of coming and going between Egypt and Judah. Some of these settlements must have been well established before the refugees from Mizpah came to Egypt.

The passage begins by pointing to the tragedy that had befallen the Judean homeland, the result of religious apostasy and the repeated failure of the people to heed the warnings that the Lord had persistently sent through his "servants the prophets" (verse 4, a characteristic phrase to describe the true prophetic tradition in the Book of Jeremiah, cf.7:25; 25:4; 29:19). Why then should the settlers in Egypt continue in the same tradition of religious apostasy by fitting easily into their religious environment, by "burning incense to other gods in the land of Egypt" (verse 8)? Had the lesson of the past not sunk in? Such conduct had sealed the fate of Judah and Jerusalem; it would seal the fate of the Jewish settlers in Egypt. They were lining up for themselves an inevitable rendezvous with the terrible three scourges, "sword, famine . . . and pestilence" (verses 12–13), the agents of God's retribution. Any hopes that the settlers may have been harbouring of one day returning to their Judean homeland were doomed to come to nothing. None of them would return. The last three words of verse 14, "except some fugitives", should probably be regarded as a later addition to the text, holding out a glimmer of hope, or should be translated as in the New English Bible, "not one [shall] escape".

We should try to understand the situation in which these Jewish settlers in Egypt found themselves. They were a minority, at best a tolerated minority, in a foreign land. As we know from the Elephantine documents, relationships with the local native population were not always easy. It surely made sense for them to adapt *as far as possible* to local Egyptian customs. The women in particular seem to have felt the need for social acceptance and integration. But how far is "as far as possible"? It is a question with which many minority ethnic groups in Britain and elsewhere have had to struggle, in the light of their traditional family, social and religious customs. For the Jews in Egypt, if acceptance meant paying respect to Egyptian gods and goddesses in the local temples, was there any real harm in it? Why give unnecessary offence? No-one likes to be branded as 'different', an odd-ball. We can alwaays come up with what seem to be good reasons for compromise, none better than "what's the harm in it, if everyone else in the community is doing it?" It was an argument that cut no ice with Jeremiah.

A CLASH OF VIEWS

Jeremiah 44:15-30

[15]Then all the men who knew that their wives had offered incense to other gods, and all the women who stood by, a great assembly, all the people who dwelt in Pathros in the land of Egypt, answered Jeremiah: [16]"As for the word which you have spoken to us in the name of the Lord, we will not listen to you. [17]But we will do everything that we have vowed, burn incense to the queen of heaven and pour out libations to her, as we did, both we and our fathers, our kings and our princes, in the cities of Judah and in the streets of Jerusalem; for then we had plenty of food, and prospered, and saw no evil. [18]But since we left off burning incense to the queen of heaven and pouring out libations to her, we have lacked everything and have been consumed by the sword and by famine." [19]And the women said, "When we burned incense to the queen of heaven and poured out libations to her, was it without our husbands' approval that we made cakes for her bearing her image and poured out libations to her?"

[20]Then Jeremiah said to all the people, men and women, all the people who had given him this answer: [21]"As for the incense that you burned in the cities of Judah and in the streets of Jerusalem, you and your fathers, your kings and your princes, and the people of the land, did not the Lord remember it? Did it not come into his

F

mind? [22]The Lord could no longer bear your evil doings and the abominations which you committed; therefore your land has become a desolation and a waste and a curse, without inhabitant, as it is this day. [23]It is because you burned incense, and because you sinned against the Lord and did not obey the voice of the Lord or walk in his law and in his statutes and in his testimonies, that this evil has befallen you, as at this day."

[24]Jeremiah said to all the people and all the women, "Hear the word of the Lord, all you of Judah who are in the land of Egypt, [25]Thus says the Lord of hosts, the God of Israel: You and your wives have declared with your mouths, and have fulfilled it with your hands, saying, 'We will surely perform our vows that we have made, to burn incense to the queen of heaven and to pour out libations to her.' Then confirm your vows and perform your vows! [26]Therefore hear the word of the Lord, all you of Judah who dwell in the land of Egypt: Behold, I have sworn by my great name, says the Lord, that my name shall no more be invoked by the mouth of any man of Judah in all the land of Egypt, saying, 'As the Lord God lives.' [27]Behold, I am watching over them for evil and not for good; all the men of Judah who are in the land of Egypt shall be consumed by the sword and by famine, until there is an end of them. [28]And those who escape the sword shall return from the land of Egypt to the land of Judah, few in number; and all the remnant of Judah, who came to the land of Egypt to live, shall know whose word will stand, mine or theirs. [29]This shall be the sign to you, says the Lord, that I will punish you in this place, in order that you may know that my words will surely stand against you for evil: [30]Thus says the Lord, Behold, I will give Pharaoh Hophra king of Egypt into the hand of his enemies and into the hand of those who seek his life, as I gave Zedekiah king of Judah into the hand of Nebuchadrezzar king of Babylon, who was his enemy and sought his life."

It is always possible to give different explanations of what happens to us in life and to come up with strong arguments to support our different views. Here is a classic example. The Jewish settlers, and particularly the women who had been deeply involved in popular religious cults in Jerusalem, including the worship of "the queen of heaven" (see comment on 7:16-20 in vol.1, pp.75-76), argue that their troubles really began when they gave up such cults (verses 15-19). It was Josiah's reformation, and the banning of all religious cults in Jerusalem with the exception of the worship of the one God, the Lord, which in their eyes, had led to national disaster. In a sense they were right. That reformation, whatever else it was, was an expression of religious nationalism. The banning of all other cults in Jerusalem was part of the movement for national independence, one nation under one God. It meant throwing down the gauntlet to any power with imperialistic ambitions in the area. You can argue that the mood it reflected, and the religious nationalism it fostered, led inevitably to the clash with Babylon which brought the destruction of Jerusalem. So Jerusalem would have been better off tolerating the worship of many gods and goddesses in its streets. That was how King Manasseh had kept his country at peace for many years, by being a faithful lackey of his Assyrian overlords, and if that meant the worship of some Assyrian gods in Jerusalem, what of it? You can usually have security and prosperity if you are prepared to pay the price. (For the story of the reigns of Manasseh and Josiah, see 2 Kings chs.21-23.)

To Jeremiah, however, there was—maddeningly no doubt in the eyes of the settlers—only one issue: the total obedience, or disobedience, of the nation to the voice of the Lord (verse 23). He was not prepared to argue the niceties of politics. Divided religious loyalties in any shape or form were an anathema. They were responsible for the tragedy, the evil that had befallen the community.

It is hard to see how these two views could ever be reconciled. Jeremiah makes no attempt to do so. He turns to the settlers and says in effect: 'Right, if you want to continue in religious practices which you think pay dividends, go ahead and do it [verse 25]. Only remember that you have the Lord to deal with, the Lord who is "watching" [see comment on 1:12 in vol.1, p.16], who is in control of all events. You are in his hands, "for evil and not for good" [verse 27]. You think your conduct will guarantee prosperity; it will in fact guarantee disaster'. As a "sign" (verse 29) that this is not merely his own view but the verdict of the God who controls all history, Jeremiah declares that Pharaoh Hophra, who controlled Egypt from 587–570 B.C., would meet with a similar fate to that of Zedekiah. Pharaoh Hophra was in fact, as we know, overthrown by an internal revolution led by an army general.

Jeremiah, however passionately he believed certain things, knew well that he could not force other people to share his beliefs. He could only remind them that beliefs are important; that what they believed influenced the choices they took in life, and that these choices had inevitable consequences. And that is still true.

A GLIMPSE OF BARUCH

Jeremiah 45:1–5

[1]The word that Jeremiah the prophet spoke to Baruch the son of Neriah, when he wrote these words in a book at the dictation of Jeremiah, in the fourth year of Jehoiakim the son of Josiah, king of Judah: [2]"Thus says the Lord, the God of Israel, to you, O Baruch: [3]You said, 'Woe is me! for the Lord has added sorrow to my pain; I am weary with my groaning, and I find no rest.' [4]Thus shall you say to him, Thus says the Lord: Behold, what I have built I am breaking down, and what I have planted I am plucking up—that is, the whole land. [5]And do you seek great things for yourself? Seek them not; for, behold, I am bringing evil upon all flesh, says the Lord; but I will give you your life as a prize of war in all places to which you may go."

This chapter is very oddly placed in the book. As verse 1 makes clear, it has to be read in conjunction with chapter 36, the story of the offending scroll. The clue to its present position may lie in the concluding words of verse 5, with their promise to Baruch that his life will be preserved "in all places to which you may go". Baruch was in Egypt with Jeremiah. Chapters 43 and 44 have had some harsh words of judgement to declare against the Jews in Egypt: "all the men of Judah who are in the land of

Egypt shall be consumed by the sword and by famine, until there is an end of them" (44:27). Baruch is one of these "men of Judah"; but he is to be the exception. This passage suggests that he did survive. Whether he returned to Judah or joined fellow exiles in Babylon, we do not know, but he survived long enough to make his contribution to the Book of Jeremiah through his record of events in the life of the prophet.

The main interest in this passage, however, lies in what it tells us about Baruch the man back in Jehoiakim's time. Elsewhere he is very much in the background, little more than Jeremiah's secretarial shadow. But even secretaries have feelings. Here we find Baruch gripped by the kind of despair, with which Jeremiah himself was only too familiar (see 15:10ff.). The reason for his despair we are not told. Perhaps he was depressed by the harsh content of the scroll Jeremiah dictated to him; perhaps he was conscious of the dangerous situation in which he was placing himself by reading the scroll in public (36:5–6); perhaps he shared Jeremiah's despair at the nil response the prophet was getting to his message. It could be—and this would fit in with the opening words of verse 5, "do you seek great things for yourself?"—that he was beginning to realise that by throwing in his lot with Jeremiah, he was ruining his own career prospects. As an educated man, belonging to a family which had influence at court, he may have been anticipating holding high office himself. But the door to political preferment must have closed when he joined a man who was increasingly critical of the political establishment.

If Baruch was looking for sympathy, he no more got it than Jeremiah did. The reply that comes from God is twofold:

(1) If you think you have problems, what about me, says God? I am having to dismantle everything that I have built (verse 4). We agonize over our own problems, but how much greater is the agony of a God who offers his people the way of life, and sees them choosing the way of death? There are hints of that divine agony elsewhere in the Old Testament; in the God of Hosea, for example, who when faced with the blatant and continuing infidelity of his people, says:

How can I give you up, O Ephraim!
How can I hand you over, O Israel!
       . . . .
My heart recoils within me,
  my compassion grows warm and tender.

(Hos.11:8)

In all its mystery it faces us in Jesus, in whom we see God suffering with and for us. The tears that Jesus wept over Jerusalem (Luke 19:41) are tears that are there in the heart of God. However much we grieve over the suffering we experience or the suffering of others in the world, it is, at its best, but a pale reflection of God's grief.

(2) You have ambitions? Forget them. All that is guaranteed is survival. This is the pattern of a change of direction in life, of an apparent giving up of career prospects, which we can trace in Christian tradition from Paul to Albert Schweitzer, from Columba to Kagawa, and in the lives of countless other unrecorded folk who have discovered the truth in the words of Jesus: "whoever would save his life will lose it; and whoever loses his life for my sake and the gospel's will save it" (Mark 8:35).

L. RULER OF ALL NATIONS (CHS.46–51)

The next six chapters (with the exception of the final six verses of ch.51) contain a collection of poems and short prose passages dealing with a number of the nations surrounding Judah, and in particular with those deeply involved in the events which led up to the destruction of Jerusalem. They are long and complicated and need not be printed in this commentary, because we are not going to study the material in them in detail, passage by passage. Any attempt to do so realistically would involve having to explain a large number of place names and historical allusions, about many of which we know very little. Read

quickly through chapter 48, the chapter on Moab, and you will
see what we mean. To understand it fully you would have to
have an expert Moabite courier by your side—and there are not
many of these around!

The order of the material largely reflects what we have
already seen in 25:19 ff. (see comment p. 43ff.). We begin in
chapter 46 with *Egypt*: we then move up the coastal plain and
deal with the *Philistines* (ch.47); from there we turn inland to
Transjordan to pick up the kingdoms of *Moab* (ch.48), *Ammon*
(49:1-6) and *Edom* (49:7-22). The *Arabian tribes* of the eastern
desert (49:28-33) are somewhat strangely sandwiched between
Damascus (49:23-27) and *Elam* (49:34-39) in distant south-
west Iran, neither of which plays any part, as far as we know, in
the history of Judah in Jeremiah's day. The collection is
rounded off, not surprisingly, by two lengthy chapters on
Babylon (chs.50-51).

As we have already noted, this material appears after 25:12 in
the Greek text of Jeremiah, and the individual sections within it
are differently ordered in places. It must at one time have
circulated independently of the rest of the Book of Jeremiah.
This is not surprising. The material reflects a long tradition of
prophetic "oracles against the nations" which we find in other
prophetic books in the Old Testament: notably in the brief
oracles that make up Amos 1:3-2:3; in Isaiah chapters 13-23; in
Ezekiel chapters 25-30; in Nahum which deals with the
Assyrians; and in Obadiah which deals with the Edomites.
There are many close links in language and in thought between
the material in these chapters in Jeremiah and what we find in
the oracles against the nations in other prophetic books. To
take but two examples, chapter 48 on Moab has many
similarities with Isaiah chapters 15-16, while the section on
Edom (49:7-22) and the Book of Obadiah, read like a series of
variations on the same theme.

Moreover we are dealing with material which, because it is
basically on the same theme and probably circulated for a while
by word of mouth, can be used in different contexts. We have
probably all at one time or another heard the same story told

about different people, and set in a different place. Thus in
49:19-21 we have verses directed against Edom and the people
of Teman, while in 50:44-46, virtually the same words are used
against Babylon and the land of the Chaldeans. Given the
tradition of prophecy in which Jeremiah stood, and the stormy
political history of his country during his own lifetime, it would
have been surprising if one who had been called to be a
"prophet to the nations" (1:5) had not drawn on the oracles
against nations that other prophets had used, and made his own
contribution to them. The two nations that did most to decide
the fate of Judah in Jeremiah's day were Egypt and Babylon. It
is therefore appropriate that the collection begins with Egypt
and ends with Babylon.

Although we are not going to look at these chapters in detail,
this must not be taken to mean that we underestimate their
importance. We are in touch here with certain convictions
that are basic to the outlook of all the major prophetic figures in
the Old Testament, not least Jeremiah.

There are certain dangers to which all religious people are
exposed, and the more passionately they believe, the greater the
dangers. One of them is the danger of converting the God in
whom we believe, the God whom we worship, into our own
patron saint; a God who exists primarily to meet our needs, to
protect our interests and to answer our prayers. We go in for a
type of religious privatization. It happened again and again in
the history of Israel. Amos met it in the attitude of a people who
believed that to be God's people meant that they were given an
unconditional passport to national greatness and prosperity
(Amos 3:1-2; 5:18-20). Jeremiah met it in the message of the
prophets of *shalom*, in the expectations that gathered round the
Jerusalem Temple. God was here in their midst; Jerusalem
could never be destroyed (see ch.7). But such a God is little
more than a personal or national idol. Prophets from Amos to
Jeremiah insisted that to believe in the Lord is to believe in a
God who has the whole world in his hands, a God who is the
ruler of all nations.

This is a God whose purposes all nations exist to serve,

whether they know it or not; a God whose universal standards of justice and righteousness nations, including Israel and Judah, ignore at their peril. Although the prophets are men of their own day and age, and look out on world events primarily as they touch the life of their own people—and nowhere is this more true than in what is said about Babylon in chapters 50–51—they are not merely concerned with what other nations may do to their own people. Their vision goes much deeper. Human pride, the lust for power, the belief that might is right, that other people may be sacrificed on the altar of imperialistic ambitions—such are the things that in God's world bring inevitable nemesis. Thus if Egypt, confident in its big battalions, pursues a policy summed up in the words (46:8):

> I will rise, I will cover the earth,
> I will destroy cities and their inhabitants;

then it is signing its own death warrant, and the Pharaoh who dreams of world conquest is going to be given a new name:

> Noisy Braggard Who Missed his Chance
> (46:17,GNB)

It is no different today.

There is in the present an idolatry of power which often masquerades in our world as national self-interest. There is an idolatry of repression which often masquerades as the defence of law and order. There is an idolatry of economic exploitation which often masquerades as the protection of our living standards. There is the idolatry of "my God" which retreats into a cosy world of personal spirituality, and believes that the complex and difficult issues in the world have little to do with Christian faith. But every idolatry means placing at the centre of life someone or something—most dangerously an image of God—other than the God who is the ruler of all nations and of every facet of life. As long as this is true of our world, we are going to be left facing the disturbing questions that occur in the word concerning the Philistines (47:6-7):

Ah, sword of the Lord!
How long till you are quiet?
Put yourself into your scabbard,
rest and be still!
How can it be quiet,
when the Lord has given it a charge?

In the oracle against the Philistines, the sword of the Lord is directed against one of the Philistine cities, Ashkelon; is it not equally directed today against apartheid, against food mountains in a world of hunger, against the arms race in a world of poverty, against economic systems that rob people of their rightful human dignity?

BABYLON IS SUNK

Jeremiah 51:59-64

[59]The word which Jeremiah the prophet commanded Seraiah the son of Neriah, son of Mahseiah, when he went with Zedekiah king of Judah to Babylon, in the fourth year of his reign. Seraiah was the quartermaster. [60]Jeremiah wrote in a book all the evil that should come upon Babylon, all these words that are written concerning Babylon. [61]And Jeremiah said to Seraiah: "When you come to Babylon, see that you read all these words, [62]and say, 'O Lord, thou hast said concerning this place that thou wilt cut it off, so that nothing shall dwell in it, neither man nor beast, and it shall be desolate for ever.' [63]When you finish reading this book, bind a stone to it, and cast it into the midst of the Euphrates, [64]and say, 'Thus shall Babylon sink, to rise no more, because of the evil that I am bringing upon her.'"

Thus far are the words of Jeremiah.

The oracles against the nations climax in two long chapters dealing with Babylon, 50-51. They anticipate and celebrate the downfall and destruction of Babylon. Just retribution falls upon a nation which had been used by God to punish his people, but which had "proudly defied the Lord, the Holy One of Israel" (50:29). It had earned a reputation for ruthless violence and an insatiable lust for power. It may flaunt its power in the face of the world, but:

> Though Babylon should mount up to heaven,
>   and though she should fortify her strong height,
> yet destroyers would come from me upon her,
>   says the Lord.

                                                          (Jer. 51:53)

To the chapters on Babylon there has been attached the account of a symbolic act of Jeremiah's which underlines that the same message had been part of Jeremiah's ministry for many years. The date is 594 B.C. Zedekiah, in the aftermath of the abortive anti-Babylonian plot (see ch. 27), seems to have been summoned to Babylon; there no doubt to have the impropriety of any such action forcibly pointed out to him. Seraiah, the king's "quartermaster" (literally, "the officer of the resting place"), is told by Jeremiah to read in Babylon a scroll on which the prophet has written "all the evil that should come upon Babylon" (verse 60). Seraiah, by the way, may well be the brother of Baruch, Jeremiah's other convenient mouthpiece; at least both are described as "the son of Neriah, son of Mahseiah" (verse 59;for Baruch see 32:12). After reading the words of judgement, Seraiah is to take the scroll, tie it to a stone and throw it into the middle of the Euphrates. As it sinks, the accompanying word declares, "Thus shall Babylon sink, to rise no more, because of the evil I am bringing upon her" (verse 64).

The date of this symbolic act is interesting. Earlier in the same year, as we know from chapters 27–28, Jeremiah had strenuously opposed any attempt by the small vassal states, including Judah, to rebel against their Babylonian overlord. This may well have led some people to consider that his political sympathies lay with Babylon. They did not. He showed his opposition to the planned revolt by a symbolic act, appearing in the streets of Jerusalem with a yoke across his shoulders to proclaim the futility of any attempt to throw off the yoke of Babylon (ch. 27). By this present symbolic act he indicates that Babylon, as well as Judah, stands under the judgement of God. To try to measure Jeremiah's activities in purely political terms, is wholly to misunderstand him. It is a mistake that many people in Jerusalem seem to have made; just as prophetic voices in the Church today, for example in South Africa and Latin America, are attacked for 'political statements' and branded as Marxist.

M. EPILOGUE (CH.52)

THE CURTAIN COMES DOWN

Jeremiah 52:1-34

[1]Zedekiah was twenty-one years old when he became king; and he reigned eleven years in Jerusalem. His mother's name was Hamutal the daughter of Jeremiah of Libnah. [2]And he did what was evil in the sight of the Lord, according to all that Jehoiakim had done. [3]Surely because of the anger of the Lord things came to such a pass in Jerusalem and Judah that he cast them out from his presence.

And Zedekiah rebelled against the king of Babylon. [4]And in the ninth year of his reign, in the tenth month, on the tenth day of the month, Nebuchadrezzar king of Babylon came with all his army against Jerusalem, and they laid siege to it and built siegeworks against it round about. [5]So the city was besieged till the eleventh year of King Zedekiah. [6]On the ninth day of the fourth month the famine was so severe in the city, that there was no food for the people of the land. [7]Then a breach was made in the city; and all the men of war fled and went out from the city by night by the way of a gate between the two walls, by the king's garden, while the Chaldeans were round about the city. And they went in the direction of the Arabah. [8]But the army of the Chaldeans pursued the king, and overtook Zedekiah in the plains of Jericho; and all his army was scattered from him. [9]Then they captured the king, and brought him up to the king of Babylon at Riblah in the land of Hamath, and he passed sentence upon him. [10]The king of Babylon slew the sons of Zedekiah before his eyes, and also slew all the princes of Judah at Riblah. [11]He put out the eyes of Zedekiah, and bound him in fetters, and the king of Babylon took him to Babylon, and put him in prison till the day of his death.

[12]In the fifth month, on the tenth day of the month—which was the nineteenth year of King Nebuchadrezzar, king of Babylon— Nebuzaradan the captain of the bodyguard who served the king of Babylon, entered Jerusalem. [13]And he burned the house of the Lord, and the king's house and all the houses of Jerusalem; every great house he burned down. [14]And all the army of the Chaldeans, who were with the captain of the guard, broke down all the walls round about Jerusalem. [15]And Nebuzaradan the captain of the guard carried away captive some of the poorest of the people and the rest of the people who were left in the city and the deserters who had deserted to the king of Babylon, together with the rest of the artisans. [16]But Nebuzaradan the captain of the guard left some of the poorest of the land to be vinedressers and ploughmen.

[17]And the pillars of bronze that were in the house of the Lord, and the stands and the bronze sea that were in the house of the Lord, the Chaldeans broke in pieces, and carried all the bronze to Babylon. [18]And they took away the pots, and the shovels, and the snuffers, and the basins, and the dishes for incense, and all the vessels of bronze used in the temple service; [19]also the small bowls, and the firepans, and the basins, and the pots, and the lamp-stands, and the dishes for incense, and the bowls for libation. What was of gold the captain of the guard took away as gold, and what was of silver, as silver. [20]As for the two pillars, the one sea, the twelve bronze bulls which were under the sea, and the stands, which Solomon the king had made for the house of the Lord, the bronze of all these things was beyond weight. [21]As for the pillars, the height of the one pillar was eighteen cubits, its circumference was twelve cubits, and its thickness was four fingers, and it was hollow. [22]Upon it was a capital of bronze; the height of the one capital was five cubits; a network and pomegranates, all of bronze, were upon the capital round about. And the second pillar had the like, with pomegranates. [23]There were ninety-six pomegranates on the sides; all the pomegranates were a hundred upon the network round about.

[24]And the captain of the guard took Seraiah the chief priest, and Zephaniah the second priest, and the three keepers of the threshold; [25]and from the city he took an officer who had been in command of

the men of war, and seven men of the king's council, who were found in the city; and the secretary of the commander of the army who mustered the people of the land; and sixty men of the people of the land, who were found in the midst of the city. ²⁶And Nebuzaradan the captain of the guard took them, and brought them to the king of Babylon at Riblah. ²⁷And the king of Babylon smote them, and put them to death at Riblah in the land of Hamath. So Judah was carried captive out of its land.

²⁸This is the number of the people whom Nebuchadrezzar carried away captive: in the seventh year, three thousand and twenty-three Jews; ²⁹in the eighteenth year of Nebuchadrezzar he carried away captive from Jerusalem eight hundred and thirty-two persons; ³⁰in the twenty-third year of Nebuchadrezzar, Nebuzaradan the captain of the guard carried away captive of the Jews seven hundred and forty-five persons; all the persons were four thousand and six hundred.

³¹And in the thirty-seventh year of the captivity of Jehoiachin king of Judah, in the twelfth month, on the twenty-fifth day of the month, Evil-merodach king of Babylon, in the year that he became king, lifted up the head of Jehoiachin king of Judah and brought him out of prison; ³²and he spoke kindly to him, and gave him a seat above the seats of the kings who were with him in Babylon. ³³So Jehoiachin put off his prison garments. And every day of his life he dined regularly at the king's table; ³⁴as for his allowance, a regular allowance was given him by the king according to his daily need, until the day of his death as long as he lived.

Chapter 51 ends with the words, "Thus far are the words of Jeremiah". In the context of the present book this statement is true, insofar as 51:59–64 gives us our last glimpse of Jeremiah, his words and his actions. But that symbolic act was neither his last word historically—it comes from the middle of his ministry—nor is it the end of the book. Since much of Jeremiah's ministry had been pointing to the inevitable destruction of Jerusalem, it is an account of this event that brings down the curtain on the book. The account, with minor modifications, has been taken over from 2 Kings 24:18–25:30.

Detailed comment on this material belongs to the volume on 2 Kings. This account differs from 2 Kings mainly in the list it gives in verses 28-30 of the numbers involved in three different deportations of Jews to Babylon: the *first* in 598 B.C., the *second* in 587 B.C., the *third* in 582 B.C., this last probably as the result of punitive measures taken by the Babylonians after the assassination of Gedaliah. The numbers given are not large, and they vary considerably from what we find in 2 Kings. In the *first* deportation in 598 B.C., 2 Kings 24:14,16 lists over ten thousand men, while this chapter gives just over three thousand (verse 28). At most, if the total number given in verses 28-30, four thousand six hundred, refers only to able-bodied men, some fifteen to twenty thousand Jews (men, women and children) must have been deported over a period of sixteen years. Many others, however, must have died during the Babylonian attacks, and in particular in the final siege and sack of the city in 587 B.C. Once the deportations had taken place, the centre of life for the Jewish community moved for fifty years from Judah to Babylon, and led to a fundamental rethinking and reshaping of Jewish life and faith (although it is worth remembering that the Book of Lamentations, which we will be studying next, stems from the depleted population left behind in the ruined capital). It has been well said that in this chapter we find history bearing its silent witness to the truth of the prophetic word.

As we cast an eye back along the journey we have taken through the Book of Jeremiah, what remains most vividly in the mind? A man's courage? ... a man's honesty? ... a man's loneliness? ... a man's faithfulness? ... yes, all of that, but surely more. What are the lasting theological truths and challenges in the book? It will speak, as all the books in the Bible do, to different people in different ways, but two things seem to stand out.

(1) There is the challenge to be careful that we do not confuse the essentials of our faith with the often congenial forms in which it comes to us. Much of the busy religiosity that Jeremiah saw around him, he dismissed as meaningless and indeed an affront to God. There were many things that his people

considered essential to their religious life: a temple in Jerusalem, God's dwelling place on earth, with its impressive ritual; and a city which was indestructible, the city of God. Such things, said the prophet, you must learn to live without. In the end, only God is indispensible, and he cannot, and must not, be imprisoned within even the most hallowed and sacred traditions with which we surround him. Sometimes it seems that we would sooner die for our traditions, than live for God. That is not to say that traditions, patterns of Church life, forms of worship, are unimportant; they are not. But neither are they God, and woe betide us if we assume they are.

(2) How are we to know what the word of God is for us today? There were many people, including prophets, in Jeremiah's day, convinced that they knew what the word of God for them was—and they were wrong. They were not insincere, they reflected the consensus of religious opinion in their day—but they were wrong. The book provides us with no easy answers as to how we can know the true word of God, but abundant warnings that it is fatally easy, in all sincerity, to confuse the will of God with our own desires, or with the interests of our own country, or our own Church. To know the word of God, was for Jeremiah to walk along an exposed road, vulnerable to misunderstanding, open to self-doubt. The word came, and comes,to those prepared to wait and to wrestle with God, rather than to those who speak with easy assurance and untroubled certainty.

LAMENTATIONS

INTRODUCTION

"After Israel was carried into captivity and Jerusalem deserted, Jeremiah sat weeping and composed this lament over Jerusalem." With these words the Greek (*Septuagint*) text of the Old Testament introduces the book we now call Lamentations; and this accounts for the book being placed where we find it in our English Bibles, immediately after Jeremiah. The Greek text is probably here following a clue in 2 Chronicles 35:25 which says that, on the death of Josiah in 609 B.C., "Jeremiah also uttered a lament for Josiah", and that this, and other similar pieces, appeared in a book called "Laments". There is, however, nothing about Josiah in the Book of Lamentations and the remark in Chronicles must refer to one of several now lost books to which we find reference in the Old Testament.

In one sense then the Greek text is wrong in attributing the Book of Lamentations to Jeremiah. The Hebrew text of the Old Testament does not make this mistake. In the Hebrew Bible it is found, not after Jeremiah, but among the miscellaneous collection of books that makes up the third section of the Hebrew Bible, called "The Writings". There it is placed alongside four other books — Ruth, Song of Songs, Ecclesiastes and Esther — all of which were used in public worship at important Jewish religious festivals. Lamentations found its natural setting in the festival on the ninth day of the month of Ab (usually July) when the Jewish community relived the catastrophes that had befallen the people — the destruction of city and temple — not only at the hands of the Babylonians in 58 B.C. but also at the hands of the Romans in A.D. 70. The

Book of Lamentations may not indeed have been written by one person at all. It is a collection of five poems, corresponding to the five chapters in the book, and it is hard to be sure whether one author—or more than one author—was responsible for the poems.

There is, however, another and deeper sense in which the Greek text is right. Had it not been for Jeremiah, and prophets like him, there would have been no Book of Lamentations. For what we find in Lamentations is not only moving and passionate expressions of grief and sorrow, but also of faith rising, Phoenix-like, from the ashes of Jerusalem. And the faith, it should be emphasized, is that of the people left behind in the city, not those taken into exile in whom, as a whole, the Old Testament shows more interest. Such faith was only possible for those who took seriously what Jeremiah had all along said about the inevitable working out of God's judgement upon Jerusalem; and about hope, based on the steadfast love of God, beyond disaster. The poems in Lamentations, which were probably for the most part first composed shortly after the destruction of the city by the Babylonians in 587 B.C. bear eloquent witness to the fact that Jeremiah's teaching did not fall entirely on stony ground. That we do not know the name of the poet or poets, need not surprise us. There are very few books in the Old Testament whose authors are known to us.

ALPHABETIC POEMS

Look at the five chapters in Lamentations and you will see that they all have twenty-two verses or, in the case of chapter 3, a multiple of twenty-two, namely sixty-six verses. The reason for this is that there are twenty-two letters in the Hebrew alphabet. The poems in Lamentations are what we call *acrostic* poems, poems which in one way or another run through the alphabet from *A* to *Z*, or in Hebrew from *Aleph* to *Taw*. Thus in chapter 1 there are twenty-two three-line verses; verse 1 beginning with the first letter in the Hebrew alphabet, verse 2 with the second letter... and so on. Chapter 2 is similar, but at one point the order of the letters in the alphabet seems to be mixed up, as in chapter 1, *O* comes before *P*, but in chapter 2, *P* comes before *O*. Chapter 3 is the most elaborate poem. Its sixty-six verses are grouped into twenty-two units: thus verses 1, 2 and 3 each begin with the first letter of the alphabet; verses 4, 5 and 6 each begin with the second letter in the alphabet—and so on. Chapter 4, although it has only two-line verses, follows the pattern of chapter 2, with again *P* coming before *O*. Chapter 5 does not go through the alphabet in this way—perhaps ingenuity failed at this point—but at least it has twenty-two verses, as if it were imitating an alphabetic poem.

What is the reason for such alphabetic poems? There have been many suggestions ranging all the way from ideas of magic associated with the alphabet to an aid to memory, but we do not really know. What we do know is that there are other examples of poems of this type, known to us from the ancient Near East and from within the Old Testament. Proverbs 31:10–31, for example, has been called 'The Golden A B C of the Perfect Wife', while Psalm 119 contains the longest, and perhaps not the most inspired illustration. It is possible that when Lamentations was being written, the alphabetic poem was already well established as a literary convention, just as you find people today who write fourteen-line sonnets. You will see an attempt to reproduce such an alphabetic poem in English in the translation of Lamentations by Ronald Knox in *The Holy Bible*, 1955.

However conventional, the alphabetic form may have served an important purpose in Lamentations. Let us change the picture for a moment. Think of a piano. It has a keyboard with a fixed number of notes in it. A skilled composer will make full use of the keyboard to explore every shade of sound and harmony. The fact that there are a fixed number of notes places a certain discipline upon him. He has to work with these notes and no others; and the mark of a great composer is that, within these limits, he can explore a wide range of human emotions. What we find in Lamentations is a poet—or poets—exploring, as it were, every note on the keyboard of grief and tragedy, searching for harmony within discord. Yet the poems are not self-indulgent. The alphabet provides a framework within which the poet works. The depth and intensity of the emotions expressed are all the more effective, because they are not allowed to ramble on and on and on.

VARIETY IN UNITY

Although the poems in Lamentations share the common feature that they are alphabetic, or imitation alphabetic, poems, there is in other respects a rich variety in them. Poems one, two and four are, in the main, funeral songs, each introduced by a word typical of such songs: the Hebrew word *eka*, translated "How!" You find a similar word in David's famous lament over the death of Saul and Jonathan, with its echoing "How are the mighty fallen!" (2 Sam. 1:19,25). Such funeral songs were often sung by women, skilled in traditional, public expressions of mourning, as they are in many eastern countries right down to the present day (see Jer.9:17). The poet takes such traditional funeral songs, adapts them and uses them, but not slavishly, to lament the fate of Jerusalem. City and temple, once throbbing with vitality, are now as good as dead. But this is a strange funeral being celebrated, because more than once the corpse sits up and speaks: for example 1:12ff.

Poem three is different. It is not in the form of a funeral song. It is similar to many of the intensely personal psalms which we call "individual laments" in which the psalmist describes and lives through a crisis experience, often of grief and despair, and in the darkness, reaches out to God to seek reassurance in the unchanging character of God. The person who speaks in this poem is someone whose experience is typical of that of the community as a whole, and so the poem switches back and forward from "I" in verses 1–39 to "we" in verses 40–47, and back again to "I" in verses 48ff.; a feature again typical of some of the Psalms: for example, Psalm 102.

Poem five throughout is a prayer of the community, reliving the horror of its present plight, acknowledging the reason for it—"our fathers sinned" (verse 7) . . . "we have sinned" (verse 16)—and pleading for God's help.

There is therefore variety in the different kinds of poems; but there is also variety *within* the poems. The Hebrew word for a lament is *qinah*, and this word is also used to describe a certain kind of line of poetry, often used to express strong emotions, not least grief. It is a line which divides into two, with the first half longer than the second half, which gives the impression of dying away. Thus:

> How lonely sat the city
>   once full of people! (1:1)

> I am the man who has seen affliction
>   under the rod of his wrath. (3:1)

But this is by no means true of the whole book. In many cases the second half is just as long as the first half and, as often in Hebrew poetry, echoes its meaning

> Her gates have sunk into the ground;
>   he has ruined and broken her bars. (2:9)

Yet in the midst of all this variety, there is an underlying unity of thought and experience. The fall of Jerusalem to the Babylonians in 587 B.C., as we have seen in our study of Jeremiah, was a traumatic experience for the people of Judah. For many it was a crisis of faith. The poems in Lamentations were a creative response to this crisis. They enabled the community, openly and healingly in worship, to live through their tragedy and bitterness and to bring the questions they raised to God. This they have continued to do for the Jewish community, faced across the centuries, as it has so often been, by similar experiences. It is not surprising that the poems have found their place in Christian tradition in the events of Holy Week, and have become readings appropriate for the

Thursday, Friday and Saturday of that week. But it is a mistake to confine them to that week. Their healing power is open to all who are prepared to live through tragedy and grief and to share it with God and their fellow believers.

TRAGEDY OBSERVED

Lamentations 1:1–11

[1]How lonely sits the city that was full of people!
How like a widow has she become,
   she that was great among the nations!
She that was a princess among the cities has become a vassal.

[2]She weeps bitterly in the night, tears on her cheeks;
among all her lovers she has none to comfort her;
all her friends have dealt treacherously with her,
   they have become her enemies.

[3]Judah has gone into exile because of affliction and hard servitude;
she dwells now among the nations, but finds no resting place;
her pursuers have all overtaken her in the midst of her distress.

[4]The roads to Zion mourn, for none come to the appointed feasts;
all her gates are desolate, her priests groan;
her maidens have been dragged away,
   and she herself suffers bitterly.

[5]Her foes have become the head, her enemies prosper,
because the Lord has made her suffer
   for the multitude of her transgressions;
her children have gone away, captives before the foe.

[6]From the daughter of Zion has departed all her majesty.
Her princes have become like harts that find no pasture;
they fled without strength before the pursuer.

[7]Jerusalem remembers in the days of her affliction and bitterness
all the precious things that were hers from days of old.

When her people fell into the hand of the foe,
    and there was none to help her, the foe gloated over her,
  mocking at her downfall.

[8]Jerusalem sinned grievously, therefore she became filthy;
  all who honoured her despise her,
    for they have seen her nakedness;
  yea, she herself groans, and turns her face away.

[9]Her uncleanness was in her skirts;
    she took no thought of her doom;
  therefore her fall is terrible, she has no comforter.
    "O Lord, behold my affliction, for the enemy has triumphed!"

[10]The enemy has stretched out his hands
    over all her precious things;
  yea, she has seen the nations invade her sanctuary,
    those whom thou didst forbid to enter thy congregation.

[11]All her people groan as they search for bread;
  they trade their treasures for food to revive their strength.
  "Look, O Lord, and behold, for I am despised."

We have all had the experience of watching on our TV screens the results of a tragedy, such as an air crash. Within a short time of the accident, the TV commentators are on the scene, or flying over the site of the disaster, giving us a graphic account of what has happened. A skilful commentator can paint a very vivid picture, discussing the reasons for what happened, analysing the human emotions involved, the shattered dreams, the stunned grief of survivors and relatives. This is what we are given in this opening section of Lamentations; a commentary on the tragedy that was the destruction of Jerusalem, the city of God, and the desolation of the Temple on Mt Zion.

But one word of warning that applies throughout Lamentations: don't go looking for any clear or neat argument running through the chapters. Rather, you will find a series of pictures, placed side by side, describing from different angles the one shattering event. This reflects the mood of bewilderment which is often part of the healing process of living through grief. A person who has lost someone who has been very close, be it husband or wife or child or friend, will keep talking almost disjointedly about their sorrow, coming back again and again to say the same things about that loved one; not aware that he or she is repeating things already said, but with a desperate need to share it with anyone prepared to listen. So it is in Lamentations.

The commentary begins by talking about Jerusalem, in verses 1–3, as being like a "widow", alone in her grief. The same picture is used by another prophet to describe the people's experience of exile, "bereaved and barren" (Isa.49:21). As often in grief, it is the memory of what once was that makes the present so hard to take. Once "great among the nations", once a "princess among the cities" (or better "the states"), once, in other words, a people treated with respect and honour, now merely "a vassal", a subject people to be treated with contempt. Once an independent nation, she now "dwells among the nations" and finds no security or rest. The promises of the past, God's promises, had collapsed, for in Deuteronomy 12:10 Israel was promised a land to dwell in and rest from all her enemies. Now there is neither land nor rest. Deserted by "lovers" and "friends", a reference to Judah's former political allies who had left her in the lurch (see Jer.30:14), she can only weep bitter tears. This picture of the city as a "widow" not only highlights her grief, but underlines how vulnerable and defenceless she is, since widows along with orphans were often at risk in ancient Israel (see Lam.5:3 and the comment on Jer.5:28).

Verses 4–7 provide further illustrations of this painful contrast between the past and the present:

—the Temple, once thronged with pilgrims and worshippers, empty;
—the priests, who used to lead the people in worship, left sighing;
—the young women, who had a joyful part to play in some

of the great religious festivals (see Ps.68:25), stunned into silence (verse 4);

—the "princes", the political leaders in the community, like stags ("harts"), weakened by lack of food and easily hunted down (verse 6);

—the enemy has come out on top (verse 5) and gloats over the fate of the city (verse 7).

In the midst of it all, we hear for the first time the beginnings of an answer to the question that tragedy almost always prompts: Why . . . why did it happen?

> Because the Lord has made her suffer
> for the multitude of her transgressions.
>
> (Lam.1:5)

"Rebellions" is probably a better translation than "transgressions", since the Hebrew word usually implies a revolt against authority. Here Lamentations is picking up where Jeremiah left off. To think of the country's ruin as the triumph of a foreign enemy, was wholly to misunderstand; the enemy was the Lord, this was his judgement upon a rebellious people. This is a view from which Lamentations never wavers and which it never tires of repeating (see verses 8,12–15). Gone entirely is the belief that the Lord lived in a holy city which he would protect for ever against all enemies. The "enemy" had been in the midst of the people, the God whom they had fondly believed to be only their protector. There is no mystery in Lamentations as to why it happened; the real problem to be faced is, where do we go from here?

(We must be careful at this point. Lamentations, like the prophet before it, can look at what happened to Jerusalem and say, rightly, it was richly deserved. But this is not always true of life. There are tragedies in life in face of which people say, "I wonder what he—or she—did to deserve that?"; and the only honest answer is "nothing". The Old Testament elsewhere is well aware of this. Nowhere is it more passionately argued than in the Book of Job.)

Verses 8–9 underline the sinfulness of the people by using words like "filthy" (although the Hebrew here might equally well be translated "an object of scorn"), and "nakedness". In ancient Israel nakedness, particularly the exposure of the private parts, was a sign of disgrace. Incestuous marriage relationships are described in Leviticus 20:17ff. as "uncovering the nakedness of . . . ", and being stripped naked in public was one of the penalties inflicted upon a prostitute (Ezek.16:35–39). The phrase "uncleanness in her skirts" refers to menstrual blood, which rendered a woman and everything she touched ritually unclean, and therefore debarred her from having contact with holy or sacred things. So the community is being described as totally unacceptable to God. Happily oblivious of this fact, it went to its doom. Into this dark picture there breaks, at the end of verse 9, an urgent cry from the community, a plea to the Lord to show that he is aware of the depth of his people's plight.

Side by side in verses 10–11 there is placed the picture of what the enemy has done, destroying everything which Judah cherished, trampling through the Temple which no foreign foot was ever meant to enter—and the picture of the plight of the people, weakened by famine, prepared to sell "their treasures", probably their children, their darlings, for food. Survival at all costs is their sole concern. Again there comes from the people an almost despairing cry, in which the critical situation of the people, "I am despised", is made the basis of an appeal to God.

TRAGEDY RELIVED

Lamentations 1:12–22

> [12]"Is it nothing to you, all you who pass by?
>   Look and see if there is any sorrow like my sorrow
>   which was brought upon me,
>   which the Lord inflicted on the day of his fierce anger.

¹³"From on high he sent fire; into my bones he made it descend;
he spread a net for my feet; he turned me back;
he has left me stunned, faint all the day long.

¹⁴"My transgressions were bound into a yoke;
by his hand they were fastened together; they were set upon my
neck;
he caused my strength to fail;
the Lord gave me into the hands of those whom I cannot
withstand.

¹⁵"The Lord flouted all my mighty men in the midst of me;
he summoned an assembly against me to crush my young men;
the Lord has trodden as in a wine press
the virgin daughter of Judah.

¹⁶"For these things I weep; my eyes flow with tears;
for a comforter is far from me, one to revive my courage;
my children are desolate, for the enemy has prevailed."

¹⁷Zion stretches out her hands, but there is none to comfort her;
the Lord has commanded against Jacob
that his neighbours should be his foes;
Jerusalem has become a filthy thing among them.

¹⁸"The Lord is in the right,
for I have rebelled against his word;
but hear, all you peoples, and behold my suffering;
my maidens and my young men have gone into captivity.

¹⁹"I called to my lovers but they deceived me;
my priests and elders perished in the city,
while they sought food to revive their strength.

²⁰"Behold, O Lord, for I am in distress,
my soul is in tumult, my heart is wrung within me,
because I have been very rebellious.
In the street the sword bereaves;
in the house it is like death.

²¹"Hear how I groan; there is none to comfort me.
    All my enemies have heard of my trouble;
        they are glad that thou hast done it.
    Bring thou the day thou has announced,
        and let them be as I am.

²²"Let all their evil doing come before thee;
        and deal with them as thou hast dealt with me
            because of all my transgressions;
        for my groans are many and my heart is faint."

We thought of the first eleven verses of the chapter as the words of a commentator describing a tragedy. But however skilful such a commentary may be, its emotional impact is much less than the words and thoughts of someone who has lived through the tragedy. The horror of the crash of the JAL flight from Tokyo to Osaka was depicted at length by commentators, but what lingers in the mind are the hastily scribbled notes by those on board minutes before disaster struck, and the halting words of a stewardess who survived. So now, following on the brief cries in verses 9 and 11, we are invited to listen to the words of the doomed city herself, speaking as a person about "my sorrow" (verse 12), "my rebellion [transgressions]" (verse 14), "my tears" (verse 16), "my suffering" (verse 18), "my distress" (verse 20). This lament by Jerusalem is divided into two sections—(1) verses 12-16, (2) verses 18-20—divided in verse 17 by a word from the poet-commentator, echoing and emphasizing what is being said, as if to say "just listen to that!"

(1) The *first* section begins with an appeal to others to recognize the depths of the sorrow being experienced. There is some doubt as to how we ought to translate the opening words: the New English Bible has, "Is it no concern to you who pass by?"; the Good News Bible has, "Look at me, she cries to everyone who passes by". Those who pass by are simply anyone who happens to be there; anyone could surely see how tragic this is. Behind these words we can see the fear that often lurks in the minds of those facing grief and sorrow. They feel isolated. No matter how kind or helpful others try to be, they just don't

understand. There is a private, desolate world into which others can't enter.

From people, who may not understand, Zion turns to the Lord, acknowledging that what has happened is God's doing. This is "the day of his fierce anger" (verse 12), that "day of the Lord" that many of the prophets said would come; not a day of gladness and prosperity for Israel, which was what the people thought it would be, but a day of judgement and disaster (see Amos 5:18-20 and the comments on Jer.4:9-10 in vol.1, pp. 47-48). It is (verse 13) "fire", a common symbol of God's anger and judgement in the Old Testament (*eg* Amos 1:3-2:3); it is God "the hunter" ensnaring the people in his net (cf. Hos.7:12); it is God putting a strength-sapping yoke upon the shoulders of his people (verse 14); it is God reaping a grim harvest, the blood of his people squeezed out like the juice from the grapes trampled underfoot in the wine press (verse 15). Picture after picture comes tumbling out in what is a personal confession. The language we use may be different, but the need for such confession, and the acknowledgement that we are in the hands of God and under his judgement, remains.

(2) The *second* section, verses 18-22, begins by echoing this theme. What has happened is the Lord's doing and he was justified in doing it. "The Lord is in the right" is a legal expression indicating that in the case at issue God is the innocent party and his people are the guilty. Yet to say that what had happened was justified did not make it any easier to bear. So what we find in this section is Zion, recognizing that no human help is available, turning increasingly to the Lord who is the source of her grief, but who alone can bring healing; appealing to the Lord to "look at [behold]" his people's agony (verse 20), to "listen to [hear]" the cries of suffering (verse 21), and to deal with the human enemies who gloat over what has happened to Zion. This last plea (verses 21-22) must not be mistaken as merely a cry for vengeance. As in the case of the oracles against the nations in Jeremiah chapters 46-51, we have here a declaration of faith that God's rule is universal, and that evil practised by anyone or any state will receive its due reward.

Before we leave this first chapter let us notice two things; the one a matter of words, the other a pointer to a lasting truth.

(a) Twice in the chapter there occurs a phrase which you will come across frequently in Lamentations; the phrase translated "the daughter of Zion" (verse 6), or the slightly longer phrase translated "the virgin daughter of Judah" (verse 15). These translations are somewhat misleading. The Good News Bible, for example, simply says "Jerusalem" in verse 6, and "my people" in verse 15. It is not "the daughter *of* Zion" that is meant, but "daughter Zion", a phrase that helps to portray the city as a person and also points to the close relationship between the city and the Lord, even when this is a daughter in trouble.

(b) Three times in the chapter we hear the words "she has none to comfort her", or similar words (verses 2,9,17); once Zion herself says "there is none to comfort me" (verse 21); and there are other phrases like "a comforter is far from me" (verse 16) and "there was none to help her" (verse 7). To "comfort" does not mean to sit and hold her hand, to be sympathetic to her. It means to bring new hope, encouragement, help. These phrases are all pointers to the fact that Jerusalem now recognizes what she took a long time to face; that she has come to the end of her tether, where there are no human resources to change her situation or to open the way ahead. She is left facing the truth, that if there is to be any hope for the future, it can only come from the God whom she had long ignored and disobeyed to her cost. Desperation drives her back to God, as it was desperation that had led the prodigal to take the first hesitant steps on the homeward road (Luke 15:17ff.). Sometimes we must be broken before we can return to the God we need, the God who all along has been waiting for us.

WHAT THE LORD HAS DONE

Lamentations 2:1-10

[1]How the Lord in his anger
   has set the daughter of Zion under a cloud!
   He has cast down from heaven to earth
      the splendour of Israel;
   he has not remembered his footstool in the day of his anger.

[2]The Lord has destroyed without mercy
      all the habitations of Jacob;
   in his wrath he has broken down
      the strongholds of the daughter of Judah;
   he has brought down to the ground in dishonour
      the kingdom and its rulers.

[3]He has cut down in fierce anger
      all the might of Israel;
   he has withdrawn from them his right hand
      in the face of the enemy;
   he has burned like a flaming fire in Jacob,
      consuming all around.

[4]He has bent his bow like an enemy,
      with his right hand set like a foe;
   and he has slain all the pride of our eyes
      in the tent of the daughter of Zion;
   he has poured out his fury like fire.

[5]The Lord has become like an enemy.
      he has destroyed Israel;
   he has destroyed all its palaces,
      laid in ruins its strongholds;
   and he has multiplied in the daughter of Judah
      mourning and lamentation.

[6]He has broken down his booth like that of a garden,
      laid in ruins the place of his appointed feasts;
   the Lord has brought to an end in Zion
      appointed feast and sabbath,
   and in his fierce indignation has spurned king and priest.

⁷The Lord has scorned his altar,
    disowned his sanctuary;
  he has delivered into the hand of the enemy
    the walls of her palaces;
  a clamour was raised in the house of the Lord
    as on the day of an appointed feast.

⁸The Lord determined to lay in ruins
    the wall of the daughter of Zion;
  he marked it off by the line;
    he restrained not his hand from destroying;
  he caused rampart and wall to lament,
    they languish together.

⁹Her gates have sunk into the ground;
    he has ruined and broken her bars;
  her king and princes are among the nations;
    the law is no more,
  and her prophets obtain
    no vision from the Lord.

¹⁰The elders of the daughter of Zion
    sit on the ground in silence;
  they have cast dust on their heads
    and put on sackcloth;
  the maidens of Jerusalem
    have bowed their heads to the ground.

The second poem begins with the poet-commentator describing what the Lord in his anger has done to the land, the city and the Temple. We can only enter fully into the dilemma in the poet's mind when we realise that what the Lord has now done seems to call into question everything that he once did. Many must have thought that God's character had changed, that the promises he had once made to his people had been irrevocably broken.

In the past "the cloud" had been the symbol of God's gracious and protecting presence among his people (see Exod. 13:21; 14:19-20); now the people were under the storm cloud of his anger (verse 1). The land, with its towns and forts, once promised by God to his people, had now been ruthlessly devastated by God (verses 2,5). The warrior God, who had once fought on behalf of his people against their enemies, had now himself turned into enemy number one (verses 3–4). The God who had once promised that the dynasty and kingdom of David would last for ever (2 Sam. 7:12ff.), had ruined the kingdom and sent king and royal family into exile (verses 2,9). Jerusalem, the city of God that could never be destroyed (Pss. 46;48), was no more, its walls and gates smashed to pieces. It had been carefully measured out for destruction, as a builder measures out a site (verses 8–9). The Temple on Mt Zion, which was to be God's resting place on earth for ever (Ps.132:14), the place where God's feet touched earth, "his footstool" (verse 1), the place to which his people came to bring their sacrifices, to celebrate his goodness at the great religious festivals, that place was in ruins, the joyful songs of the worshippers silenced before the victory cries of the enemy; the place where God met with his people had become like a rough temporary hut or shelter, "booth", left to fall into decay by a gardener who had no longer any use for it (verses 6–7). The people had been abandoned, with no longer any access to God; the law (*torah*), God's instruction and teaching, was no longer heard; prophets no longer claimed to have any "vision" or revelation from God (verse 9).

This was not only physical devastation; it was spiritual annihilation. This was the death of their God, as Auschwitz and the holocaust signalled the death of God for many Jews in our time. Perhaps the urgent questions it raised would only come home to us with full force if we found ourselves among the stunned survivors of a nuclear attack, with all the old landmarks of our life obliterated. What was left? Nothing, but for the whole community, from its leading citizens, "the elders", to its young girls, to go into silent mourning (verse 10).

GRIEF AND UNANSWERED QUESTIONS

Lamentations 2:11-17

¹¹My eyes are spent with weeping;
    my soul is in tumult;
  my heart is poured out in grief
      because of the destruction of the daughter of my people,
  because infants and babes faint
      in the streets of the city.

¹²They cry to their mothers,
    "Where is bread and wine?"
  as they faint like wounded men
      in the streets of the city,
  as their life is poured out
      on their mothers' bosom.

¹³What can I say for you, to what compare you,
    O daughter of Jerusalem?
  What can I liken to you, that I may comfort you,
    O virgin daughter of Zion?
  For vast as the sea is your ruin;
    who can restore you?

¹⁴Your prophets have seen for you
    false and deceptive visions;
  they have not exposed your iniquity
    to restore your fortunes,
  but have seen for you oracles false and misleading.

¹⁵All who pass along the way
    clap their hands at you;
  they hiss and wag their heads
    at the daughter of Jerusalem;
  "Is this the city which was called
    the perfection of beauty,
    the joy of all the earth?"

¹⁶All your enemies rail against you;
    they hiss, they gnash their teeth,

they cry: "We have destroyed her!
Ah, this is the day we longed for;
    now we have it; we see it!"

[17]The Lord has done what he purposed,
    has carried out his threat;
as he ordained long ago,
    he has demolished without pity;
he has made the enemy rejoice over you,
    and exalted the might of your foes.

There comes a point when to describe a tragedy is to share it, and the poet who was himself probably a survivor of the final agony of Jerusalem, can no longer contain his own emotions. He is in anguish—for the expression "my heart" [Hebrew "my bowels"] is poured out . . . " see comment on Jeremiah 4:19 (vol.1, p.51). He breaks down, particularly when he remembers the children, their emaciated bodies lying in the streets, or dying of hunger in their mother's arms (verses 11-12). It is a picture only too sadly familiar to us today from the famine-devastated lands in Africa. The poet finds himself at a loss for words. Questions flood into his mind; but there are no answers. The extent of the tragedy goes beyond anything he has experienced. Any conventional words of hope are drowned in the immensity of what has happened (verse 13). Are there not situations in our world today which have the same numbing effect on us?

Yet it all might have been so different. Like Jeremiah, Lamentations fixes a major responsibility for what has happened upon the religious leadership of the community, and in particular upon the prophets who ought to have remedied the situation (for the phrase "restore your fortunes" in verse 14, see comment on Jer.30:3), by making the people face up to the evil of their ways instead of indulging in "false and deceptive visions". The word translated "deceptive" in this phrase is the Hebrew word for "whitewash". You will find in Ezekiel 13:8ff. a biting attack on the prophets who say "Peace" when there is no peace, and who "when the people build a wall . . . daub it with whitewash". We still use the same expression when we talk of a cover-up job as a whitewash. All that these prophets had done—to use a similar expression—was to paper over the cracks with their misleading words. The result is fatal. The voice of these prophets is now silent; the only voices heard are the voices of the jeering, sneering enemy, pouring scorn (verse 15) on a city that was once thought of as "the perfection of beauty" (Ps.50:2) and "the joy of all the earth" (Ps.48:2). The latter phrase comes ironically from a psalm which claimed that Jerusalem could never be conquered by an enemy. Now the enemy gleefully claims, "We did it . . . we have destroyed her. . . this is the day we longed for" (verse 16).

Perhaps if it had been just the triumph of such enemies it would have been bearable; but as the poet is quick to point out, it is not. It is the Lord who "demolished without pity". His writing had been on the wall for a long time. This was not "the day the enemy longed for"; it was more seriously for Jerusalem, "the day of the Lord" (verse 17).

APPEAL AND RESPONSE

Lamentations 2:18–22

> [18]Cry aloud to the Lord!
>> O daughter of Zion!
> Let tears stream down like a torrent
>> day and night!
> Give yourself no rest, your eyes no respite!

> [19]Arise, cry out in the night,
>> at the beginning of the watches!
> Pour out your heart like water
>> before the presence of the Lord!
> Lift your hands to him
>> for the lives of your children,
> who faint for hunger
>> at the head of every street.

²⁰Look, O Lord, and see!
 With whom hast thou dealt thus?
Should women eat their offspring,
 the children of their tender care?
Should priest and prophet be slain
 in the sanctuary of the Lord?

²¹In the dust of the streets
 lie the young and the old;
my maidens and my young men have fallen by the sword;
in the day of thy anger thou has slain them,
 slaughtering without mercy.

²²Thou didst invite as to the day of an
 appointed feast
 my terrors on every side;
and on the day of the anger of the Lord
 none escaped or survived;
those whom I dandled and reared
 my enemy destroyed.

Although the first half of verse 18 can be taken in several
different ways (see, for example GNB) it is best to see it as the
beginning of an appeal that the poet makes to Zion to turn
urgently and penitently to the Lord. The time for the niceties of
conventional religion is over. It is now all or nothing; a total
pouring out of grief to the God who is the source of their
trouble, but the God in whom alone any hope rests. Their whole
future—"the lives of your children", dying in the streets (verse
19)—is at stake.

In verses 20–22 we hear Zion's response. It is an appeal to the
Lord, but it is an appeal in which there is a good deal of pent-up
bitterness and anger close to the surface. "Look, O Lord, and
see" in verse 20, is immediately followed by a stream of accusing
questions. How can you justify what you have done to us, your
people? Look at its ghastly consequences: women driven to
cannibalism, eating their own children to survive; priests and
prophets massacred in the Temple. It is hard to be calm when
the streets are littered with dead bodies, and the religious

festivals, to which the worshippers once joyfully thronged, have been replaced by a festival of terror where the Lord's invited guests are those who come to attack and destroy his people. The prayer ends with Zion, the mother, sadly and bitterly lamenting the death of her children, the children she had fondled and brought up.

Let us not try to conceal the bitterness in this appeal. It is typical of the piety of the Old Testament, as we find it, for example, in the Psalms, in Job and in the "Confessions" of Jeremiah (see comments in vol.1, pp.5, 98-99), that people are not afraid to pour out their honest, often angry, accusations and complaints to God. If the bitterness and perplexity was there in the heart, it was there for God to hear, to share and to heal.

SUFFERING AND DESPAIR

Lamentations 3:1-20

1I am the man who has seen affliction
  under the rod of his wrath;
2he has driven and brought me
    into darkness without any light;
3surely against me he turns his hand
    again and again the whole day long.

4He has made my flesh and my skin waste away,
    and broken my bones;
5he has besieged and enveloped me
    with bitterness and tribulation;
6he has made me dwell in darkness
    like the dead of long ago.

7He has walled me about so that I cannot escape;
    he has put heavy chains on me;
8though I call and cry for help,
    he shuts out my prayer;
9he has blocked my ways with hewn stones,
    he has made my paths crooked.

¹⁰He is to me like a bear lying in wait,
  like a lion in hiding;
¹¹he led me off my way and tore me to pieces;
  he has made me desolate;
¹²he bent his bow and set me
  as a mark for his arrow.

¹³He drove into my heart
  the arrows of his quiver;
¹⁴I have become the laughingstock of all peoples,
  the burden of their songs all day long.
¹⁵He has filled me with bitterness,
  he has sated me with wormwood.

¹⁶He has made my teeth grind on gravel,
  and made me cower in ashes;
¹⁷my soul is bereft of peace,
  I have forgotten what happiness is;
¹⁸so I say, "Gone is my glory,
  and my expectation from the Lord."

¹⁹Remember my affliction and my bitterness,
  the wormwood and the gall!
²⁰My soul continually thinks of it
  and is bowed down within me.

As we have seen in the Introduction, chapter 3 has the most complex alphabetic pattern of all the poems, with verses 1–3 each beginning with the first letter of the alphabet, verses 4–6 each beginning with the second letter, and so on through the alphabet. It is also the poem in which, at least in this opening section, the experience of suffering seems to be most intensely personal. Who is the "I" who speaks and introduces himself as, "I am the man who has seen affliction under the rod of his wrath"? Suggestions have ranged all the way from Zion the community, to the prophet Jeremiah or to some otherwise unknown sufferer whose experience is regarded as typical of what others have had to face. The view taken here is that the "I" is still the poet-commentator. He is responding to the hurt and bitter cry of Zion at the end of the last chapter, by reliving his own experience which took him to the verge of despair before he came to terms with it. He shares the bitterness. He knows what it is to have to say, "I have forgotten what happiness is" (verse 17), and because he knows, because he has been through the mill himself, he has something of help to say to others.

If this view is correct, then we have here something which is very close to what the writer of the Letter to the Hebrews has to say to us about Jesus:

> For we have not a high priest who is unable to sympathise with our weaknesses, but one who in every respect has been tempted as we are, yet without sinning. Let us then with confidence draw near to the throne of grace, that we may receive mercy and find grace to help in time of need.
>
> (Heb.4:15–16)

Lamentations speaks to a time of need, and comes from a man who was tempted to despair, but finds help.

In verses 1–20 the poet not only describes his suffering but in picture after picture insists that God is responsible for it. There are close links here with Job, another man at the end of his tether, with the "Confessions" of Jeremiah (see comments in vol.1,pp.98–99), and with many a Psalm in which a worshipper, in a situation of crisis in his or her life, pours out his complaint to God (*eg* Ps. 13). Instead of following up such parallels in detail—you can trace them in any concordance—let us notice how time and time again God is accused of acting in a way which seems to call into question much that people in Israel had been brought up to believe.

God, the good shepherd (Ps.23), who leads his people to life-restoring water, has now led this man not into light (symbol of joy and salvation), but into darkness (symbol of judgement and disaster), where his body wastes away. The shepherd's protecting and reassuring rod or staff has become the "rod of his wrath" (verses 1–4). The God who was to be with his people

in the darkest experiences of life, has left this man in intolerable
and unceasing darkness, heedless of his cries of need and his
prayers (verses 6-8).

The God who had released his people from the chains of
slavery in Egypt, has now, like an enemy, thrown him into a
crowded prison and "put heavy chains on [him]" (verse 7). The
God who prepared the way ahead for his people, has placed
insuperable obstacles in the way, and, instead of protecting, is
lying in wait to pounce like a bear or a lion (verses 9-11).

The God who had encouraged his faithful people not to fear
"the arrow that flies by day" (Ps.91:5) has used this man as a
target for his arrows, just as Job similarly complains (6:4):

> The arrows of the Almighty are in me,
>   my spirit drinks their poison.

The God, who was the guardian of his people, had made this
man, like Jeremiah, "a laughing stock" (see comment on
Jer.20:7, vol. 1, pp.161-162), the object of the mocking songs of
enemies (verses 12-14).

The God who had promised his people abundant food and
water, now feeds him with unpalatable "bitterness" and gives
him poison, "wormwood" (see vol.1, p.89) to drink (verse 15).
The food picture continues when it is said (verse 16) "my teeth
grind on gravel", probably a reference to bread crudely baked
with bits of sand and gravel caught up in it; the sort of thing that
today you would send back to the manufacturer, asking for a
refund. Indeed the poet feels like that about his whole life, a life
devoid of *shalom* (peace) and happiness (verse 17); his strength
(rather than "glory" in verse 18) sapped, his hope in the Lord at
an end. He is wandering in a strange and bitter world. (Retain
"wandering" with the RSV footnote in verse 19 instead of the
RSV "bitterness"; so the New English Bible renders the first
half of verse 19, "the memory of my distress and my
wandering".) Whenever this man thinks of what he has gone
through—and he cannot help but think of it—he ends up
baffled and despondent. He is struggling not only against

physical suffering, but wrestling with a real crisis of faith. If God is not responsible for what has happened to him, who is? And if it is God, how can this be squared with belief in a loving, caring God? These are questions that still haunt people and lead them often to the brink of despair. It is good to know that many of the people we meet in the Bible have been there before us.

REVIVING FAITH (i)

Lamentations 3:21–39

21But this I call to mind,
    and therefore I have hope:

22The steadfast love of the Lord never ceases,
    his mercies never come to an end;
23they are new every morning;
    great is thy faithfulness.
24"The Lord is my portion," says my soul,
    "therefore I will hope in him."

25The Lord is good to those who wait for him,
    to the soul that seeks him.
26 It is good that one should wait quietly
    for the salvation of the Lord.
27It is good for a man that he bear
    the yoke in his youth.

28Let him sit alone in silence
    when he has laid it on him;
29let him put his mouth in the dust —
    there may yet be hope;
30let him give his cheek to the smiter,
    and be filled with insults.

31For the Lord will not
    cast off for ever,

³²but, though he cause grief, he will have compassion
　according to the abundance of his steadfast love;
³³for he does not willingly afflict
　or grieve the sons of men.

³⁴To crush under foot
　all the prisoners of the earth,
³⁵to turn aside the right of a man
　in the presence of the Most High,
³⁶To subvert a man in his cause,
　the Lord does not approve.

³⁷Who has commanded and it came to pass,
　unless the Lord has ordained it?
³⁸Is it not from the mouth of the Most High
　that good and evil come?
³⁹Why should a living man complain,
　a man, about the punishment of his sins?

The end of the previous section leaves unanswered the question:
If the Lord is responsible for the suffering and the tragedy being
experienced, to whom does the poet turn for help? The answer,
as in so many of the Psalms, is to no-one other than the Lord,
the same God who is the source of his trouble. Let us follow this
answer through four stages in verses 21–39.

(1) The answer begins in verses 21–24 by recalling what alone
can be the foundation of hope, the true character of God as
Israel had known him in the past. All the great words of
assurance come tumbling out: God's "steadfast love" (*hesed*),
that constancy which means that he could never walk out on his
people (see comments on Jer.2:2 in vol.1, pp. 24–25); his
"mercies", his warm compassion (*raham*, a Hebrew word that
basically means the womb); and his "faithfulness", that
dependable support which will never let anyone down. The
words recall the description of God given, according to Exodus
34:6, to Moses when he received the stone tablets with the
commandments: "The Lord, the Lord, a God merciful and
gracious, slow to anger, and abounding in steadfast love and
faithfulness ... ".

This is the story of the past, but it is a past which in faith can be relived to become part of present experience. Notice how after mentioning "the steadfast love of the Lord" and "his mercies", the poet suddenly turns to grasp what is still there, and new day by day, "*your* faithfulness" (verse 23). This is no longer merely the God of the past, this is the God who is dealing with him personally now. Therefore he can say, "The Lord is *my* portion" (verse 24), source of hope for me. The description of the Lord as "my portion" probably goes back to the story of the settlement in Canaan, when the land was portioned out among the different tribes. The priestly family of Aaron was given no portion of land, because (said the Lord), "I am your portion and your inheritance among the people of Israel" (Num.18:20). The priests were different, they existed to serve God and stood in a special relationship with him. It is this sense of a personal relationship with the Lord which enables the poet to say, "The Lord is my portion"; as it enabled a psalmist to face a world in which evil seemed to triumph, to live through a crisis of faith and yet affirm, "God is my portion for ever" (Ps.73:26). The God about whom this man had been taught, the God whom he had known with his mind, had become a personal reality in his life—and that is the essence of faith. So for the Christian the Crucifixion and Resurrection are not merely events that happened once in the past; they are present, relived now in that experience of dying and rising with Christ of which Paul speaks in Romans 6:5-11.

REVIVING FAITH (ii)

Lamentations 3:21-39 (*cont'd*)

(2) Such a relationship with God leaves many questions unanswered. Verses 25-30 try to describe what the attitude of such faith ought to be amid the unanswered questions. It centres around three "goods"; verses 25, 26 and 27 each

beginning with the Hebrew word for "good". The *first* is how "good" the Lord is to those who "wait for him". Such a waiting is far from a passive acceptance of things as they are; it is a waiting marked by an eager looking forward to the fulfilment of God's purposes. The same word is to be found in Isaiah 40:31 which declares that "they who wait for the Lord shall renew their strength". It is like that alert and eager "watching" for God's coming which is commended by Jesus; see Mark 13:32-37.

It is perhaps unfortunate that the *second* "good" in verse 26 uses again in the RSV the word "wait", because underlying it is a different Hebrew word already translated "hope" in verses 21 and 24, and to be translated "hope" again in verse 29. What is commended here is that quiet, but unquenchable, hope or optimism which looks forward, believing that nothing can ultimately prevent God's purposes from being fulfilled.

The *third* "good" in verse 27 probably uses a proverbial saying—there are similar sayings in Proverbs, *eg* 22:15—stressing the element of discipline in life and in the way God deals with us. The kind of discipline here envisaged is spelled out in verses 28-30. It involves an honest facing of the situation in which God has placed us, a humble recognition of the fact that we are not the masters of our own fate; "putting one's mouth in the dust" (verse 29) denotes an act of humble submission before a superior (cf.Isa.49:23). But when we have no answers, that does not mean that there *are* no answers. This is expressed in the words "there may yet be hope", words which are not intended to indicate any doubt, but rather the conviction that the future lies not in our hands, but in God's. When we cannot see the way ahead, that does not mean that there is no way ahead. In the light of this hope there then can be a willing acceptance of suffering, believing that it can have a creative place in God's purposes. Verse 30 is echoed in the picture of the Servant of the Lord in Isaiah 50:4-9 as one who, through the acceptance of suffering, fulfilled his God-given mission.

Waiting . . . hoping . . . accepting . . . all are words which can sometimes have about them a rather dreary note of resignation. But not here; here they are offered to us as positive and creative elements in faith.

(3) The appeal to the past and to a present continuing faith depends, however, on believing that God can still be trusted and that his purposes are constructive. Throughout verses 31-36 there runs the conviction that suffering and grief, and the sense of rejection they bring are not things the Lord "willingly" sends. They are indeed alien to his true character, abhorrent to him. This is a God who does not trample upon those who are already down, "the prisoners of the earth", a God who does not, like many all too human judges, condemn the innocent; and if there are any people who believe that God neither sees nor cares about such things, they are wrong. This is the note on which, according to Luke, Jesus began his ministry, with that sermon in the synagogue in Nazareth based on the reading from Isaiah 61:1-2;

> The Spirit of the Lord is upon me,
>   because he has anointed me to preach good news to the poor.
> He has sent me to proclaim release to the captives
>   and recovery of sight to the blind,
> to set at liberty those who are oppressed,
>   to proclaim the acceptable year of the Lord.
>
> (Luke 4:18-19)

And that is the note on which, in word and deed, it continued. To believe in such a God is to live with hope, even in the midst of much in the world and in ourselves which tells a different story.

(4) But if the suffering this man experiences is not something God "willingly" sends, why is he experiencing it? Here he has two things to say in verses 37-39; (a) That all of life, "good and evil", comes from the God who is the creator of the world and who is free to do what he wishes. The language of verse 37 reminds us of the creation hymn in Genesis 1, with its recurring phrases. "And God said, 'Let X happen'. . . . and it was so". In spite of tragedy, in spite of unanswered questions, this is still God's world, a world which we can face without fearing that it is

a hideous mistake devoid of meaning. In God's world we are in God's hands in "good and evil". We are reminded of the words of Jesus:

> For only a penny you can buy two sparrows, yet not one sparrow falls to the ground without your Father's consent. As for you, even the hairs of your head have all been counted. So do not be afraid; you are worth much more than many sparrows.
>
> (Matt. 10:29-31, GNB)

(b) Also, that, in his case, suffering is the just punishment for his sins. He is recognizing that what is being called into question is his own life, not the character of God.

The opening verse of the chapter began with the words, "I am the man [Hebrew, *gever*] who has seen affliction"; this intensely personal part of the poem closes with words which literally would be rendered "a man [*gever*], on account of his sin". These closing words look back to tell us that what began with a man complaining to God ends with a man confessing his sins. He has moved from thinking of himself and his problems as being at the centre of life, to seeing himself in the light of God. This is a true pilgrim journey. But the closing words also look forward to the next part of his poem in which, out of his own experience, this man calls upon his people similarly to confess their sins.

TEARS OF REPENTANCE

Lamentations 3:40-51

40Let us test and examine our ways,
   and return to the Lord!
41Let us lift up our hearts and hands
   to God in heaven:
42"We have transgressed and rebelled,
   and thou hast not forgiven.

⁴³"Thou hast wrapped thyself with anger and pursued us,
  slaying without pity;
⁴⁴thou has wrapped thyself with a cloud
  so that no prayer can pass through.
⁴⁵Thou hast made us offscouring and refuse
  among the peoples.

⁴⁶"All our enemies
  rail against us;
⁴⁷panic and pitfall have come upon us,
  devastation and destruction;
⁴⁸my eyes flow with rivers of tears
  because of the destruction of the daughter of my people.

⁴⁹"My eyes will flow without ceasing,
  without respite,
⁵⁰until the Lord from heaven looks down and sees;
⁵¹my eyes cause me grief
  at the fate of all the maidens of my city."

The poet now calls upon his people to acknowledge that they have rebelled against the Lord and rejected his authority. They must change and such a change involves three things (verses 40-41):

(a) self-examination, which takes an honest look at life in the light of what God expects;

(b) repentance, that right about turn (*shuv*) which all the prophets, not least Jeremiah, demanded (see comment on Jer.3:1-5 in vol.1, pp.36-37);

(c) renewed faith, which can never be merely a matter of outward appearance ("our hands" lifted to God), but must also involve a total inner renewal ("our hearts"). It is possible to make this point even more strongly by translating verse 41 as in the New English Bible: "Let us lift up our hearts, *not* our hands, to God in heaven".

These three things do not always go together. We can take an honest look at ourselves, see the need for change, yet do nothing about it either because we can't or don't want to. We may claim that we have repented or been converted and show all the outward signs of such an experience, yet remain inwardly unchanged. An aggressive, self-centred atheist can become an aggressive self-centred Christian—and the one is no more attractive or easy to live with than the other.

The urgency of the call for a radical change on the part of the community is underlined by the words, "and thou hast not forgiven" (verse 42). The Lord had obviously not forgiven, because true forgiveness is never simply a matter of words. It must take tangible form. It is no use saying you forgive someone for what they have done, if your attitude towards them remains harsh and hostile. That remained God's attitude to his people; a God so enveloped in anger that he was beyond the reach of his people's prayers, a God who had cast off his people as if he had no further use for them ("offscouring and refuse" as they are called in verse 45). The harsh reality of mocking enemies and a devastated land remained. Verse 47, in its description of this harsh reality, plays on the similarity in sound of two pairs of Hebrew words, a similarity impossible to render into English. Perhaps we can get no nearer to it than to give, as the RSV does, pairs of English words that begin with the same letter, "panic and pitfall' and "devastation and destruction".

Will God forgive? Here the poem switches from the "we", "us" and "our" of verses 40–47 to the "I", "me" and "my" in verses 48–51. Zion, the community, now speaks as a person pouring out her heart in grief, in tears that "will flow without respite" (verse 49). There is a door that needs to be knocked on, and knocked on again and again until it opens and God's answer comes (cf. Luke 11:5–10). The tears that flow are both tears of continuing repentance and tears that are the only possible response to the tragedy that has happened. There are times when the stiff upper lip needs to give, and the tears should be allowed to flow freely and unashamedly. This was such a time for Zion as she looked at "the fate of all the maidens of [her] city" (verse 51). This could either be a reference to the young women of Jerusalem, raped in all probability by the victorious enemy troops, and carried off into captivity, or it could be a reference to the fate that had befallen all the other towns throughout the land, towns thought of as the daughter towns of mother Jerusalem. Where in the midst of this are the signs of God's forgiveness?

THE ANSWER

Lamentations 3:52–66

52"I have been hunted like a bird by those who were my enemies
    without cause;
53they flung me alive into the pit and cast stones on me;
54water closed over my head;
    I said, 'I am lost.'

55"I called on thy name, O Lord,
    from the depths of the pit;
56thou didst hear my plea, 'Do not close
    thine ear to my cry for help!'
57Thou didst come near when I called on thee;
    thou didst say, 'Do not fear!'

58"Thou hast taken up my cause, O Lord,
    thou hast redeemed my life.
59Thou hast seen the wrong done to me, O Lord;
    judge thou my cause.
60Thou hast seen all their vengeance,
    all their devices against me.

61"Thou hast heard their taunts, O Lord,
    all their devices against me.
62The lips and thoughts of my assailants
    are against me all the day long.
63Behold their sitting and their rising;
    I am the burden of their songs.

64"Thou wilt requite them, O Lord,
    according to the work of their hands.
65Thou wilt give them dullness of heart;
    thy curse will be on them.

⁶⁶Thou wilt pursue them in anger and destroy them
from under thy heavens, O Lord."

Now we hear on the lips of Zion a lament, which like many
other such laments in the Psalms (*eg* Pss. 16 and 55), moves
from a situation of crisis in a person's life, through an appeal to
God, to the certainty that the appeal has been answered.

It is also typical of such laments that judgement is called
down upon the enemies who are held to be responsible for the
crisis. The crisis is described in verses 52–54 and culminates in
the despairing cry "I am lost", or as the New English Bible has
it, "My end has come", literally "I am cut off". The pictures used
are vivid: hunted like a bird; like an animal, or a prisoner,
thrown into a pit and stoned; almost drowned in water, the
threatening waters that are traditional symbols of a desperate,
near death situation. So a Psalmist cries out:

> The waters have come up to my neck.
> I sink in deep mire . . . . .
> I have come into deep waters,
> and the flood sweeps over me.
>
> (Ps. 69:1–2; cf.Jon. 2:5–6)

Zion's appeal is made "from the depths of the pit" (verse 55),
out of a situation in which she feels herself as good as dead, the
"pit" being one of a series of words which are used to describe
the vague, shadowy, no-life world of Sheol to which the dead
go. It is a place of no hope. As Job protests (Job 17:14–15):

> If I say to the pit, "You are my father",
>   and to the worm, "My mother," or "My sister",
> where then is my hope?
>   Who will see my hope?

Into this no-hope situation there comes God's answer, "Do not
fear!" (verse 57), words that echo reassuringly across the Bible
as the answer to many of the doubts and the pain-filled
questions which haunt people (see comment on Jer.30:10). But

these words, "do not fear", only make sense to someone who knows that the Lord is not an enemy, as some of the earlier verses in this chapter suggest, but an advocate for the defence, pleading Zion's case in court, and acting as her "redeemer" (*go-el*; verse 58; see comment on Jer. 31:11). For Christians the seal is set on these pictures of God by what we see in Jesus, our "advocate with the Father" (1 John 2:1); Jesus in whom we receive our "redemption" (Rom. 3:24).

The lament closes in verses 59–66 with the longest passage in the book demanding that the Lord sees to it that the cruel, mocking enemies get what they have coming to them. More briefly we have already heard the same plea in 1:21–22; we shall hear it again, directed specifically against the Edomites, in 4:21–22. Such enemies, as well as Zion, must know the reality of God's judgement. The thought and language of these verses should by now be familiar, though it is not clear what is meant by the words, "Thou wilt give them dullness of hearing" (verse 65). It may mean, "make them stubborn", or make them experience "anguish", or as the NEB translates, "Show them how hard your heart can be". We have already discussed the meaning and importance of such prayers directed against other people in our comments on the oracles against the nations in Jeremiah chapters 46–51. That remains; but in the light of all that we know of God in Jesus, and with the words "love your enemies" (Matt. 5:44) ringing in our ears, dare we pray, "show them how hard your heart can be"? Zion's prayer cannot be the final answer; but neither is the answer that we too often give in our dealings with other people, particularly those whom we regard as in some way posing a threat to us.

MISERY ABOUNDS

Lamentations 4:1–16

> [1]How the gold has grown dim,
>   how the pure gold is changed!
> The holy stones lie scattered at the head of every street.

²The precious sons of Zion,
    worth their weight in fine gold,
how they are reckoned as earthen pots,
    the work of a potter's hands!

³Even the jackals give the breast and suckle their young,
    but the daughter of my people has become cruel,
        like the ostriches in the wilderness.

⁴The tongue of the nursling cleaves to the roof of its mouth for
        thirst;
The children beg for food,
    but no one gives to them.

⁵Those who feasted on dainties perish in the streets;
    those who were brought up in purple lie on ash heaps.

⁶For the chastisement of the daughter of my people has been
        greater than the punishment of Sodom,
    which was overthrown in a moment, no hand being laid on it.

⁷Her princes were purer than snow,
        whiter than milk;
    their bodies were more ruddy than coral,
        the beauty of their form was like sapphire.

⁸Now their visage is blacker than soot,
        they are not recognised in the streets;
    their skin has shrivelled upon their bones,
        it has become as dry as wood.

⁹Happier were the victims of the sword
        than the victims of hunger,
    who pined away, stricken by want of the fruits of the field.

¹⁰The hands of compassionate women
        have boiled their own children;
    they became their food in the destruction of the daughter
        of my people.

¹¹The Lord gave full vent to his wrath,
    he poured out his hot anger;
and he kindled a fire in Zion,
    which consumed its foundations.

¹²The kings of the earth did not believe,
    or any of the inhabitants of the world,
that foe or enemy could enter the gates of Jerusalem.

¹³This was for the sins of her prophets
    and the iniquities of her priests,
who shed in the midst of her the blood of the righteous.

¹⁴They wandered, blind, through the streets,
    so defiled with blood
that none could touch their garments.

¹⁵"Away! Unclean!" men cried at them;
    "Away! Away! Touch not!"
So they became fugitives and wanderers;
    men said among the nations,
    "They shall stay with us no longer."

¹⁶The Lord himself has scattered them,
    he will regard them no more;
no honour was shown to the priests,
    no favour to the elders.

In this fourth alphabetic poem the mood has changed. We no longer hear any agonizing questions. The struggle for faith seems to be over, at least for the moment. There are no more urgent appeals to God. It is quietly accepted that what has happened is the Lord's doing, the outpouring of his anger, the expression of his displeasure (verses 11 and 16). But the tragedy remains, misery abounds. Imprinted in the poet's mind is the painful contrast between the city as he once knew it, and as it is now.

The gold, that once gleamed in temple and palace (see Jer. 52:19), is tarnished; jewels, "holy stones", lie scattered in the streets, poignant reminders of a people once worth their weight in gold, but now no more valuable than cheap crockery, those clay pottery jars that were ten a penny in the ancient world, frequently broken and thrown out as worthless (verses 1–2). It is the picture of hunger and famine, however, which seems to be most deeply etched in the poet's mind (see also 1:11; 2:11–12). The jackals of the desert provide milk for their cubs, but the women of Jerusalem cannot. They are more like the ostriches who, so it is said, lay their eggs in the sand and then abandon them, as if they do not care about the chicks (see Job 39:13–16). Children vainly search for food (verses 3–4). Those accustomed to living in the lap of luxury, "lie on ash heaps" (verse 5) or perhaps "pick through garbage", like the down-and-outs in our city centres who scavenge in the litter bins. A quick death by the sword would have been preferable to the slow lingering death by starvation which drives even compassionate women to cannibalize their own children (verses 9–10; see also 1:11). "Her princes", the aristocracy, once immaculately groomed and a picture of health, are now scarcely recognizable, with their wizened, blackened skin revealing every bone in their bodies (verses 7–8; you can follow up some of the language of beauty and the comparison of various parts of the body to jewels, in Song of Solomon 5:10–15). Worse than what happened to Sodom, is the poet's verdict (verse 6; see comment on Jer. 23:14): worse than Hiroshima, we might say.

There is widespread incredulity that it should have happened to this city of God that was to last impregnable for ever (see Pss. 46 and 48). The blame for it, however, is firmly fixed—as in 2:14 and as so often in Jeremiah—upon the religious leadership, priests and prophets "who shed in the midst of her the blood of the righteous" (verse 13). This is probably an accusation that by default, by their failure in God's name to challenge the corruption and injustice in society, they had in fact encouraged it and were responsible for it. To turn a blind eye to evil is often the surest way to guarantee that it will flourish. Ironically, those who were supposed to guide the nation, are now depicted as wandering "blind through the streets" (verse 14); those whose duty it was to examine various skin infections and to pronounce the dreaded word "unclean" (see Lev. 13), now hear others directing at them the words "Away! Unclean!" (verse 15); those who were once recognized as having a vital part to play in the religious life of the community, are now condemned to become "fugitives and wanderers", welcomed by no-one.

It is almost as if, having come to terms with the questions that had led him to rethink his faith, the poet needs to remind himself that what prompted the questions in the first place is still there in all its challenging pathos and horror. He cannot, he must not forget. Any faith that turns a blind eye to the misery and injustice in our world, to the ever increasing divide between rich and poor, to the nuclear threat to life, is not a faith rooted in the witness of the Bible, however personally comforting it may be.

LAST DAYS AND BEYOND

Lamentations 4: 17–22

> [17]Our eyes failed, ever watching vainly for help;
>   in our watching we watched for a nation which could not save.
>
> [18]Men dogged our steps so that we could not walk in our streets;
>   our end drew near; our days were numbered;
>   for our end had come.
>
> [19]Our pursuers were swifter than the vultures in the heavens;
>   they chased us on the mountains,
>   they lay in wait for us in the wilderness.
>
> [20]The breath of our nostrils, the Lord's anointed,
>   was taken in their pits,
>   he of whom we said, "Under his shadow
>   we shall live among the nations."

²¹Rejoice and be glad, O daughter of Edom,
 dweller in the land of Uz;
but to you also the cup shall pass;
 you shall become drunk and strip yourself bare.

²²The punishment of your iniquity,
 O daughter of Zion, is accomplished,
  he will keep you in exile no longer;
but your iniquity, O daughter of Edom, he will punish,
 he will uncover your sins.

This section, which switches to the first person plural ("our eyes"), reads as if it were written by someone who was closely associated with the royal court in the final days of the independent Judean state; and that may be as close as we can get to the author of much of Lamentations. The section begins in verse 17 by recalling the vain hope of help from "a nation which could not save". Almost certainly this is a reference to the hopes placed in the Egyptians as the Babylonians tightened their stranglehold on Jerusalem, hopes that seemed at one point as if they might be realized, hopes which Jeremiah consistently declared to be an illusion (see Jer. 37:5-11 and the comments on the passage). There follows a picture of the ever increasing anarchy in the streets of Jerusalem, and the danger perhaps of being picked up by enemy patrols, signs that "our end had come" (verse 18).

Verses 19-20 describe the unsuccessful attempt by Zedekiah, the last king of Judah, to escape from the Babylonians (see Jer. 39:4-5). The poignancy of what happened is underlined by the way in which the king is referred to in a series of phrases in verse 20, all of them stressing the great expectations which surrounded the king:

(1) "*The breath of our nostrils*", a traditional Egyptian royal title, although nowhere else found in the Old Testament, a title which indicates the indispensible role the king played in the life of the community. He was their life-support system.

(2) "*The Lord's anointed*", words that point to the special

relationship between the king and God, words that have their origin in a rite of anointing to office, such as we find in the narrative in 1 Sam. 16:13 where Samuel anoints David. Although people could be anointed to a variety of roles in the life of ancient Israel, the ruling king was *par excellence,* "the Lord's anointed", from the moment of his coronation (see Ps. 2:2). The Hebrew word translated "anointed", *mashiah,* gives us our English word "messiah". It is important to remember that for the Old Testament the "messiah" is not, in the first instance, a future king. The word describes the king who sat on the throne in Jerusalem.

(3) "*Under his shadow*" are words usually found referring to God in the Old.Testament, particularly in the Psalms. Psalm 91 speaks of the man, "who abides in the shadow of the Almighty" (Ps. 91:1; cf.Ps. 63:7). But the same phrase is used in ancient Egypt to describe the way in which the king, sometimes depicted as a falcon, protects his subjects under the shadow of his wings.

Great expectations, destroyed at a stroke! It is out of such hopes dashed that there came, with ever increasing conviction, the belief that one day there would come a true king, who would give meaning to all the hopes centred on kingship: a future messiah (see comment on Jer. 23:5–6).

The passage ends with (a) a word to the Edomites (verses 21–22) who, as the Book of Obadiah reminds us, took full advantage of the Babylonian attack on Jerusalem to pay off old scores. Let them rejoice; their joy will only be temporary. They will soon experience the same judgement which has befallen Jerusalem, and for the same reason. For the picture of the potent "cup" of the Lord as the symbol of judgement, see the comments on Jer. 25:15ff.

And (b), a word to Zion (verse 22), a word of hope that she has paid the penalty for her sins and will not have to go through the horror of national catastrophe and exile again: "he will keep you in exile no longer" is better translated, as in the New English Bible, "never again shall you be carried into exile". This is perhaps the most specific word of hope to the community in the entire book. It is a modest hope, but it gleams brightly against the dark background of mocking enemies and national ruin; modest, yet providing a basis for the future. To a drowning man the life-line which pulls him to the shore is more welcome and attractive than the wildest dreams he has ever cherished.

A PRAYER OF DISTRESS

Lamentations 5:1–18

¹Remember, O Lord, what has befallen us;
  behold, and see our disgrace!
²Our inheritance has been turned over to strangers,
  our homes to aliens.
³We have become orphans, fatherless;
  our mothers are like widows.
⁴We must pay for the water we drink,
  the wood we get must be bought.
⁵With a yoke on our necks we are hard driven;
  we are weary, we are given no rest.
⁶We have given the hand to Egypt,
  and to Assyria, to get bread enough.
⁷Our fathers sinned, and are no more;
  and we bear their iniquities.
⁸Slaves rule over us;
  there is none to deliver us from their hand.
⁹We get our bread at the peril of our lives,
  because of the sword in the wilderness.
¹⁰Our skin is hot as an oven with the burning heat of famine.
¹¹Women are ravished in Zion,
  virgins in the towns of Judah.
¹²Princes are hung up by their hands;
  no respect is shown to the elders.
¹³Young men are compelled to grind at the mill;
  and boys stagger under loads of wood.
¹⁴The old men have quit the city gate,
  the young men their music.
¹⁵The joy of our hearts has ceased;
  our dancing has been turned to mourning.

¹⁶The crown has fallen from our head;
　woe to us, for we have sinned!
¹⁷For this our heart has become sick,
　for these things our eyes have grown dim,
¹⁸for Mount Zion which lies desolate;
　jackals prowl over it.

The final poem in the book is different in several respects from the others. It is not an alphabetical poem, although it nods in that direction by having twenty-two verses. Even in the English translation it is clear that the poetic structure is different from that of the previous poems; no longer any lines of unequal length, in the *qinah* style, but lines of more or less equal length throughout. Although superficially verses 1–18 have much in common with 4:1–17 in that they contain harrowing and graphic descriptions of the plight of the people, they are different in as much as they are part of a prayer, beginning "Remember, O Lord . . . ".

Chapter 5 has many of the marks of a typical community lament, such as we find in Psalms 44 and 74. There is the use throughout the first person plural, "we", "us", "our"; there is the description of the tragedy that has befallen the people; there is the appeal to God and the nagging questions "Why? . . . Why?". Look at Psalms 44 and 74 and you will see that they divide almost equally between a description of the national crisis and an appeal to the Lord. But here the account of the crisis takes up eighteen verses, while the appeal to God is very brief, verses 19–22. Against that we must balance the fact that verses 1–18 are in themselves an appeal to the Lord, because if he accepts the invitation in verse 1 to "remember", "look [behold]" and "see", how can he fail to be moved by the plight of his people?

Here are people once free, now living in occupied territory; lacking security (verse 3; see comment on 1:1); forced to buy some of the basic necessities of life—water and wood—from the occupation regime (verse 4); going into the country in search of food, their lives at risk because of the rampant lawlessness (verse 9); their bodies wracked by famine (verse 10); their women raped (verse 11); some of their former leaders caught by the occupation troops and publicly executed (verse 12); their young men forced to do the most menial tasks (see verse 13, grinding of corn being a job only normally done by women in Israel); ruled over by petty and insolent officials ("slaves", verse 8): it is a story that could have come from many an occupied country in Europe in the 1940s, under the heel of the Nazis.

What had previously been taken for granted as normal life is gone. The city gate, where the elders used to meet to decide community affairs and to do business, is deserted (verse 14). Joy and laughter are no more (verse 15). This is a community in the grip of shame, a community which has lost heart, not least when it looks at the desolated Temple on Mt Zion, once the centre of a joyful, confident religious life, once the symbol of the Lord's presence in their midst—now the haunt of jackals (verse 18).

If the pitiful destruction of the community is central to this prayer, there is also the recognition that what has happened is understandable. "Our fathers sinned" (verse 7) and we are still reaping the bitter harvest of their mistaken belief that security and prosperity were to be found, not by trusting in the Lord, but through alliances with Assyria or Egypt (verse 6). "Our fathers sinned. . ." but "woe to us, for we have sinned" (verse 16). There is no attempt here to wriggle out of personal responsibility (see comment on Jer. 31:29); instead, a frank recognition that if the seeds of disaster had been sown in the past, the present generation had actively cultivated them. There is a healthy realism that neither pretends that we live in isolation, uninfluenced by the past, nor claims that we are simply victims of the past. "Our fathers sinned" . . . "we have sinned".

CERTAINTIES AND QUESTIONS

Lamentations 5:19–22

> [19]But thou, O Lord, dost reign for ever;
> thy throne endures to all generations.

20Why dost thou forget us for ever,
   why dost thou so long forsake us?
21Restore us to thyself, O Lord, that we may be restored!
   Renew our days as of old!
22Or hast thou utterly rejected us?
   Art thou exceedingly angry with us?

As in many of the community laments, the move from describing the nation's present darkness to an appeal to God is marked by a celebration of who God is, a recalling of his wonderful deeds and of that power which controlled the past and will shape the future. You will see this clearly in Psalm 74:12. There is nothing like a good rousing hymn of praise to help us to see ourselves and our problems in a new light. The Temple on Mt Zion may be in ruins, but that does not mean that God's kingdom has collapsed. There may no longer be any Judean king sitting on the throne in Jerusalem, but "thy throne endures to all generations" (verse 19).

There is a kingship which is not of this world (John 18:36), a kingship which nothing that happens in this world can ever destroy. This is the great certainty to which Lamentations clings, and on which it seeks to build for the future: but it cannot stop the questions coming. There may, as we have seen, be a satisfactory answer to the question, "Why did it happen?"; but what about, "Why does it continue?" Does it mean that the Lord has forgotten, abandoned us "for ever" (verse 20)? We hear the same troubled question in the opening words of Psalm 74:

   Why hast thou cast us off, O God. Is it for ever?

                                                 (verse 1, NEB)

And questions about the future often seem more pressing and unanswerable than questions about the past.

The appeal in verse 21, "Restore us to thyself, O Lord, that we may be restored", may be more literally rendered, "Cause us to turn to you, O Lord, that we may turn": it is that word *shuv* again (see comment in vol.1, p.36). It is an appeal to God to bring the people back to himself in true repentance so that the covenant relationship, which was the foundation of the nation's life from the beginning, may be renewed. If that happens, then the question in verse 20 will be answered; the Lord will not have forgotten or abandoned his people.

But will it happen? This is the issue raised by the last verse in the book. There has been a great deal of discussion as to how we ought to translate it. The RSV and the Good News Bible assume that it contains two further questions that consider the possibility that the Lord has "utterly" rejected his people, and that there may be no limits to his anger. The NEB translates:

> For if thou has utterly rejected us,
>> then great indeed has been thy anger against us.

This has the attraction of eliminating the questions, but it still leaves open the possibility that the Lord in his anger has totally rejected his people. Other translations tend to leave the people facing the same awesome possibility.

It is hardly surprising that this ending has troubled many people. The Jewish rabbis insisted that when Lamentations was read in worship, verse 21 should be repeated after verse 22, to end the book on a more positive and hopeful note, the appeal to the Lord to renew his people. But we should learn from many parts of the Old Testament that we do not necessarily strengthen our faith by suppressing our doubts. Let us not underestimate the depth of the crisis of faith through which the writer of these words had lived. The destruction of Jerusalem and the Temple had swept away many of the familiar landmarks in his spiritual life. He struggled to find his bearings and, with the help of a prophetic compass, he was able to resume his journey. Some of the questions he had faced were answered, but were there no lingering doubts? Perhaps he is telling us that faith may have to go on living with questions unanswered. Why should we be slow to admit this or try to avoid it?

FURTHER READING

The books marked with an asterisk are suitable as an introduction to the study of Jeremiah and Lamentations.

JEREMIAH

S. H. Blank, *Jeremiah: Man and Prophet* (Cincinnati 1961)

J. Bright, *Jeremiah* (Anchor Bible Vol. 21, New York 1965)

R. P. Carroll, *From Chaos to Covenant: Uses of Prophecy in the Book of Jeremiah* (London 1981)

*R. K. Harrison, *Jeremiah and Lamentations* (Inter Varsity Press 1973)

*W. L. Holladay, *Jeremiah, Spokesman Out of Time* (Philadelphia 1974)

*E. W. Nicholson, *Jeremiah 1–25* (The Cambridge Bible Commentary on the NEB, Cambridge 1973)

*E. W. Nicholson, *Jeremiah 26–52* (The Cambridge Bible Commentary on the NEB, Cambridge 1975)

J. Skinner, *Prophecy and Religion, Studies in the Life of Jeremiah* (Cambridge 1922)

J. A. Thompson, *The Book of Jeremiah* (Grand Rapids 1980)

A. C. Welch, *Jeremiah, His Time and His Work* (Oxford 1951)

LAMENTATIONS

B. Albrektson, *Studies in the Text and Theology of the Book of Lamentations* (Lund 1963)

N. K. Gottwald, *Studies in the Book of Lamentations* (London 1962)

*R. K. Harrison, *Jeremiah and Lamentations* (Inter Varsity Press 1973)

D. R. Hillers, *Lamentations* (Anchor Bible, New York 1972)

*G. A. F. Knight, *Esther, Song of Songs and Lamentations* (SCM Press, London 1955)

*T. J. Meek and W.P. Merrill, *The Book of Lamentations* (Interpreters Bible Vol. VI, New York 1956)

*S. Paul Reemi, *Amos and Lamentations* (International Theological Commentary, Grand Rapids 1984)